TO
A NEW GENERATION
OF SCHOLARS

Lyn Graybill and Harry G. West

AFRICA'S SECOND WAVE OF FREEDOM

Development, Democracy, and Rights

Edited by

**Lyn Graybill
Kenneth W. Thompson**

**Volume XI
In the Miller Center Series on
A World in Change**

UNIVERSITY
PRESS OF
AMERICA

Lanham • New York • Oxford

The Miller Center

University of Virginia

Copyright © 1998 by
University Press of America,® Inc.
4720 Boston Way
Lanham, Maryland 20706

12 Hid's Copse Rd.
Cummor Hill, Oxford OX2 9JJ

All rights reserved
Printed in the United States of America
British Cataloging in Publication Information Available

Copublished by arrangement with
The Miller Center of Public Affairs,
University of Virginia

The views expressed by the author(s) of this publication do not necessarily represent the opinions of the Miller Center. We hold to Jefferson's dictum that: "Truth is the proper and sufficient antagonist to error, and has nothing to fear from the conflict, unless by human interposition, disarmed of her natural weapons, free argument and debate."

Library of Congress Cataloging-in-Publication Data

ISBN: 0-7618-1070-6 (cloth: alk. ppr.)
ISBN: 0-7618-1071-4 (pbk: alk. ppr.)

∞™ The paper used in this publication meets the minimum requirements of American National Standard for Information Sciences—Permanence of Paper for Printed Library Materials, ANSI Z39.48–1984.

Contents

PREFACE vii
Kenneth W. Thompson

INTRODUCTION xiii
Lyn Graybill

1. AFRICA IN A WORLD IN CHANGE 1
   Pauline H. Baker

2. CIVILITY, INCIVILITY, AND DEMOCRATIZATION:
   THE POLITICS OF CIVIL SOCIETY IN AFRICA 23
   Robert Fatton

3. THE CONSTRAINTS ON DEMOCRACY IN SUB-SAHARAN
   AFRICA: THE CASE FOR LIMITED DEMOCRACY 43
   John F. Clark

4. TRADITIONAL AUTHORITIES AND THE MOZAMBICAN
   TRANSITION TO DEMOCRATIC GOVERNANCE 65
   Harry G. West

5. MOBUTU SESE SEKO OF ZAIRE AS A
   NONDEMOCRATIC PRESIDENTIAL LEADER 81
   John F. Clark

6. THE NIGERIAN PRESS UNDER THE MILITARY:
   PERSECUTION, RESILIENCE, AND POLITICAL
   CRISIS (1983–1993) 103
   Adeyinka Adeyemi

7. THE SUPREME COURT OF ZIMBABWE 157
   Anthony B. Gubbay

CONTENTS

8. **THE ROLE OF CHRISTIANITY IN THE TRANSITION TO MAJORITY RULE IN SOUTH AFRICA** 173
   Peter Walshe

9. **THE IMPACT OF CHRISTIANITY ON THE STRUGGLE AGAINST APARTHEID** 193
   Lyn Graybill

Preface

KENNETH W. THOMPSON

Africa is the hope and fascination of almost every Westerner who has looked for new worlds to conquer. So it was for my colleagues and me at the Rockefeller Foundation in the late 1950s. We had read Frederick Jackson Turner's history of the frontier, but the last frontier within the territorial limits had been crossed. The Foundation had managed a brilliantly successful program with country representatives in the important countries of Europe. A stunning percentage of Nobel Prize winners in science and medicine have been former Rockefeller fellows. It would be difficult to imagine more fertile soil for assisting the development of young scientists. I doubt if the yield from philanthropic dollars has ever been higher.

Why, then, did the Foundation turn away from Europe and reach out to Africa and Asia? Was this shift the first wave of large-scale institutional interest in Africa, and if so, why did it occur when it did? One answer was that Africa needed help. The decision rested on half-a-dozen factors, no one capable by itself of bringing about dramatic change. A first factor was leadership. Change comes, as is almost always the case, because of effective leadership. But what is leadership, and from whence does it come? Political leaders emerged with newfound political power to hold their own with the leaders of the West. Because many had been educated in Western educational institutions, they shared up to a point a common universe of discourse. But only time, we believed, would tell whether, and if so in what form, they shared common interests. We told ourselves that they shared the world's interest in food and shelter, education and progress, and development and health. Yet, diversity manifested itself in different cultures, social organization, hierarchies of leadership, and economic needs. We found that those who mediated change were often the traditional leaders and chiefs rather than graduates of Oxford and Harvard, who were more often in demand in the West or the international community than in their own countries. Those who remained had to demonstrate their national credentials by sometimes opposing the West.

A second factor was the need for that minimum political and economic infrastructure on which cooperation would be based. Development in health, agriculture, and education presupposed at least rudimentary roads and transportation and a communication system. Funding organizations thought in terms of matching and counterpart funds. Where this was lacking, trained leaders from abroad who came to serve were unable to contribute in significant ways, as the British learned with their groundnut scheme in the Sudan. The same was true of others who followed, including agricultural specialists from the Rockefeller Foundation.

Third, not every underdeveloped country has the energy, resources, and what economists call human capital to become a less-developed or a developing nation. The Belgian Congo had only seven university graduates, and Tanzania only 13 when they achieved independence. As a result, the Congo's vast energy potential, for example, remained largely undeveloped, and Tanzania had to await Nyerere's strong emphasis on education. Chad and Niger wholly lacked the national resources for development for which no amount of external assistance would compensate. The dynamics of change proceed in response to natural and human factors, and their absence limits what an underdeveloped nation can do.

Fourth, political instability and turbulence is often an obstacle to development. Countries that experience a succession of internal revolts and coups d'etat are unlikely to successfully harness their national resources for nation-building. Some observers will insist that countries that fail to achieve political development are high-risk choices for economic development. Political development is doubtful when corrupt and unstable regimes remain in power. In such cases, the creation of more stable regimes becomes a precondition to economic development.

Fifth, it would be as unrealistic to think that every nation in Africa was capable of the development that has taken place, say, in

PREFACE

Uganda and Ghana, nor has the growth rate of these two nations been uniform and without setbacks. Ghana squandered the resources that had been accumulated before independence. The Gold Coast was plundered in the extravagances of building an Ghanian airline and in the policies of Nkrumah and his economic minister, Gbedemiah. A succession of regimes failed before one came to power that paid stricter attention to the principles of economics. What countries such as Ghana achieved is likely beyond the reach of the poorer countries in the region where economic realities come into play, but the postcolonial period for Ghana under military and academic rulers was hardly a success.

The hope remains that the more fortunate countries will not only succeed but will match the developing countries of Asia. In the 1950s, this was the hope, and it determined the selection of countries that it was assumed had the best chance for growth. At that time several countries had the same income level as South Korea. Today, South Korea has a per capita income of $10,000, while the Congo has remained at $150. Part of the loss of interest in Africa has its cause in the standing of this factor. Research into development in Asia and Africa, however, has suggested that this condition may be changing. Countries such as Uganda, one of the first selected in the Rockefeller Foundation program, are among the fastest-growing economies in the world. Other countries in the region are experimenting with market-based economic policies, privatization, and stock markets. They are renewing their emphasis on education, agriculture, and health care. They are trying to learn from examples in Asia. Sixteen countries fall into this category. Studies by the World Bank show that at least four countries— Uganda, Angola, Lesotho, and Malawi—are achieving growth rates of 10 percent, matching the peak rates of the so-called Asian tigers: Hong Kong, Taiwan, Singapore, and South Korea. Yet the top African countries start from a much lower base and clearly the best have suffered from leaders such as Idi Amin and neglect of education and health. In the period of 1967 to 1973, savings as a percent of gross domestic product, including government and private savings, was 21.1 percent in the four Asian countries and 15.7 percent in Sub-Sahara Africa. Tariffs in the Asian countries were 5.7 percent and in Africa 22.5 percent. Direct foreign investments in billions of dollars to build factories and stimulate economic growth was 60 percent in Asia and a little over 2 percent in Africa. The percentage of school-age children attending primary or secondary schools was 59.5 in Asia and 41.5 in Africa, with a literacy rate of 82.7 percent compared with 55.1 percent in Africa. Climate, Asian Confucianism, the greater burdens of colonialism in Africa, and the lack of financial prudence by Africans are all cited as the reason for Asian superiority. Even some World Bank officials are optimistic about Africa's economic and educational future, and this optimism may herald the dawn of new hope and fascination for the region in the rest of the world.

It is against this background that we have organized a series of forums on Africa. They touch themes such as leadership and governance that are at the core of the Miller Center's program. They are in response to some of the changes reported above that are affecting at least part of the continent. For a host of reasons from the spread of AIDs, malnutrition, and epidemics of all kinds the United States cannot afford to isolate itself from Africa. There are humanitarian and ideological reasons for resuming the relationship. Countries such as Uganda, the site of the Rockefeller Foundation's first postwar initiative in Africa, are providing examples of economic and social progress. If the 1960s were the crest of the first wave of American interest in Africa, the end of one millennium and the beginning of another may be a time to renew U.S. commitments. It can be called the second wave of postwar interest in Africa.

To explore these topics and others we invited colleagues from the University of Virginia and friends from the international community of scholars to address urgent problems in various African countries. Dr. Pauline Baker was a leader of the Aspen Institute's Congressional Program and a faculty member at Georgetown. Later she was named president of the Fund for Peace. The Honorable Chief Justice of the Supreme Court of Zimbabwe, Anthony R. Gubbay, came to the Miller Center at the initiative of University of Virginia law professor Dick Howard. Adeyinka Adeyemi, who was formerly correspondent with the Pan African News Agency, made a presentation on the Nigerian press under the military at the Joan Shorenstein Center at Harvard's

PREFACE

Kennedy Center. John F. Clark was earlier a fellow and editor at the Miller Center and is now a faculty member in international relations at Florida International University. Peter Walshe is director of the African Studies Program at the University of Notre Dame and a professor of government. Since Professor Robert Fatton delivered his paper on "Civility, Incivility, and Democratization," he has become chairman of the Department of Government and Foreign Affairs at the University of Virginia. Harry West was completing his doctorate at the University of Wisconsin and a visiting scholar at the Miller Center when he wrote his paper. He also worked at the Miller Center as an undergraduate at the University of Virginia. He since has become an assistant professor at Sweet Briar College in Lynchburg, Virginia.

As we were completing the present volume, Professor Lyn Graybill came to the Miller Center. Earlier, she had been an editor and writer at the Center. She was teaching in the government department at the University of Virginia at the time and shortly thereafter became a scholar-in-residence at the Virginia Foundation of the Humanities. In the final stages of this study, she took over the writing of the introduction to the volume and is primarily responsible for its organization. A married woman with children, she must commute to the University of Virginia from Culpeper, Virginia. She has been limited not by talent but by family in the academic opportunities available to her. Nonetheless, as her introduction and final paper on "The Impact of Christianity on the Struggle Against Apartheid" demonstrate, she possesses extraordinary writing and analytical skills. As she struggles to maintain a scholarly and teaching career balanced against responsibility to her two children and a husband who works in Washington, D.C., her problem is not unique. Somehow a way must be found to give opportunities to women of such remarkable talent who are seeking to raise a family.

xi

Introduction

LYN GRAYBILL

Not too long ago a journalist writing in a leading journal of foreign affairs commented that when the Cold War ended, setting America free to pursue its own interests in Africa, we found, lo and behold, that we did not have any! A more accurate statement would be that now that geopolitical "interests" surrounding the fight against communism do not predominate, Africa can be viewed on its own terms and not merely as a pawn in U.S.-Soviet rivalries. Perhaps in the past a choice had to be made between interests and values (with interests trumping values), but surely now these two can complement, not compete with, each other. This means practically that it is in the U.S. national interest to support efforts at democratization, the building up of a human rights culture, and the strengthening of civil society in Africa—efforts that have always been at the core of American liberal values.

The scholars represented in this volume share a concern with the development of civil society in Africa. The first three chapters by Pauline Baker, Robert Fatton, and John Clark deal theoretically with these issues.

Pauline Baker has devoted a lifetime to the study of Africa. She inaugurates this series with a discussion of "Africa In a World in Change." She points to the impossibility of the United States barricading itself against environmental decay, refugee problems, spiralling debt, and health epidemics (including AIDS) that are endemic in Africa—problems that are no respecters of national boundaries. "As the problems become overwhelming," she argues, "there will be some awareness that we have something at stake in dealing with the problems of Africa." She warns that in the United States' own self-interest, Africa—which controls one-third of the United Nations votes—cannot be ignored. Africa will be the

INTRODUCTION

development challenge of the 21st century, and "the sooner we own up to the fact, the better."

Robert Fatton in "Civility, Incivility, and Democratization: The Politics of Civil Society in Africa," contends that the end of the Cold War will lead to the end of support for dictators and the ascendance of liberal democratic values. Yet, he maintains that democracy in Africa is fragile and contradictory—often involving the establishment of alliances by predatory rulers with the middle sector—in order to resist full democracy. For true democracy to take hold, popular civil society represented by the subordinate classes must wrest power from the predatory rulers and middle sectors. The consolidation of democracy can only occur when the forces of civil society are institutionalized. There is no predictable outcome, according to Fatton, and reversion to dictatorship is always a possibility.

John Clark analyzes the barriers to the consolidation of democracy in "The Constraints on Democracy in Sub-Saharan Africa: The Case for Limited Democracy." He asserts that for democracy to work in Africa, it will have to be limited in a number of ways. Beyond providing basic services, efforts to create social equality (as opposed to political equality) are infeasible and will send capital out of the country and discourage foreign investment. "To try to deliver too much too soon only promises future rounds of instability," he argues. In the areas of human rights, progress will be slow. Clark points out that it took Western countries a long period to make their democracies real, noting that it took 100 years for American democracy to eliminate slavery. Therefore, one should not expect more from African countries than "democratic incrementalism." Flawed as they are, African democracies should be supported by the West, and in time democratic practices perhaps will be entrenched and broader social welfare policies may be attempted.

What follows the introductory pieces on the prospects for democracy and stability in Africa are case studies of various aspects of civil society from Mozambique, Nigeria, Zimbabwe, and South Africa.

Harry West assesses the prospects for a democratic transition in Mozambique following nearly 20 years of civil war in "Traditional

INTRODUCTION

Authorities and the Mozambican Transition to Democratic Governance." West begins his forum with a discussion of the tragic war between FRELIMO and RENAMO forces in which a million were killed and over six million displaced. When the election campaigns began in 1993, the international community wondered about the possible role of traditional chiefs in a democratized Mozambique. FRELIMO historically had sought to eliminate traditional chiefs, viewing them as "collaborators" with the former Portuguese regime. RENAMO, too, had ruthlessly exploited chiefs in areas they controlled for crops and soldiers for the war effort against FRELIMO. Yet chiefs hold sway over the loyalty of thousands of Mozambican peasants. Admittedly, a "nondemocratic" institution—determined not by elections but by inheritance—chieftaincies are powerful institutions in the absence of a strong civil society, and local politics is expressed through them.

The new constitution protecting individual human rights is at odds with the authority of chiefs with unlimited power and ability to extract tribute, which poses a problem for democracy. West admits that there are no simple answers; the language of democracy spoken in Mozambique will be different from the models imported from the West and must take into account the reality of the power of chiefs in the countryside. West doubts that a Western model of multiparty electoral politics will be reproduced, but instead trusts that the "people in Mozambique show a tremendous capability to deal with changes that are thrust upon them and to make the effects of those changes their own."

John Clark in "Mobutu Sese Seko of Zaire as a Nondemocratic Presidential Leader" analyzes authoritarian rule under the corrupt regime of Mobutu and the prospects for a vibrant opposition arising against him. Supported by the United States during the Cold War years, Mobutu has survived also because of support bases in the army, the police class, his home province, and the chiefs in rural areas. Mobutu, who has systemically plundered $5 billion of his country's wealth, has been able to use this wealth to buy off and co-opt the opposition, leaving few resources for national development. Some of his excesses might be forgiven, argues Clark, if he had managed the economy better as did other authoritarian leaders such as Houphouët-Boigny of the Ivory Coast.

INTRODUCTION

Following the two country studies are chapters on various agents of civil society in sub-Saharan Africa: the press in Nigeria, the Supreme Court in Zimbabwe, and the church in South Africa.

Former correspondent with the Pan African News Agency, Adeyinka Adeyemi, examines the role of the press in Nigeria in "The Nigerian Press Under the Military: Persecution, Resilience, and Political Crisis (1983-1993)." With 66 major newspapers, 50 television stations, and 40 radio stations, Nigeria boasts the largest active press community on the continent. Yet what was once claimed to be the freest press in Africa is under assault by the Abacha regime. Adeyemi traces the fluctuations between subtle and not-so-subtle forms of coercion, co-optation, and seduction of the press under a series of military governments since the early 1980s. Following General Sanni Abacha's coup to power, Nobel laureate Wole Soyinka predicted, "This is going to be the worst and most brutal regime that Nigeria ever had. This regime is prepared to kill, torture, and make opponents disappear." The Nigerian press began echoing this sentiment. Adeyemi's predictions of early government toleration of press criticism, followed by repression of press opposition once Abacha consolidates power, appears to have been borne out by recent events in Nigeria.

Still, Adeyemi argues for an important role for the Nigerian press in steering Nigeria toward a democratic culture. Technological advances in communication, the growing popularity of desktop publishing, and the increasing interest of the world media in Nigeria will draw attention to the autocratic maneuvers of the Abacha regime. Editors of influential media should write editorials in support of journalists who are being persecuted and harassed. Finally, the United States needs to expand its definition of "national interest" to include democracy and respect for human rights and "act decisively on the side of democracy at all times."

The Honorable Chief Justice of the Supreme Court of Zimbabwe, Anthony R. Gubbay, is well qualified to speak on "The Supreme Court of Zimbabwe." Gubbay describes the situation in Zimbabwe as a de facto one-party state headed by Robert Mugabe and his ZANU-PF Party. Government funding of candidates only goes to parties with 15 seats in the house. Only Robert Mugabe and ZANU have had the requisite number of seats and hence are the only ones to benefit from public funding, which serves to entrench the party against any challengers. Gubbay recounts the story of the 1996 presidential campaign, in which Sithole abruptly withdrew his candidacy, and Muzorewa asked the Supreme Court to postpone the election because of inadequate funding of his party. The Supreme Court rejected the application, the elections proceeded, and Mugabe was reelected president for the next six years.

In addition to the recent elections, Gubbay describes the court systems, including the customary law courts based on traditional law. A major problem he sees with the legal system is that the government can pass amendments to the constitution with a two-thirds majority, which is a simple process since one party nearly dominates the government. Many amendments have overruled the judgments of the courts on important issues of human rights.

"The Role of Christianity in the Transition to Majority Rule in South Africa" is the subject of a forum presented by Peter Walshe of Notre Dame. Walshe paints a broad history of repression in South Africa against opposition groups. He looks specifically at the period after 1988, when the United Democratic Front and COSATU (the major trade union movement) were banned. He looks at the rise of "prophetic Christianity"—expressed earlier through the Black Consciousness-inspired Christian Institute—and later through the South African Council of Churches, headed successively by Desmond Tutu, Beyers Naude, and Frank Chikane, as it moved in to fill the political vacuum in the wake of those bannings. By the late 1980s, a unified resistance movement supported by prophetic Christianity and in conjunction with the international sanction campaign forced the regime to move toward negotiations. The meshing of prophetic Christianity and the liberation movement was successful, Walshe claims, because the language of justice within the black protest movement had drawn heavily on biblical values, symbols, and terminology over the years.

Graybill's presentation, "The Impact of Christianity on the Struggle Against Apartheid," begins where Walshe's presentation ends. After briefly reviewing the importance of Christian ideas on resistance leaders—including Albert Lutuli of the ANC, Robert Sobukwe of the PAC, Steve Biko of the Black Consciousness movement, and Desmond Tutu of the United Democratic Front—she assesses Christianity's contribution in the reconciliation process in a postapartheid society.

She concurs with Walshe that economic policies that redistribute income in favor of the poor—those devastated by decades of apartheid—are essential. She quotes Tutu, who says that repentance must be followed by restitution: "Those who have wronged must be ready to make what amends they can. They must be ready to make restitution and reparation. If I have stolen your pen, I can't really be contrite when I say, 'Please forgive me,' if at the same time I still keep your pen. If I am truly repentant, then I will demonstrate this genuine repentance by returning your pen."

Christianity, Graybill believes, can contribute to the continuing struggle for justice in South Africa by inspiring white South Africans to repent for their past complicity in maintaining an evil system, fostering forgiveness on the part of black South Africans, and invoking a sense of unity among the races.

CHAPTER ONE

Africa in a World in Change*

PAULINE H. BAKER

NARRATOR: Pauline Baker completed her undergraduate work at Douglass College, Rutgers University; her master's degree at the University of California, Los Angeles; and her doctorate with distinction at the University of California, Los Angeles. She has been senior associate at the Carnegie Endowment for International Peace and director of the Carnegie Endowment's South Africa forum. In January 1992, she joined the Aspen Institute's Congressional International Program. She is also a faculty member at Georgetown University's School of International Affairs.

Ms. Baker lived in Africa for 11 years and travels there frequently. Her books range from such topics as the military, politics, and federalism in Africa to, most recently, the book *The United States and South Africa: The Reagan Years*. No one could be better qualified with a richer background for a discussion of Africa in a world in change than Ms. Baker.

MS. BAKER: I will begin by citing recent dramatic quotations from two leaders. The first one is as follows:

> If we do not act decisively and urgently, surely the present economic problems, economic strife, and divisive nationalism will eventually lead our countries to anarchy, bloodshed, civil war, and bickering over territories.

Presented in a Forum at the Miller Center of Public Affairs on 9 December 1991.

1

That statement was made by Robert Mugabe, the president of Zimbabwe, in Harare last August at a meeting of party leaders from 20 African states.

The second quote may be more familiar:

> Disintegration will bring misfortune to millions of those who live outside their national republics. Disintegration is fraught with ethnic interrepublic clashes and even wars. It would be catastrophic for the international community.

These words were spoken by Mikhail Gorbachev in a televised message to parliaments of the former Soviet republics earlier this month.

I cite these two quotes because of their striking similarities. They suggest that as the world stands on the threshold of a new but yet to be defined international order brought on by the collapse of the Soviet empire, it may be useful to reflect on a time when another empire collapsed. Roughly 30 years ago, when European colonialism in sub-Saharan Africa unraveled, dozens of new states burst on the world stage with an exuberance akin to that in Eastern Europe and the Soviet republics today. In a sweeping wave of political change that commenced in 1957 with Ghana and swelled in the 1960s with countries as varied as Nigeria and Swaziland, Africans claimed their independence from British, French, Belgian, Spanish, and, in the 1970s, Portuguese overlords. "It was," one observer stated, "a revolutionary shift in 20th century politics."

The cry for self-determination that was once invoked by the indigenous peoples of Africa is now reverberating with equal or greater fervor throughout a string of territories throwing off Soviet imperialism. To most observers, however, the collapse of European colonialism and Soviet communism share only superficial similarities. Conventional wisdom tells us that cultural disparities and vast geopolitical differences put Africa and the former Soviet Union in totally different camps.

Our acceptance of this hypothesis can be seen by the differing responses of the West to the end of the empire in both territories. Periodic concerns about Soviet expansionism in the Third World had underlain U.S. policy toward Africa for decades, but it was never so great a threat as to make the continent a priority in our foreign policy or to justify opposition to European withdrawal.

Widespread disputes in Africa—from lingering colonial wars in Portuguese territories to coups d'état, border disputes, secessionist movements, ethnic clashes, and the quest for majority rule in southern Africa—never posed a risk to the vital national interests of the West. A possible exception might be South Africa, where some stressed the importance of U.S. access to strategic minerals and to the sea route around the Cape of Good Hope.

History, however, tells us that concern over the Cape sea route and strategic minerals was exaggerated. No sub-Saharan country has ever denied the United States access to a vital strategic resource as a matter of policy. Even in Angola, where a local power struggle escalated into one of the most intense proxy wars on the continent involving military intervention from five countries, business carried on as usual. American companies continued to pump oil from installations protected from guerilla attacks by Cuban troops backing the Marxist government.

From the time of independence to the end of the Cold War, then, the geopolitical stakes remained low in Africa. They still are minimal in the minds of most observers, perhaps more than ever before. Unlike the former Soviet republics, Africa does not present the world with critical choices, such as what to do with leftover nuclear arsenals, looming international migration problems, or demands for massive financial bailouts. Nor did Africa ever present an extraterritorial threat to the global status quo; its sovereignty could be celebrated on its merits. Even in the 1960s, in the height of the Cold War with flashpoints of confrontation such as the Congo crisis, America identified with African anticolonialism.

African independence appealed to American values of individuality and freedom, to the sense of racial pride among the 12 percent of Americans who traced their ancestry to Africa, and to the Wilsonian ideal of self-determination—a principle whose moral validity at that time was not questioned and whose practical implementation, once the political winds had shifted, was accomplished by a stroke of the pen.

The collapse of the Soviet empire in the late 20th century, however, occurred in entirely different circumstances and triggered a totally different response than the collapse of the European colonial African empire in the mid-20th century. Initially thrilled by the demise of communism, America soon became deeply ambivalent about its aftermath. The universal desirability of the principle of self-determination so evident in African decolonization is no longer self-evident. As Mikhail Gorbachev warned, "The breakup of the largest country on the globe with 100 nationalities and sizable ethnic minorities in each of the republics could create new Yugoslavias."

Thirty-odd years after independence, that observation applies to Africa as well, a continent with twice the population, 20 times the number of nationalities, and deeper ethnic divisions than the former Soviet Union. Indeed, African "Yugoslavias" have already erupted in places like Liberia and Somalia, and more could be on the way.* It is no accident that Gorbachev and Mugabe have sounded similar alarms about the future.

The potential for conflict arising from the disintegration of the Soviet state has produced one of the biggest historical ironies of the century. When the empires of the United States' European allies shrank, people applauded without reservation; but when the empire of the United States' most menacing Cold War adversary dissolved, people began worrying immediately.

America responded to the birth of dozens of new nations in Africa by creating the Peace Corps, establishing the United States Agency for International Development (USAID), and launching a foreign aid program to help develop the world's poor. The birth of nations from the former Soviet Union, by contrast, has not spawned any initiatives of comparable importance. Rightly or wrongly, Americans are questioning their own national priorities and, consequently, not developing a coherent, confident response to the momentous changes underway. Who could have imagined in the 1960s, when Americans had a robust approach to the world despite the terror of nuclear brinkmanship, that paralysis would set in during the 1990s, following a historic ideological breakthrough?

The irony stems in large part from our misreading of underlying international realities. One of the contemporary realities not

---

*Written before events in Rwanda and Zaire.

fully appreciated is that, contrary to conventional wisdom, Africa and the Soviet Union have much in common. Their geopolitical significance to the West still is very different, but the internal sociopolitical and cultural characteristics of these two vast territories offer striking parallels. Ethnic and religious divisions, the scope of the economic crisis, the depths of popular discontent, the revolt against centralized authority, the lack of internal resources to meet looming calamities, and the fragility of emerging democracies are features common to both regions. The former Soviet Union is becoming Africanized to a degree never thought possible.

The long-range international implications of this development could be significant. If current trends continue, turmoil and fragmentation in African and former Soviet territories could create a new fault line in world politics. On the one side, a cluster of countries could arise and undergo what Gorbachev termed a "crisis of statehood," which puts borders, leadership structures, and sovereignties of entire regions in flux. On the other side, there could be a cluster of countries consolidating their statehood into supersovereignties or transnational associations, large power centers flexing muscles through either giant trading blocs, new political alignments, or revamped international organizations. The split, as Nelson Mandela recently warned, would also have an international economic dimension—a division between the abysmally poor and the superrich.

If this turns out to be the new world order, the North-South divide would be transformed. A smaller North, not necessarily united, would be dominated by Europe, the United States, and Japan. It would confront a New South, consisting of what Zbigniew Brzezinski once called an "arc of instability," stretching from Africa, as the poverty core, through the Middle East, the Persian Gulf, Soviet Central Asia, and South Asia. Islam would find fertile ground there, not as the crescent of Islamic fundamentalism that Brzezinski postulated, but rather as a wider belt of have-nots, some of which would be fundamentalists, others not. What would unite them is their common status; they would be more marginalized and alienated from the West than during the Cold War.

If such a chasm in world politics emerges, Africa will be at its bottom. In terms of the number of people whose lives are at risk,

Africa is worse off economically than any other region today. The Russian economy in free-fall is raising the specter of a former superpower sliding back toward the Middle Ages, as the *Washington Post* recently described the desperate situation. Moscow, it was reported, has houses that are now lit by candles and people who are bartering for necessities, an image that conveys the specter of a time bomb ready to explode.

In Africa, the lack of electricity is common and barter is a well-established form of trade; yet no one is pointing to these trends with alarm. This is not to ignore the urgency of the situation or diminish in any respect the problems of the Soviet republics. It is merely to note that in Africa, we ask not whether people can survive the season, after which things may calm down, but whether people can survive the decade.

To give you some idea of how deep the survival questions are in Africa, I will list briefly some of the major issues confronting the continent.

Low Economic Growth Rates. Breaking down the economic growth rates of the world by region shows great disparities. The overall gross national product (GNP) growth for developing countries in 1989 was 2.9 percent. It fell to 2.3 percent in 1990 because of Africa and what used to be the U.S.S.R. Between 1989 and 1990, GNP rose in Latin America (except in Brazil), the Middle East, and in East Asia, but dropped in Eastern Europe, Africa, and the former Soviet Union, counterbalancing the progress made elsewhere.

Population Pressure. At one time population pressure was a low priority in Africa because overall population density was considered low and land is abundant. Now population pressure is undermining Africa's economic progress, even in countries that have implemented structural reforms. This is because population density, land availability, and arability of the soil vary immensely on the continent.

About one-third of Africa is desert. Migration is increasing onto marginal lands and causing soil degradation, deforestation, desertification, and falling agricultural output. Eighty percent of

Africa's energy needs are supplied by firewood, which is in short supply. Poverty alongside population pressure will not lower the population growth rate. In fact, the greater the poverty, the greater the motivation to have children as an insurance policy in old age. Africa has the highest birthrate in the world, hovering around 3 percent. Current estimates indicate that the African population is going to double every 20 years, and by the year 2010, it will rise to one billion people.

Economic Isolation. Africa is the only region, apart from the emerging states in the former Soviet Union, not yet included in the process of regional economic integration and cooperation into multinational trading blocs. There is lip service for an African common market, but those who know Africa do not think it will come to pass very soon. There are emerging markets in the developing world, but they are mainly confined to Asia and Latin America, where flight capital is beginning to return.

Foreign investment was promised by the World Bank and the IMF to Africa when several countries adopted structural reform policies in the mid-1980s, but the capital has not materialized. The IMF asserts that good reformers who have adopted its recommended structural adjustment programs are performing well and have shown progress. That progress, however, is canceled by the population growth rate and the fact that external resources are not flowing back into the continent.

AIDS. AIDS is an enormous problem that has been severely ignored in Africa. A new study released this year reports that AIDS is spreading so rapidly that the most affected areas will show a net population loss within a few decades. Since AIDS disproportionately strikes the well-educated, productive urban workers, deaths would hit the economic elites, having a statistical impact on national per capita growth for years to come.

AIDS is spreading fastest in the middle states of Africa, where population density is high. Malawi, Rwanda, Uganda, Tanzania, and Zambia are now estimated by British researchers to have a staggering 24 to 37 percent of their population infected with AIDS. In the worst affected areas, the AIDS infection rate is doubling every one to three years, while in less affected regions, the rate is doubling every five years—a startlingly high rate.

The World Health Organization (WHO) estimates six million people are already infected with the HIV virus in sub-Saharan Africa—or one in 40 adults—and the number will increase to ten million by 1995. Two-thirds of the world's AIDS cases are in Africa, a continent with only 12 percent of the world's population. Next year, the total number of children infected with AIDS in Africa is expected to reach one million. By the middle of the decade, WHO says that AIDS will cause more deaths in sub-Saharan African children than either of the present top killers, malaria and measles. AIDS patients comprise 20 to 40 percent of inpatients of large urban hospitals in Central and Eastern Africa. One recent report stated that in Brazzaville, 70 percent of the hospital patients are AIDS-related cases. Tragically, the political violence in some countries jeopardize AIDS medical research projects. In Zaire, where a particularly important program was being conducted to find vital information to help fight the disease, foreign personnel have been evacuated after unpaid soldiers rioted throughout the country.

Debt. Africa's debt is crushing its ability to recover, even though the absolute sum, roughly $270 billion, is relatively small in absolute terms. Africa is in a debtor's prison: It cannot earn the foreign exchange necessary to repay its debt, since it has a falling share of world trade—from 3 to 2.5 percent over the past 30 years. Africa's debt is now greater than its total economic output. Because of debt service, more money is flowing out of the continent than in.

Famine. The United Nations estimates that 25 to 27 million people are at risk of starvation from famine caused by drought and war. In some countries, such as the Sudan, the government refuses to own up to the disaster, saying merely that there are "food deficits." Yet the Sudan represents roughly one-third of the total of African famine victims.

Corruption. Corruption is a universal complaint in Africa, but the extent of it varies widely. The political unrest that swept Africa in the last couple of years often was aimed against those who have enriched themselves at the expense of the people. President Mobutu Sese Seko of Zaire, for example, whose political future is now very much in doubt, is regarded as one of the world's richest men. His country is one of the world's poorest. In Mali, the fortune of an ex-president, General Moussa Traore, who was overthrown, was estimated to be over $2 billion. Swiss authorities confirmed that half of it was deposited in Switzerland. The total public funds embezzled from Mali is nearly the equal to the country's external debt.

Cases like this raise the specter of "dishonest debtors," those whose debt is the result of swindlers and autocrats as opposed to "honest debtors"—those who fell into bankruptcy because of external factors over which they had no control. Because of this image of "dishonest debtors," the rest of the world is reluctant to bail out or cancel debt in Africa, even for states that have changed governments, conducted elections, or otherwise tried to clean house.

External Disengagement. Another problem facing Africa is the trend of outside powers to disengage. Despite protests to the contrary, all former extraterritorial powers are lowering their presence in Africa. Former African allies that have been close to the United States, for example, have been left to fend for themselves. Witness what happened in Somalia and Liberia, two former close allies of the United States. The United States did little but watch these countries deteriorate into anarchy.

The big players in Africa now are the World Bank and the IMF. They are the driving forces behind the economic reform programs in 30 out of 47 sub-Saharan countries. Donor fatigue, preoccupation with other problems, and the primacy of domestic issues in the Western world will mean that bilateral donors will be unlikely to respond on their own to African needs that will cost money.

Refugees. One-third of the world's refugee population is in Africa, roughly 5.5 million out of an estimated 17 million people. Including displaced persons, there are actually 19 million refugees in Africa, some of whom are pouring into Europe, causing racial problems. The Liberians are knocking on the doors of the United States and claiming there is a racial preference that denies Liberians access to the United States—a refrain similar to that which is heard from the Haitians.

The United States is the largest single financier of international refugee assistance. Washington pays 25 percent of the United Nations program and 20 percent of the International Committee of the Red Cross program. Unless there is a major turnaround in Africa, the refugee burden on the international community will increase.

Failed Development Strategies. A recent review of development strategies by Doug Porter, Bryant Allen, and Gaye Thompson estimated that one in three agricultural projects funded with outside economic assistance failed in West Africa and more than five in ten failed in East Africa. The reasons are mixed. Political considerations sometimes overrode economic rationality. Sometimes the project design and implementation by outside experts was poor, and sometimes the wishes of the local population were not taken into account. In any event, there is a consensus that the billions of dollars poured into African development efforts have not yet worked.

Political Turmoil. News of some rather stunning events in Africa has led commentators to conclude that the continent is entering its second stage of independence with a shift toward democracy. While some countries, such as Benin and Zambia, have broken new ground in the field of democracy, it is premature to declare Africa democratic. There is an encouraging trend underway, but it is very fragile. The movement could result, in some instances, in open government, but that does not necessarily translate into good or stable government. Elections in Africa must be seen against other harsh realities that are undermining the quest for accountability and representative government.

For example, ethnic clashes have erupted again in Burundi, where there have been some of the biggest ethnic massacres in Africa. In Liberia, a negotiated settlement after a brutal civil eruption and collapse of government is only limping along.

Pauline H. Baker

Nigeria, Africa's most populist country, is promising to turn military rule over to the civilians, but old habits are beginning to emerge. There has been vote buying, communal riots, and corruption.

The Sudan is becoming a repressive, fundamentalist Islamic state. As the largest country in Africa, it could be a gateway for the spread of fundamentalist Islamic governments elsewhere on the continent.

Zaire has no real government. The economy is in ruins as the country runs out of food and fuel. A big explosion could occur right in the heart of Africa.

Southern Africa has a chance of turning things around, if settlements in Angola, Mozambique, and South Africa come to fruition.

This litany of survival issues depicts a continent living on the razor's edge. An article by Vladimir Titov published in *International Affairs* spelled out some of the implications of this dire situation. He was the former acting deputy director of the Directorate of International Organization in the Soviet Ministry of Foreign Affairs. After returning from a trip to Africa, he made three key points: First, he stressed that of all of the regions in the world, Africa was the least prepared for the dissolution of the bipolar world. It still has not gotten a bearing on how it fits into the global environment. Second, Africa sees itself as now confronting a dispassionate and self-absorbed North; it worries that the North's economic confrontation with the disunited South could become the principal component of the future. Finally, he warned that in our own self-interest, Africa cannot be ignored: "No stable international order can be set up or efficiently managed through global cooperation mechanisms without the participation of the continent which disposes of a nonaligned majority and a third of the United Nations votes."

On the map of international politics, Africa is oversaturated with destabilization problems. In many respects, it is the vulnerable link without which positive global change on issues ranging from democratization to AIDS, can occur. Mr. Titov urged new mechanisms of economic cooperation with Africa based on real interests and he postulated a future of direct links between republics of the former Soviet Union and their African partners. Whether there is economic compatibility in that relationship is questionable. But if Africa is left out of the equation, it could create a new protest platform in world politics.

What is clear is that Africa will be the development challenge of the 21st century. The sooner that people own up to that fact, the better. Otherwise, the North will face mounting financial, refugee, environmental, health, and possibly revolutionary political problems of an entire continent in distress.

QUESTION: I was struck by the realism of your survey of the continent and wondered whether there is any cause for optimism on what is going on in southern Africa in the last two years, specifically, the resolution of that 15-year war in Angola and the 50-year confrontation in South Africa. You addressed Zambia in the context of the AIDS epidemic, but for the moment there appears to be some progress there towards reasonably democratic political processes.

There are people on the economic side who talk about sustainable development, and in spite of the overwhelming environmental and demographic factors you have outlined, they are proposing development schemes that are more locally ruled and imbedded in the communities. These development projects depend less on borrowing foreign capital and technology. Can you suggest any windows through which to look for solutions?

MS. BAKER: To deal with your last point first, I believe the West deals with these problems in a very fragmented way. People who work on AIDS or environmental issues do not usually work on general problems of economic development in Africa. In a fragmented, highly specialized, and compartmentalized policy community, few are assessing the big picture.

Last month I conducted an informal survey in which I asked a number of Africanists who work on economic development what work they had done on the impact of AIDS on economic development, and they said they were not doing anything. Only the health specialists were working on it. People simply are not factoring in

AIDS, which is going to have a tremendous impact on Africa's growth potential.

My recommendation would be to have a meeting similar to the Bretton Woods meeting, where specific resources are allocated to Africa, targeting particular objectives and problems, such as AIDS. Unfortunately, however, I do not think that an international response on this scale is around the corner. Preoccupation with the former Soviet Union and other crises is going to dominate world action for a while.

To address your larger point, however, there are some grounds for optimism. Even if the emerging African democracies do not last, there is a growing movement for dissent, change, and multi-party government, at least among the urban elites. After living in Africa for 11 years and watching it closely for nearly three decades, I have seen this before. Sometimes democracies become worse than military rule if they are characterized by irresponsible elites, corruption, and people disenchanted with democracy. So patience is required. Democracy needs to be nurtured, but the stirrings are there.

Those democracies that are created in Africa are born poor and therefore are at grave risk. Zambia is a good illustration. As the most highly urbanized state in Africa, the structural adjustment program is inevitably going to increase discontent because, to many, democracy also means not tolerating any more economic pain. Economic deliverance is not going to happen right away; structural reforms shift resources from urban areas to the agricultural sector, which still has not developed a political voice. Zambia is in for some hard times ahead.

Angola and South Africa are two other bright spots on the horizon, South Africa more than Angola. Like Namibia, once Angola has an election, everyone will probably pull out and the country will be on its own. South Africa has many resources and is of great symbolic importance, but it still has a long way to go. People think that because apartheid laws have been repealed, it is all over. This country represents the vortex of the ideological spectrum in the world today. Everything is represented in South Africa—from a Communist Party on the left to a neo-Nazi Party on the right; from a very poor, landless class in rural areas to wealthy elites and powerful corporate conglomerates in the cities.

Squatters are pouring into South African towns by the millions; the unemployment rate among blacks is 40 percent and rising. The white population is supporting the change, for now. There are those, however, who want to bring back apartheid and have their own white homeland. Apartheid is one form of tyranny that is not going to be ended merely with a stroke of a pen.

Nevertheless, people regard South Africa as the savior of the continent with its vast wealth and talent. African countries must recognize that they cannot benefit from South Africa without first correcting their own domestic problems.

Moreover, pent-up demands in South Africa among its own black population is great. Demands to redistribute wealth internally and to generate more social equity will have to be met if South Africa is going to be an anchor upon which others can build on the continent.

QUESTION: When I was head of the African side of the British Foreign Office and later ambassador to some dozen countries at once, I felt that decolonization, the main job of the European powers, was to find markets for African products. After all, the African countries had been built up as colonial economies designed to market African products in Europe. Europe now buys less coffee, bananas, and other products from Latin America and more from Africa. Therefore, to list grounds for optimism, you might list the conscientious policy of the European Community to ensure that markets exist for African produce. For the foreseeable future, Africa will have to buy not only medical equipment, but electric light bulbs, transport equipment, and everything else, and it is essential for Europeans to provide markets.

There will possibly be some markets for African products in Asia. The United States is unlikely to provide large markets for African produce. Therefore, considerable responsibility rests on Europe to make economic transition possible. As a non-European, what do you believe to be the European contribution to the development of Africa? What is the future of the commercial agreements between the Lomé powers and the European Community?

Pauline H. Baker

MS. BAKER: Africa is very concerned about the issue of whether or not the Lomé Convention would be sustainable after 1992, particularly when the poorer countries in Europe are already saying they come first. You are right about the contribution that Europe has made to Africa in terms of developing markets, although many Africans say that was self-serving in order to fuel its own industrial growth.

The debate now is whether to stress export-led growth or food security. Most African countries cannot feed themselves, and if they continue to supply products to feed Europe, they are victimized by fluctuating commodity prices. A one-crop economy is destroyed when the price plummets. The argument has been that dwelling on one commodity exported to Europe or other markets has made African countries even more vulnerable; they have to diversify and stress food security—the ability to grow their own grains.

Nigeria banned the importation of American rice and wheat, for example, in order to grow its own to feed its people. The United States, however, has a trade dispute with Nigeria because it imports oil and is blocked from selling grain, causing a huge trade imbalance. The Africans have a point when they say they cannot continue to stress only export of primary commodities without having any control over the price. Perhaps price stabilization can be reached or a package deal could be put together that would include debt and economic reform. To deal with it in isolation, just in terms of markets, is a mistake. It leaves Africans at a complete disadvantage.

COMMENT: The Lomé negotiations of the European Community included educational, health, and other foreign aid. France does much more than Britain does in Africa, but they are beginning to pull out because of the lack of African response. France would be willing to jack things up again if there could be, as you suggest, a package deal.

When I last talked to some of the African embassies in Paris, they stressed that it must remain global and include health and educational aid; you cannot deal with trade alone.

QUESTION: The burden of arms purchases and the military rests on all of these countries. The taxation, either in kind or in money, on the economies and on the people must be enormous to buy munitions and maintain armies. Is there something the United States can do to alleviate that burden?

MS. BAKER: Efforts in the past to get coordinated arms transfers policy have never worked because no one respects them. The Africans claim to have a legitimate right to mount a defense like anyone else. Though many are conscious of the economic drain this creates, the reality is that African armies are very important to the domestic stability (or instability) of these countries. The straw that broke the camel's back in Zaire, for example, was that the army was not being paid. Soldiers started rioting with popular discontent pouring out on top of it.

COMMENT: You gain the impression that every teenager has a machine gun!

MS. BAKER: In some places, it is close to being just that sort of situation. You cannot count the number of armies left by the legacies of the Cold War in Somalia, for example. Children operate sophisticated arms because of the stockpiles accumulated from U.S. and Soviet aid, the latter almost exclusively military. When Somalia switched superpower patrons with Ethiopia, the United States became the new patron and began stocking arms. Warlords have armories there now, which anyone strong enough to open the door can seize.

QUESTION: As bilateral donors pull out, can private volunteer organizations, both from the United States and from other countries, play a significant role? Will that be a problem as far as not having a global perspective?

MS. BAKER: There are two kinds of private voluntary organizations. One are the humanitarian organizations trying to hang in there as much as possible, but when the lives of their own technical workers are at stake, they also must pull out, which is what happened in Zaire and Sudan. Warring bands fire on Red Cross trucks as easily as they fire on anyone else, but humanitarian organizations are making breakthroughs at least on relieving famine. For them, there might be some optimism because there is growing consensus about the legitimacy of humanitarian intervention because of what happened in Iraq with the Kurds. That principle might also be employed in Africa where warring sides do not allow food in for starving people.

The other kind of private voluntary organizations are those that help entrepreneurs or train and educate people. That group is definitely moving toward Eastern Europe and the former Soviet Union. Someone involved in monitoring the whole world of PVOs indicated recently that many of them are getting involved in Eastern Europe as an amplification of their current programs, and that they find that there is a bigger return on their investment than in Africa. The money and political interest are there to sustain those kinds of projects now, so many are shifting away from Africa and jeopardizing PVO development assistance in Africa.

QUESTION: One of the greater problems is being able to support themselves on the food they can produce. While desert and dry land characterize much of Africa, I observed considerable lushness and fertility in western Africa. Why is it not possible to support home agriculture and have enough papaya, tropical fruits, and fish from the rivers by making more of a continental effort?

MS. BAKER: First of all, the image of Africa having unlimited fruit to pick from the trees is misleading. One of the environmental disasters beginning to appear in Africa as a result of population pressure is that the area that actually has a tropical rain forest—which actually represents only about 10 percent of the land mass—is small and diminishing. The desert is moving, particularly the Sahara.

One of a number of complicated reasons why existing resources have not been exploited, however, is economic mismanagement. In most postcolonial African countries, the state dominated the economy, whether leaders called themselves socialists or not. State marketing boards did not pay a sufficient price to farmers because the state took the difference between the world price and the producer price. This situation, combined with falling world prices of certain products like cocoa, diminished production.

In Nigeria, one of the few countries that had a diversified agricultural base, oil took over. Nigeria used to be the second largest producer of groundnuts (peanuts) in the world. When I lived in Nigeria during the 1960s, there used to be giant pyramids of bags of peanuts in the north. Groundnuts were the country's biggest foreign exchange earner. Then oil completely wiped out the groundnut industry. Combined with failed development projects, disease, and so forth, farmers have gotten the short end of the stick.

QUESTION: Many things about Africa are truly disheartening, but the root cause would seem to be low levels of education, making it difficult for the people to govern themselves properly or develop any kind of economy. Also, tribal culture intrudes on reasonableness within given countries or between countries. We hear about it in South Africa and throughout West Africa. Since that has gone on for centuries, what is the hope of bridging the gap?

MS. BAKER: I am not so sure which comes first. With development comes diminished ethnic conflict, but many believe that there needs to be diminished ethnic conflict before development. Obviously, they probably go together.

Education is the one area since the 1960s in which Africa has made some real progress. Many governments channeled money into health and education, but because of failing economies, even those social expenditures are drying up.

When I first started teaching in the 1960s at the University of Lagos, I had night classes, and the university did not even have money to change the light bulbs in the room. I brought my own light bulbs and had to change them myself. That is a measure of the poverty. Nonetheless, elites were educated. They are largely heading the demand for more open government today.

COMMENT: The more thoroughly one studies African problems, the closer to insolubility they become. The magnitude of the problem of AIDS can be compared to the 14th century plague.

Because it is such an enormous epidemic, there seems to be no likelihood that any organized effort by the rest of the world will be sufficient.

The one optimistic thing you mentioned was that one country's huge debt was equal to the amount of the previous ruler's wealth. Perhaps there is hope if they could find an honest ruler and could keep some revenue.

MS. BAKER: I hope that is the case.

QUESTION: How many farmers did the United States put out of action all over the world by dumping its excess agricultural production in the Food-for-Peace program? There is a great deal of propaganda in the Congress about that.

MS. BAKER: There are mixed arguments about Food-for-Peace. On one hand, it put some local farmers out of work, as essentially it was a subsidy program for our own farmers. On the other hand, you cannot deny the overwhelming humanitarian needs in Africa.

Again, it comes back to fragmentation. The food program should be administered in such a way that it does not devastate the local economy of the recipient countries. The Food-for-Peace program operates independently. Rarely do the local communities, USAID, and Food-for-Peace closely coordinate actions. There is dialogue, but not an actual implementation of programs that involves them all.

COMMENT: Before things broke down too much in Zaire, the British military had a proper statistical base testing the army in Zaire, which they found to be 90 percent HIV positive!

MS. BAKER: Armies are one of the main transmitters of the HIV virus.

QUESTION: If you look at the 1980s apart from Angola and South Africa, can you find areas of light in terms of economic policies—areas where states that perhaps appeared to be decomposing have bounced back and reincorporated the peasantry into the economy?

A second question is, What do you think the consequences of AIDS are actually going to be? Clearly, it is going to be catastrophic for the urban sector, but presumably if it does kill many people, there will be advantages in the rural areas in terms of pressure on ecology and the environment. Is something like the economic boom that took place in the 14th century after the Black Death possible?

If Africa in the 1960s at the height of the Cold War did not attract international attention, what factors other than the complete decomposition of Africa is likely to engender the North's interest in addressing these problems? Will people simply see the progressive marginalization of Africa?

MS. BAKER: There are examples in which the peasantry has been reincorporated into the economy. One of the effects of the IMF structural adjustment programs has been to open economic opportunities for the agricultural sector, which in some countries has resulted in increased agricultural productivity. The question is not whether the peasantry has been reincorporated into the economy, however. The question is whether the peasantry has been reincorporated into the political system. In other words, do they have a vote that counts so that more health and education benefits return to the rural sectors? That really has not happened yet.

The people who are calling the shots are still largely those in the urban areas. The question that must be asked is whether the democratization that is beginning to occur is simply a rotation of elites, with essentially the same system, or is it an institutionalization of democratic values and ideals?

As for AIDS, more and more people are beginning to understand the dimensions of the problem. They do compare it to the Middle Ages and the bubonic plague, throw up their hands, and say there is nothing they can do and that in any event, this might be the precursor of a recovery.

Apart from the moral problems I have with that, I also think realistically it is wrong. African economies and societies are so fragile that no one can escape the AIDS epidemic; institutions will be too eroded to make a comeback for some time. AIDS is also beginning to penetrate rural areas, which means that farmers will be contracting it. Many women are getting it as well. In societies that practice polygamy, women and children are going to be among the primary victims. It is best to mount an aggressive program to stop it now.

There has been some very effective AIDS education programs started in Africa, including some aimed at children. AIDS transmission in Africa is primarily heterosexual. In order to stem the epidemic, there must be a change of behavior, and that is very difficult. Sometimes you have the wrong change of behavior. For example, some older men, fearing liaisons with women who may infect them, now choose younger women with whom to have liaisons. Therefore, if the men are carriers, AIDS jumps across generations. For both moral reasons and because of what the impact might be, it is a mistake to merely sit back and let it happen.

What will interest the North in Africa? It will be when people here begin to understand that the roots of some of their problems are coming from Africa, when refugees pour out of Africa in large waves, for example, like refugees pouring over the Mexican border toward the North. This will occur mostly in Europe, but many will also call at the door of the United States. Liberians, for example, are saying, "America got so much out of Liberia; it was a special relationship. It was the closest thing to an American colony; there is a moral obligation there." That message, however, is not getting through yet.

AIDS is a global problem, and solving it in this country means conducting research in Africa and finding answers on that continent as well. The global environment is another issue. On these matters, which touch all of us, you cannot quarantine a continent. No walls can be put up on environmental decay, disease, or refugees. There will be a price to pay when the financial burden becomes too great. Americans cannot just turn their backs on these problems; eventually, the United States will have to help pay for refugees, humanitarian aid, and so forth. As the problems become overwhelming, there will be some awareness that the United States has something at stake in dealing with the problems of Africa.

QUESTION: When do you think that will be?

MS. BAKER: Perhaps in ten years time, a shift may begin to occur. I say ten years because things are changing in this country with regard to increasing racial and ethnic problems. People in the United States are also being educated about Africa. A recent survey looking at African education revealed surprisingly that the United States has a higher concentration of people studying Africa than any other country in the world.

Within the next decade, people may begin to get more consciousness and awareness, both because of what is happening in Africa and because of domestic trends toward greater racial sensitivity in this country. Awareness of the New South, which will embrace the Central Asian republics, the Middle East, South Asia, and Africa, will generate a new voice for the world's poor in international circles. Maybe people will be compelled to start paying attention.

NARRATOR: This kind of futuristic analysis could have benefited private organizations that initiated African programs during the euphoria of the 1960s. The real dimensions of the problem are now with us, and the type of realism heard during this presentation puts us on firmer ground. We thank Dr. Baker very much.

CHAPTER TWO

Civility, Incivility, and Democratization: The Politics of Civil Society in Africa*

ROBERT FATTON

NARRATOR: Professor Robert Fatton was born in Port-au-Prince, Haiti. He received master's and doctoral degrees from the University of Notre Dame. Professor Fatton has taught primarily at the University of Virginia, but has also taught at the School of Advanced International Studies in Washington.

Professor Fatton is the author of a number of well-reviewed and much-discussed books: *Black Consciousness in South Africa: The Dialectics of Ideological Resistance to White Supremacy*; *The Making of Liberal Democracy: Senegal's Passive Revolution, 1975-1985*; and *Predatory Rule: State and Civil Society in Africa*. He has also contributed to numerous books, including *The Anti-Apartheid Reader: South Africa and the Struggle Against White Rule, Women and the State in Africa*, and *Political Leaders of Contemporary Africa South of the Sahara*. He has also written many articles carrying further themes that he has developed.

What is most impressive to me about today's speaker is that he has in a relatively short time achieved a meteoric rise among African scholars. He has been recognized as one of the five or six leading scholars working in his area. His scholarship has become known to a number of professional societies, and he has spoken at

---

*Presented in a Forum at the Miller Center of Public Affairs on 27 October 1993.

conferences around the country and abroad. This kind of intellectual growth and development is something of which not only can Professor Fatton be proud, but the University of Virginia as well can feel pride in his accomplishments.

MR. FATTON: What I will discuss today is really a short version of a much longer project of civil society in Africa. For our present purposes, I will concentrate only on the relation between civil society and the ongoing processes of democratization. I argue that if civil society is to be a useful, heuristic tool in deciphering contemporary African politics, it must be conceptualized as the realm of collective solidarities generated by processes of class formation, ethnic inventions, and religious revelations. As such, civil society will not always embody the peaceful harmony of associational pluralism, nor does its opposition to the state necessarily spell freedom. In fact, civil society in Africa is conflict-ridden and prone to Hobbesian wars of "all against all" and is a prime repository of invented ethnic hierarchies, conflicting class visions, patriarchal domination, and irredentist identities that fuel deadly conflicts in many areas of the continent.

Rather than embodying coherent social projects, civil society tends to be a disorganized plurality of mutually exclusive projects that are not necessarily democratic. To this extent and in a limited sense, civil society has to be conceptualized in the plural rather than in the singular. As such, I contend that three types of civil society are vying for power in Africa, and their emergence stems from three fundamental processes encapsulating three distinct and conflicting social projects of three major political blocs: the predatory coalition, the middle sectors, and the subordinate classes that coincide roughly with the existing demarcation of class and status. These blocs thus enter into relations of struggles and compromises with each other, making politics a calculus of uncertainties. Such uncertainties, however, are not overwhelming, but are regulated by the existing distribution of endowments and the constraining presence of the state and civil society. To that extent, certain classes are clearly more equal than others. Moreover, class position is never an absolute determinant of collective and individual behavior.

Class solidarity in Africa has indeed been fragmented and altogether supplanted by other powerful identities such as religion, gender, or ethnicity.

In contemporary Africa, these identities have shaped decisively the process of class formation, but they have neither obliterated the realities of class politics nor denied the increasing salience of class hierarchies, which in turn reflect profound inequalities in life, resulting in what Basil Davidson has described as "the absolute hostility between rulers and ruled."

By the early 1990s, however, that stultifying and often deadly impasse, where power and participation had become sore enemies of one another, was suddenly overcome in an unexpected series of *conferences nationales* and democratizing pacts throughout much of Africa. This is how the process of democratization began, but it is exceedingly fragile and contradictory and has no predetermined outcome.

Confronting a massive and devastating fiscal crisis of their own making, predatory rulers in Africa are bent on systematically contracting out services previously performed by the state and on benefiting from the corresponding enlargement of private property rights. They use their entrenched positions in the state in an effort to shape the growth of civil society as an arena over which they can impose what in French is called *le projet disciplinaire*, the disciplinary project, and pursue their own private corporate interests.

The goal of those predatory rulers is a controlled liberalization that would not evolve to full-scale democratization. They seek to revamp and consolidate the old system of constitution without constitutionalism in which civil society is a zone of limited pluralism and functions as their own private estate. Such revamping is difficult to achieve, for however reformed, a constitution without constitutionalism is ultimately incompatible with liberalization, let alone democratization. It is not easy to conceive how a system that presupposes a shrewd political arena, lorded over by a presidential monarch whose power is personalized and immune from all legal processes, can tolerate the renewal of perfect debate and civil freedoms for a long or even a modest period of time.

Liberalization of predatory rule is inherently short-lived, terminating in either the process of re-dictatorialization or leading to full-scale democratization, while holding forth the catastrophic alternative of descending into a hellish war of all against all. This is not to say that liberalization (of predatory rule) cannot temporarily assuage the opposition and preserve the predator's power. Predatory rulers are not all incompetent, and the degree of their predatoriness varies. Some may possess the statecraft that allows them to develop preemptive strategies of co-optation through which an imminent downfall can be avoided. They may even acquiesce to elections and national conferences, but they do so only when convinced of their capacity to maintain presidential monarchism.

Clearly, however, there can be gross miscalculations. Presidential monarchs can embark on processes of reform that rapidly escape their control and eventuate in their own demise. Former President Mathieu Kérékou of Benin acceded reluctantly to a political opening, only to face a sovereign national conference that emasculated his power and led to his ultimate electoral defeat. Kenneth Kaunda, the father of Zambia's independence, legalized multipartisan politics in an effort to regain legitimacy and ended up suffering a humiliating rout at the polls.

Some miscalculations have been even more costly. For example, when Mali's President Moussa Traoré rejected popular calls for full-scale democratization, which his timid liberalization generated, he was overthrown in a violent coup and arrested.

Such outcomes, however, are not the rule. Presidential monarchs manipulate political structures and decapitate a divided opposition. Benefiting from the fragmentation of what had been earlier united democratizing coalitions, Kenya's Arap Moi, Cameroon's Paul Biya, Gabon's Omar Bongo, and Côte d'Ivoire's Houphouët Boigny emerged victorious from staged electoral dramas that were fault-ridden and reluctantly enacted. Liberalization of this kind, unlikely to offer any long-term solution to the dilemma of constitution without constitutionalism, only serves to delay the ultimate collapse of predatory rule.

Such collapse, however, does not imply necessarily an extrication from authoritarian politics, nor does the defeat of a dictatorship inevitably imply successful liberalization. In fact, the collapse of predatory rule may unleash pathos and centrifugal forces, degenerating into civil strife, ethnic violence, and personalistic confrontations. The experiences of Somalia, Liberia, Angola, and Mozambique indicate clearly that the fear and the ugly realities of hellish wars of all against all do not necessarily compel political actors into accepting democratizing pacts and "satisficing" the interests of everyone without maximizing those of any. Liberalization thus navigates between the Scylla of settling on unpredictable democratic outcomes and the Charybdis of violent chaos.

Democracy by its very nature creates uncertainties. If democracy is to succeed at all, however, it must equalize and regulate these uncertainties. It cannot tolerate the erratic, capricious, and arbitrary absolutism that characterizes presidential monarchism.

As one of the fictional heroes of Chinua Achebe's *Anthills of the Savannah* put it:

> Worshipping a dictator is such a pain in the ass. It wouldn't be so bad if it was merely a matter of dancing upside down on your head. With practice, anyone could learn to do that. The real problem is having no way of knowing from one day to another, from one minute to the next, just what is up and what is down.

Democratic governance requires a different sort of uncertainty, one contained within and structured by the predictable system of rules. Most critically, political actors at a minimum must be convinced that the uncertainties of defeat do not outweigh the gains of a possible future victory. The precondition for the establishment of such convictions is the institutionalization of uncertainty within a predictable system in which outcomes are neither permanent nor arbitrary. In Africa, such institutionalization is in turn mediated by the impact of transnational power relations and the nature of civil society. In current transnational power relations, it is clear that predatory rulers can no longer automatically depend on external forces in order to maintain their rule. The end of the Cold War has led to the dissolution of foreign support for dictatorships to a significant degree and the global ideological ascendancy of liberal democratic values.

The process of democratization in Africa, however, increasingly reflects the domestic balance of power among the differing actors.

Now isolated from their erstwhile foreign friends, predatory rulers seek to establish an alliance with the middle sector in order to contain the bold challenges of popular groups and resist full-scale democratization. It is an alliance that is by no means assured, given the middle sector's ambiguous political and material interests.

The democratic and professional class of the middle sectors that has been increasingly excluded from the prebend of predatory rule as found in the associational life of civil society—the means to acquire status, power, and money, supported by international agencies and committed to the magic of the market—seeks the democratization of authoritarian polities by entrenching itself into civil society as the watchdog that curbs the monopolizing claims of the state. The ultimate goal of the middle sectors is the implantation of constitution with constitutionalism in a system of individual rights that upholds the sanctity of private property and the pursuit of market gains.

The middle sector's commitment to democracy is largely opportunistic, tending to reflect their incapacity to share power with intransigent predatory rulers and their growing exclusion from the shrinking pool of prebendal gains. Hence, the middle sectors need to mobilize popular civil society to realize their social project. Necessity transforms them into pseudo-liberal democratizers who push for minimal liberal democracy with the support of a mobilized popular civil society. Once the predators advocate the deceits of power and gain the right to rule from the founding election, however, the middle sectors will undermine the very minimal rights of liberal democracy they helped to establish, as they feel threatened by an increasingly assertive popular civil society. The short history of national conferences and democratizing pacts seems to confirm this somber scenario.

The processes of democratization set in motion by the rage of subordinate groups in the face of intransigent and corrupt predatory regimes were soon hijacked by the middle sectors. In the following instance, however, national conferences have resulted in the electoral triumph and disproportionate empowerment of the middle sectors. After performing the initial and decisive act of resistance in what has been called "Benin's Miracle," *le peuple* (the people) lost control of its own creation when in February 1990 the authorities reluctantly convened Benin's National Conference, Africa's first and arguably most successful conference. *Le peuple* was eclipsed and supplanted by the middle sectors, *les fonctionnaires* (the functionaries), as the African social scientist, Eboussi Boulaga, calls them.

This is not to deny the therapeutic and liberating elements of national conferences. National conferences have served as the conduit through which the overwhelming and salutary critiques of the abuses, mismanagement and corruption of predatory rule can be voiced and have thus generated democratizing processes and contributed to political equalization.

The new leaders of Benin, the Congo, Cape Verde, Niger, Madagascar, Cote d'Ivoire, and Senegal, are all a part of a newly emergent technocratic class steeped in the legal and banking network of international finance. The minimal liberal state that these members of the middle sectors are seeking to implant is already facing critical challenges. The material basis of a minimal liberal state remains too fragile to effectively sustain its liberal, ideological commitments. The survival of democracy is not just a matter of ideological conviction, but the people must acquire the sense that economic performance is fair and effective and that their self-interest is not altogether scoffed out. This sense of economic fairness and efficiency is, of course, even more difficult to foster in the midst of profound structural adjustment programs. By further eroding the already fragile welfare system, promoting market rationality, and simultaneously transforming property relations, structural adjustment programs are likely to generate greater political discontent and plunge society into the uncertainties of polarized instability.

The consequences of structural adjustment are thus likely to have devastating effects on the long-term consolidation of democratic regimes. Here authoritarian temptation and/or descent into chaos are dangerous alternatives that are constantly lurking behind the curtain of the democratic premier. Given this circumstance, how can extrication from dictatorship succeed? How can democracy be implanted, consolidated, and expanded? This is the Gordian Knot of African politics, and only the empowerment of popular society can cut it. This empowerment, however, faces manifold obstacles. Subordinate groups in Africa comprising the unemployed, the poor, and the underpaid people of rural and urban areas seek to constitute the popular civil society with basic networks of survival designed to counter the devastating impact of predatory rule. These basic networks of survival are meant to replace decaying and vanishing public services and fill the gap left by an increasingly indifferent state. These structures come hesitantly into the open from the structural foundations of what James Scott has called "infrapolitics." In this infrapolitical world, demarcated from the public stage, subordinate groups express in coded words their outrage at official justice and the notoriety of those lording it over them.

In Kenya, for instance, poor and powerless Luos utter frequently among themselves the phrase *Naling' aling'a*, "I just kept quiet," to appeal to their shared sense of fairness and communicate their anger at the abuses they have suffered. As Cynthia Hoehler-Fatton has explained, "The statement can often be slightly ominous, for it suggests that the speaker may secretly be garnering the strength to strike back at a later date." Thus, when those who keep quiet muster the means, the resources, and the courage to break their silence, they explode into the public stage as relevant actors in national politics. Breaking the silence may merely result in a *reglemont de compte*, or it may acquire the potency of public protest and open revolt.

For example, in March of 1992 when Kenyan martyrs, who had been fasting in protest against the political imprisonment of their sons, were brutally assaulted by the police, they disrobed in public to voice their absolute outrage of such violence. This display of nakedness at Nairobi's Freedom Corner was meant to be in the words of the participant, "the curse to the authorities"—the time of *Naling' aling'a*, of keeping quiet, had passed. The war of words was no longer confined to the infrapolitics of subordinate groups. It became a public expression of defiance to those in power, symbolizing the public declaration of the angst of subordinate groups and the emergence of popular civil society as an effective political force.

Embedded in the informal economy, voicing utter contempt for the powers that be, and expressing a sense of communal defense against the abuses of state power, popular civil society has clear social democratic impulses. It is cognizant of the fact that without a social policy that protects at least those whose subsistence is threatened by the reforms, the political conditions for the continuation of reforms become eroded. Thus, popular civil society must be fundamentally opposed to the revamped constitution, which exists without and seeks to transcend the obdurate impairments of the minimal liberal state as advocated by predatory rulers. Popular civil society articulates the need for the protection of the democratic collective rights of subordinate groups and classes.

As we have argued previously, national conferences and democratizing pacts would have never materialized without the protests, strikes, and overall energy of the subordinates who in all cases represent the determinant social force that has compelled predatory rulers to accept transitions to more politically accountable regimes. To put it bluntly, democracy is impossible without the empowerment of subordinate classes, the working class in particular. Yet, neither predatory rulers nor middle sectors favor such empowerment, and subordinate classes have to wrest it from them. Given this fact, democracy in Africa becomes a function of the balance of power between these three political blocs. The denser and more hegemonic popular civil society, the more likely is the implantation and consolidation of democracy. In fact, it is only when the forces of civil society, in particular popular civil society, are institutionalized that such a consolidation can have a real chance of materializing.

The making of a long-lasting democracy is a virtual impossibility without the emergence of political society as an arena in which the polity specifically arranges itself for political contestation to gain control over public and state power. Unless civil society can generate an effective political society, extrication from dictatorial rule can easily degenerate into a sham democracy or a new dictatorship.

The capacity of subordinate groups to organize effective and autonomous trade unions, political parties, and other associational agencies is contingent, however, on the existence of certain spaces of political freedom, which in turn require liberalizing coalitions with the middle sectors for the conquest of at least a minimal liberal democracy. The democratic project of subordinate classes cannot be realized without a provisional or tactical alliance with the middle sectors. The alliance is necessary, given that the power of the subordinates is severely debilitated by their daily struggles for survival under conditions of extreme deprivation, by their limited organizational resources, and by their long habituation to the subalternity of infrapolitics.

The limited size of the working class and the difficulties of institutionalizing contribute to the further erosion of the already debilitated power of subordinates in Africa. Thus, popular civil society is politically weak. If it is at all feasible the democratic project entails, at least initially, the combined mobilization of both popular and liberal civil societies. The mix, however, is full of ambiguities, antinomies, and contradictions and is by no means assured. The middle sector's relation to predatory regimes tends to be tenuous as the cost of sacrificing relatively affluent lifestyles and of rejecting individual prebends mount with the passage of time.

While the middle sectors may support the idea of a liberal state, they may quickly feel threatened by the mobilization of popular society and opt for an easy compromise with the existing dictatorship. Given their ideological individualism and their fear of subordinates, they are prone to all sorts of opportunistic defections from democratizing coalitions and to personal accommodation with the authoritarian bloc. For instance, in March 1993 Faustin Birindwa, a major leader of the Sovereign National Conference that called for an end to President Mobutu's dictatorship and co-founder of the Union for Democracy and Social Progress, Zaire's most important political opposition, succumbed to temptation and became prime minister of Mobutu. In doing so, Birindwa formed a rival government to be headed by his long-time ally, Etienne Tshisekedi, whom the National Conference had appointed prime minister of the Transitional High Council of the Republic.

Birindwa's *volte-face* exacerbated this iron crisis as the country was governed by two rival governments and prime ministers. The dramatis personae in the crisis were locked in a dangerous equilibrium of forces, with neither the democratizing bloc nor the despotic Mobutu coalition capable of imposing its agenda on the other. In the interregnum, Zaire is hovering on the verge of utter catastrophe. Birindwa's journey from the opposition to capitulation to Mobutu is symptomatic of the fact that certain segments of the middle sectors are likely to enter into the most compromising agreements with authoritarianism when confronted by the vicissitudes and hardships of democratization. They are likely to turn against democratization unless the middle sectors perceive the overthrow of presidential monarchism as a rather immediate possibility involving neither a social revolution from below nor the chaos inherent in fundamental transformations. Predatory rule can thus resurrect from the ashes of failed liberalizations and from the threatening abyss of civil strife and chaos.

Finally, this specter of military intervention continues to haunt civil societies' capacity to effect a sustainable consolidation of democracy. Military intervention limits the range of options and vitiates the empowerment of subordinates. For instance in June 1993, after a decade of military rule in Nigeria, President Ibrahim Babangida and his uniformed men canceled the transition to civilian democracy that they had strictly supervised by annulling presidential elections that they had themselves organized. Their veto power hangs like the sword of Damocles over any process of democratization. Civilian authorities have yet to institutionalize their control of armed forces. Moreover, it is likely that disaffected segments of civil society will continue to knock on doors of the barracks, creating more opportunities for *bremarian* moments to turn into praetorian decades. For instance, opposition leader Bernard Kolelas, after failing to gain a parliamentary majority, pleaded for a military intervention to save, in his words, "what could be saved of the democratic process."

When military power is invoked to settle electoral outcomes, democracy has lost its meaning and becomes a tragic farce, breeding popular alienation and cynicism. Extrication from authoritarianism and founding elections are thus not synonymous with the implantation of long-lasting democracies. They have no predetermined outcome. They are at best a sign of a new beginning toward more accountable and possibly democratic systems of governance. Alternatively, they herald the resurrection of presidential monarchism where civil society is again repressed into their obtrusive confines of infrapolitics. At worst, they may degenerate into the violence of a hellish war of all against all. Africa's difficult and painful process of democratization is thus, as the French would put it, *"une affaire à suivre."*

QUESTION: In your use of the term *democracy*, do you go beyond the concept of a political regime to the concept of democracy, stressing the tensions between state and the individual and individual freedoms? How deep is this tension in various societies? Also, could you elaborate further on the groups of states that fit the various categories ranging from authoritarian to popular rule? Finally, in your concept of the popular, what leads you to believe that the popular elements coming to the fore have grasped not only the virtues of the freedoms they wish to employ but the necessity of the self-restraint that must accompany these freedoms to make democracy work?

MR. FATTON: The first question relates to the notion of civil society and the place of the individual within civil society. Civil society in the Western sense implies the individual as a centrally self-contained agent. In Africa, if one were to apply that definition, it would not work. Civil society in Africa is one where the individual is to a large extent subsumed by other forces, whether they be religious, ethnic, communal, or others. Thus, when people talk about civil society in Africa, they have to talk about a different type of civil society. The term, nonetheless, has some heuristic validity because it entails the reality of opposition to the predatory state. What I mean by this opposition is the many different defensive mechanisms that can be used to avoid the authority of the state, like the peasant, for instance, who is involved in the black market and bribes the agents so he can get his crop to the market. Corruption is also a form of resistance to the state.

QUESTION: Is this a tradition that goes back to the colonial days?

MR. FATTON: Absolutely. It is to a large degree fending for one's self and fending for one's group, which people have in Africa, but the notion of civil society here is really the notion of something that is foreign or opposed to the state. That opposition is rather complicated. On the one hand, people are opposed to the state obviously when the state represses them, but they are clearly unopposed to the state when it offers health clinics and jobs. Thus, there is a contradiction in civil society itself. For instance, many of the bureaucrats who are now members of civil society—the nongovernmental organizations—have become almost by necessity an agent of that civil society, not because they wanted to, but because they were fired from their jobs. They are no longer part of the state, so they occupy a different position, a different location in the social structure, and they now oppose the state. Thus, it is an ambiguous relationship on many levels.

When I talk about civil society, I am not talking about the individual that we have in mind in the West. It is very much a sense of everything that is not the state. Paradoxically, the notion of civil society Africans have and that I have tried to develop here is one that is quite similar to the one entertained by people in the former Soviet bloc. In the writings of such people as Havel, civil society is very much like that—the opposition to the state, the opposition to authoritarianism. The individual is there but is really not the significant actor. He is very much a part of a larger community that is opposed to the state.

The second question relates to the notion of popular. I do not think the popular civil society is any more democratic than the middle sector is democratic. I think democracy is to a large degree a compromise between conflicting actors, and it occurs only when that compromise is effected. It is not because the middle sectors are more democratic or peasants are more democratic. It is a balance of power. If that balance of power does not exist, I do not think democracy can work. So I do not think that any particular group has a privileged understanding of democracy as such. Democracy to that extent, then, is the regulation of the balance of power. What I am arguing is that when the popular sectors are completely outside of the framework, then they will be repressed. They have to be brought in, and the only way that can be done is from their own organizations. When they are brought in from without, that leads to all kinds of problems and authoritarian tendencies. Consequently, I am not claiming any democratic peculiarity for the popular sectors.

On the other hand, I would nonetheless argue that they have been the sector that has suffered the most, so they clearly have a more significant stake in the establishment of certain rules of the game, such as preventing repression. To that extent I think they know the consequences of authoritarianism better than the middle sectors do, who for a long time were part of the predatory bloc and have now moved away because the prebends are no longer there. The economic crisis has to a large degree led to the shrinkage of what the state can give away—the spoils of power, which has led to a process of defection from the state almost by necessity. Thus, I am not quite sure that they are very democratic either. I think they are very opportunistic and would become democratic if a balance of power existed. Therefore, I am not counting on the goodwill of any political actor, expecting democracy to come out as a result of a balance of power between conflicting groups in society.

QUESTION: If President Clinton or Secretary Christopher should ask you to bring your understanding of democratization in Africa to bear on the problems of Haiti and how the United States should behave toward Haiti, how would you respond?

MR. FATTON: I do not think that any type of democratic regime in Haiti can be established from outside the country. Thus, I would be clearly opposed to any foreign intervention. Ultimately, I think any foreign intervention would erode the type of support that Aristide would have because there is a strong nationalism in Haiti bordering on chauvinism—not only on the part of anti-Aristide forces, but on the part of most Haitians as well. For that reason I think continuing the pressure with even a stricter embargo is the best course of action.

The question of Haiti also raises from the issue of sovereignty. If I were to justify intervention, it would be fairly easy in the sense that Haitians are not sovereign in their own country. There is no sovereignty for the vast majority of Haitians, so when people talk about sovereignty, it is a rather farcical word, especially coming from the army. The reality is that even those who do not have that sovereignty from within are deeply nationalistic and would look at foreign intervention as an invasion. Such interference, I think, would undermine Aristide's capacity to rule.

Even if Aristide were to return, I seriously doubt that he would be able to rule effectively unless there were fundamental formations in the different structures of the political system, particularly in the army and the police, and I just do not see that as a possibility in the short term. There is the dilemma that if the army is attacked, it will retaliate, and it has the weapons, so the opposing force will be defeated. On the other hand, if the army is not undermined, it will undermine the rule. That has been the tradition in Africa and Haiti, so one is in a catch-22 situation. I believe that Haitians missed an opportunity in the immediate aftermath of Duvalier's departure. If we had moved swiftly, at that time eliminating the army would have been feasible. The army has reemerged as the only viable institution, however corrupt it may be, capable of inflicting punishment and imposing order. I do not think it is a necessary vehicle for Haiti, however. Haiti is a tiny country; it does not have enemies that are going to invade the country. The army has been used internally for repression, so I do not quite see the historical necessity of having an army. On the other hand, if a politician in Haiti made such a statement, the politician would immediately be out of a political position because that recommendation is politically incorrect.

QUESTION: What is the relation between the state and class? It seems the middle sector is detached from the state. What is the social base of the state? Second, when you say the middle sector, what is the economic base? Is it only the functionaries or some kind of professional or international organization? Third, about the popular civil society, particularly regarding different groups, are you emphasizing the ethnic aspect or the class aspect? Some social class has been organized in Africa. Different groups are organized in terms of ethnicity and tribal pluralism; on the other hand, as in the case of Somalia, there can be an entirely different outcome.

MR. FATTON: To your question about the state's relation to class, to a large degree I would argue that in Africa, in order to become a viable economic class, a political class must exist first. In other words, the state has traditionally been the arena in postcolonial Africa within which people acquire wealth and distribute that wealth. Consequently, there is a relation between the process of class formation and the capture of the state. It is not an economic mix that produces political power; it is political power that furnishes economic power in most postcolonial states in Africa.

That particular arrangement is presently facing a crisis, however, and that crisis stems from the monumental economic problems in Africa. The state no longer has the resources it used to have, so the state is no longer capable of distributing the prebend on the scale it used to. Thus, significant sectors within the state have largely left the state. This is what I call the middle sectors. They are not just functionaries; they are lawyers, journalists, and people organizing political parties. They represent a fairly small class of people, but nonetheless, they represent an important one in the urban sectors in particular. Those people have moved away from the state. It is not that they are necessarily opposed to the state per se, but they are opposed to the state because they are outside the state. If they happen to win an election, they will no longer be opposed to the state.

Examples of this are seen in the processes of transition. Even with processes of privatization, it is nice if a person is in the state because that person can arrange things in such a way that his or her cronies will benefit or he or she will receive the benefits. So the state is still central, even if that type of opposition exists between civil society and the state. In other words, there should not be a complete dichotomy between the two. What happens in the state has a fundamental impact on what happens in civil society, and what happens in civil society also has a fundamental impact on what happens in the state.

The issues of ethnicity and class are other traditional problems forced on social scientists who are studying Africa. Two conditions are occurring at the same time: the salience of ethnicity and the process of class formation. Even if people belong to the same ethnic group, that clearly does not mean all of them are in the privileged groups of that society.

Ethnicity, however, can mitigate class conflicts, and it does so in a significant way in Africa. Most conflicts in Africa are either regional or ethnic, whether one is talking about Nigeria, Somalia, or even Angola. Thus, ethnicity is very significant. On the other hand, ethnicity hides the process of stratification, which is quite important in understanding politics—in other words, what goes on in the state. Many African states have what is called *ethnic arithmetic*, whereby even if there is clearly a dominant ethnic group, to remain in power that ethnic group must disperse its spoils, which clearly goes to meet the needs of the other ethnic groups. In certain areas, this method does not appear to work very well. In Burundi, for instance, another coup has occurred. In Kenya this method worked fairly well, although the Kikuyus were the dominant group. That coalition is now disintegrating, however.

Consequently, when African politics are analyzed, the two processes of class and ethnicity often cannot be separated and in some instances may actually coincide. When they do coincide, there is a potential for real catastrophe. In South Africa, for instance, not only does the stratification of class lines exist but also that of stratification along religious or ethnic lines, which leads to more significant potential for civil strife.

COMMENT: Personally, I think the issue of ethnicity becomes more important because of the failure of the state to ignore the need for and reality of ethnicity.

MR. FATTON: On the other hand, it is difficult to contain problems associated with ethnicity. In Nigeria, many attempts have been made after the civil war to challenge the importance of ethnicity—in the manipulation of states, and so on. On one hand, it might lead to more stability or, depending on the situation, it could do just the opposite by exacerbating tensions. In addition, there is the problem of the nation-state. Some ethnic groups are in different states, as in Somalia, Kenya, and Ethiopia. These problems are significant, and I am not sure that African states have yet managed the problems successfully. The events occurring in Eritrea are certainly significant.

QUESTION: A few years ago with our participation, the United Nations was distributing food supplies in Ethiopia and Eritrea. I do not hear much about African countries helping other African countries in need, however. How do the African nations relate to each other and do they assist each other very much?

MR. FATTON: Relief for those types of disasters from other African countries is very limited. Most African states are facing severe economic crises, so they are unlikely to be partners in that particular type of venture. What they are able to do, however, is to accommodate many refugees. Kenya has welcomed a significant number of people from Somalia and Burundi.

Other forms of assistance that are not necessarily related to relief efforts toward natural catastrophes have nonetheless had an impact on them. For instance, during the 1980s many of the southern African states were clearly suffering the consequences of supporting the African National Congress in South Africa. South Africa devastated many of those states supporting anti-apartheid groups. They paid a severe price. Mozambique's plight right now is not just the result of bad policies; it is also the result of South Africa's intervention in the internal affairs of Mozambique. This had led to significant problems of malnutrition and fear of starvation. Thus, it is unlikely that many African countries will be able to economically assist other African states, but they will be able to assist in other ways. In Liberia there is an African contingent trying to reestablish some order and make the transition to a more accountable regime. In terms of food, however, assistance will not come from Africa; it must come from countries outside of Africa.

An important issue that arises from the support of other countries is, Are the recurring problems of Africa being reinforced by continuing assistance from other nations? It may well be that if no assistance was provided, Africans would have to develop their own means of surviving. The possibility exists that if assistance is continued, there is no incentive to create domestic networks that would eventually resolve the problem. This is a moral dilemma. When millions of people are facing starvation, it is difficult to refuse to help.

There are other areas in Africa, however, that are completely ignored. In Angola, for instance, there is a significant threat of massive starvation, but very little is heard about it. The same is true of certain regions in Zaire. I have always been puzzled by the fact that Somalia became such a huge concern of the international community. Not that it should not, but it has surprised me, given previous experiences.

QUESTION: Vernon Walters has suggested that it might be wise to have some leadership from Francophone countries in Africa intervene militarily or otherwise to help Haiti. What do you think about using French-speaking troops from Africa if troops have to go into Haiti?

MR. FATTON: It would be tragic for me to see troops coming from Gabon or the Ivory Coast or Senegal as protectors of democracy in Haiti. If they can help, so be it, but I do not think that would be a positive step. I think, actually, the elites would understand each other. The military from those countries would probably have better relations with Haitian military leader Cedras than with the opposition.

COMMENT: A recent article stated that when the United States had a ship traveling to Haiti, it was turned around because of potential danger from people on shore. A large contingent from the United Nations was evacuated as well, leaving hundreds of the future leaders of Haiti in danger of dying in a blood bath, which is probably coming.

MR. FATTON: Those people who constitute the future leadership of Haiti are all in hiding. The prime minister has been unable to move to his official office and is still in his private home. Aristide supporters are terrified about the possibility and probability of facing what have been called the *Attaches*, who are essentially *Macoutes*. There is a problem of security for the people who have been elected. The minister of the economy had to stay in her office for one week because *Attaches* had it surrounded. The minister of information cannot function because the national radio is controlled by the army. Thus, Haiti has a government that does not govern and ministries that are to a large degree repressed. Those are the facts, however bleak they may be.

NARRATOR: When some organizations began to work in Africa, they thought nationalism was a predominant characteristic, partly because of the application of African nations to the United Nations for recognition. Quickly, however, there was a renewal of conflicts over diverse norms and values among groups. A discussion such as this one helps us understand that there are dimensions to societal conflict not thought of 20 years ago. We are grateful to Professor Fatton for furthering our understanding of these serious problems.

CHAPTER THREE

The Constraints on Democracy in Sub-Saharan Africa: The Case for Limited Democracy*

JOHN F. CLARK

In 1990, following the wave of democratization then sweeping the globe, a number of opposition campaigns began against many of the authoritarian regimes in Sub-Saharan Africa. The path of political reform was blazed by tiny Benin, where a national conference bringing together important groups from the civil society and government produced a new constitution in 1990. Under that new constitution, Mathieu Kérékou, the nonelected president of 17 years, was voted out of office in 1991. The national conference route to political change was then taken by Congo, Gabon, and eventually almost every other francophone country on the continent.[1] In anglophone Africa, Zambia was the paradigm case. There the country's venerable president of 27 years, Kenneth Kaunda, voluntarily stepped aside and allowed free elections in November 1991, which he lost to opposition leader Frederick Chiluba. These events gave heart to opposition leaders in other anglophone African countries, including Malawi, Kenya, and Nigeria, though the results were less dramatic. Of course, in the

---

*This paper was originally published in, and reprinted with the permission of, *SAIS Review*, the journal of international affairs of the Paul H. Nitze School of Advanced International Studies, Summer-Fall 1994. John F. Clark is an assistant professor at Florida International University. He was a U.S. Department of State intern in Brazzaville, Congo, in 1990.

43

West it has been South Africa's near miraculous transformation, also beginning in 1990, that has captured most of the attention.

Since 1990 most of these movements have reached some sort of tentative resolution. In a number of countries, including Zaire and Togo, dictators have temporarily ridden out the wave of campaigns for democracy and reestablished their dominance after having apparently been rendered impotent by their opponents. In others, including Ghana and Gabon, the old rulers have remained in power by allowing minor reforms and holding new elections in order to legitimate their rule. In a third category, which includes Benin, Congo, Mali, Zambia, Nigeria, South Africa, and Malawi, long-standing authoritarian rulers have been ousted through coups or have been voted out of office. Yet even in these last cases, it is far from certain that democracy has yet been consolidated.

To many analysts, the wave of reform between 1990 and 1994 must have come as a great surprise. Among many others, for instance, Samuel Huntington argued in the mid-1980s that the prospects for more developing countries to establish democratic political systems were quite poor.[2] This pessimistic prediction coincided closely with Huntington's well-established analysis of the problems facing developing countries and the policy prescriptions that flowed from it. In his view, the major challenge for developing countries was not, at least in the short term, democratization, but rather the establishment of order.[3] In this conception, order was the prerequisite for economic growth and the expansion of state power, which in turn were the ultimate prerequisites for democracy. In the 1980s Goran Hyden masterfully applied a similar logic to the problem of politico-economic development in Africa specifically.[4] According to Hyden, there was little prospect for development in Africa until the "economy of affection," or the preindustrial, nonrational biases in microeconomic decision making could be eliminated. Other scholars explicitly argued that premature, and hence misguided, efforts at democratization only delayed development.[5] Predictably, both Huntington and Hyden have reacted very skeptically to the recent campaigns for political change in the developing world, including Africa.

While these views of Huntington and Hyden appear to spring from rather conservative assumptions about political prospects for the developing world, those on the far left were also skeptics about democracy in African and other developing societies. Indeed, quasi-Marxist analysts of Africa have generally shared the view that development must precede democracy. For them, the dominant reality of African politics has been persistent class oppression, resulting in economic privation.[6] As a result, they too have favored authoritarianism in the short term, albeit with a different vision of how African societies would achieve a more satisfactory politico-economic order. Also like their "conservative" counterparts, these analysts have reacted with skepticism to the first hints of democratization in Africa, emphasizing that "an exaggerated belief in the strength and achievement of *liberal* democracy . . . belies the democratic limitations and class impairments that cripple such democracies."[7] Thus, for the left, even if democracy were possible, it would not be desirable inasmuch as it would have little effect on the national and international capital interests controlling Africa's future.

Each of these two differing views suggested a different model for development in Sub-Saharan Africa. The conservative view implied a tough, authoritarian state, along the lines of South Korea, to develop and implement rational economic policy. This sort of state would be able to resist undue public pressures for social expenditures or premature democratic institutions. This was the model for the Western-oriented African states like Côte d'Ivoire and Kenya. The quasi-Marxist view, of course, implied one-party states committed to redistribution of existing wealth, the expansion of public services, and *étatist* economic coordination. This conception was the theoretical model for the Afro-Marxist states of Ethiopia, Angola, Benin, Mozambique, and Congo, though none had the resources and/or will to implement such programs fully. Unfortunately for the Africans, neither of these approaches produced results that met people's economic needs or fulfilled political aspirations, which explains the domestic sources of the 1990 political crises.

During the 1960s and 1970s only a small group of liberal centrists believed that democracy was both possible and desirable in Africa. These scholars reacted positively and hopefully to the first hints of political change in Africa. As the veteran Africanist

John Wiseman argued, "There is nothing inherently un-African about democracy and there is certainly nothing inherently undemocratic about Africans in general." Wiseman even suggested that it was racist to suggest otherwise.[8] Meanwhile, Richard Joseph lauded Zambia as a model to be followed by others.[9] These supporters of liberal democracy in Africa were clearly gratified that the Africans themselves had begun to take serious steps to rid their nations of long-standing dictators. Unfortunately for both them and the Africans, the luster on the newly elected regimes quickly faded after Zambia's new president, Chiluba, declared a state of emergency in 1993, after political dissidents were detained in Benin and after ethnic warfare erupted in Brazzaville, Congo. As a result of these setbacks, the historical meaning of post-1989 events in Africa has become more cloudy.

Both the course of events themselves and the scholarly reaction to them do, however, invite renewed reflection on the possibilities for democracy in Africa. The stakes for Africans are enormously high because they have largely been denied the promise of freedom that they believed independence would bring them. Moreover, African authoritarianism has utterly failed to produce prosperity of the Asian variety, leaving a majority of Africans as poor as they were in 1960. Yet one should not let emotions evoked by the unspeakable poverty and oppression of many African societies blur one's understanding of the possibilities or constraints. While democracy is both theoretically *and* practically possible in Africa, the constraints on democratic consolidation will render all democratic experiments extremely fragile. Therefore, the democratic regimes most likely to survive, even if unsteadily, will be those that promise the least, compromise the most, evolve slowly, and concentrate on basic government services.

Democratization in Africa: Possibilities and Constraints

One can understand nearly all sociopolitical struggles as contests between the deterministic social forces of history, culture, and economics, on the one hand, and of the voluntaristic force of individual and collective human will on the other. Even Adam

Przeworski, no unmitigated optimist, has argued that "objective factors constitute at most constraints to that which is possible under a concrete historical situation but do not determine the outcome of such situations."[10] This understanding applies to the current struggles for freedom and material well-being in Sub-Saharan Africa as well as anywhere else. If one reserves any room at all for the influence of free will in history, then democratization is at least theoretically possible, regardless of social circumstances.

Beyond this philosophical truism, though, there is evidence that many individuals truly are struggling for democracy in Africa. Unless one is completely cynical about the motivations of the opposition militants who have been recently engaged in campaigns to unseat African dictatorships, one has to acknowledge that at least some individuals are interested in establishing democratic regimes, rather than merely seizing power for themselves. Certainly the current campaigns are more than a spurious manifestation of some other social process like economic adjustment with the external market or underlying class struggle. Perhaps the struggle is a quixotic one, doomed to failure, or one that should be placed squarely in second place behind the imperative of providing economic sustenance, but one owes it to Africa's democrats at least to take their project seriously. Seen through their eyes, the problem of reform in African can best be understood as a series of impediments to, or constraints on, the institution and consolidation of democratic regimes.[11]

Finally, one can point to the existing democracies in the developing world, including those in Africa, as *prima facie* evidence for the position of "democratic possibilism." Though India, Mexico, and Botswana may have serious flaws in their political processes, each country does hold periodic, multiparty elections that allow some expression of popular sentiments about its government. One may speculate over time that these proto-democracies may become more truly democratic, and indeed there is some indication that they are already doing so. In any case, the presence of these democracies, however flawed, provides considerable ammunition for the democratic optimists.

Nonetheless, the constraints on democratization are daunting. The most immediate of these constraints concerns the transition to democracy, which necessarily entails the dissolution of an existing authoritarian regime. The challenge for would-be democratizers in authoritarian states is to assemble opposition coalitions, at the grass roots and/or among elites, with enough solidity, stamina, courage, and resistance to corruption to face down savvy, and often brutal, dictators. In some cases, such as that of Zaire and Kenya, this critical mass has not yet assembled, and the authoritarian rulers have been able to divide the opposition movements sufficiently to retain power for the time being.

Beyond the dissolution of authoritarian regimes is the more serious problem of democratic reformulation. As Alfred Stepan argues, "The most likely outcome of sharp crises of authoritarian regimes stemming from diffuse pressures and forces in society"— which aptly describes the crises recently generated by opposition campaigns in Africa—"is either a newly constituted successor authoritarian government, or a caretaker military junta promising elections in the future."[12] While this was certainly true of regime crises in Africa before 1990, the recent opposition campaigns have produced a number of elected regimes that have committed themselves to democratic governance. African democrats must have also been truly inspired by the case of Mali, in which a military *junta* seized power in 1991 but then allowed free elections and turned over power to a civilian regime in 1992. The true test of all of these new democracies, however, will be at the time of the *second* postauthoritarian elections.

Those who focus on the transitional part of democratization are frequently preoccupied with the political compromises and formal constitutions that follow from the termination of authoritarian regimes when there is strong sentiment for the institution of democratic forms. Theorists who have drawn extensively from case studies in Iberia, Greece, and Latin America frequently emphasize the necessity of a "class compromise" in the transition to democratic institutions.[13] In relatively more economically advanced societies this approach is justified by the observable organization of social groups along class and ideological lines. In Africa, though, where political activity (if not social oppression) along class lines has been more muted, this concern is less relevant to constitution-making and compromise. More important are the political arrangements that reconcile the leaders of ethnic and personal constituencies to democratic processes. Those who focus on the compromises and processes of democratic transitions, like Giuseppe, DiPalma, and Joseph, are generally more optimistic about the possibility of democratic consolidation.[14]

By contrast, those who focus on the "structural" problems are generally far more pessimistic. These problems act as constraints during both the periods of transition and consolidation. Though these constraints can, with sufficient Procrustean effort, be artificially separated and given discrete labels for purposes of discussion, they actually form part of an interrelated complex of concepts useful for describing political behavior in any society. Consider here, for instance, the concepts of state, civil society, political culture, level of development, and economic growth. Using these fundamental tools, authoritarian states, weak civil societies, nondemocratic political cultures, and underdevelopment may all be described as important constraints on democratization. Considering these apparent constraints on democratization, one may theorize that weak civil society and nondemocratic culture are to a large degree the *product* of underdevelopment. That is, defective political culture or weak civil society serve as "important intervening variables" in the relationship between underdevelopment and authoritarianism.

The most basic constraint on the consolidation of democratic regimes in Africa, however, is underdevelopment itself. The positive association between development and democracy is apparent to even the most casual observer, and scholars have attempted to verify this linkage between the two variables since the 1950s.[15] As noted, most scholars have typically focused on the "intervening variables" that follow from underdevelopment and impede democratization, including illiteracy, ethnic strife, fragmented civil society, and political culture. For instance, one recent study suggests that "population pressures," defined chiefly as population growth, "are related to the use of repression by policymakers."[16] Rapid population growth, of course, is a principal characteristic of developing societies.

In Africa, underdevelopment is the main contributor to the dominant political forms of the continent: patrimonialism, prebendal politics, and personal rule. Patrimonialism, as first described by Max Weber, is a political system in which a leader imbued with charismatic or traditional authority maintains power by rewarding the loyalty of important elites with advisory or administrative positions.[17] In the independence era, during which African states have nationalized foreign commercial concerns or created them outright, managerial posts in these state-owned enterprises have often served as rewards for loyal clients. Mobutu Sese Seko of Zaire, for instance, has used the distribution of his country's nationalized enterprises in precisely this way.[18] As Richard Sandbrook argues, personal rule is a form of patrimonialism that has arisen in Africa where rulers have no "constitutional, charismatic-revolutionary or traditional legitimacy." As he describes personal rule:

> A chief or strongman emerges and rules on the basis of material incentives and personal control of his administration and armed force. Fear and personal loyalties are the mainstays of a personalistic government untrammelled by traditional or modern constitutional limitations.[19]

Successful personal rule is a frequent product of underdevelopment because elites recognize that their only access to the economic rewards of state office lie in their loyalty to the ruler. Meanwhile, individual rulers often find themselves attacked by critics if they attempt to reform access to state office according to a rational, merit-based system.

This secular underdevelopment in Africa is accompanied by the short-term requirement of full-scale economic restructuring. Democratic transition and consolidation are rendered nearly impossible when they must take place simultaneously with systemic and inevitably painfully economic reforms. This has certainly been true for the relatively more developed economies of Southern and Eastern Europe and Latin America, but it is a more conspicuous truth still for the utterly collapsed economies of Sub-Saharan Africa. Virtually every country on the subcontinent is now enduring structural adjustment programs mandated by the International Monetary Fund (IMF) as a condition for relief from their debt burdens, and the near-term social consequences of these programs are devastating.[20] And ironically, while these social costs can be the source of strong opposition to autocratic regimes, they make the consolidation of the "democratic" regimes that follow them extremely difficult.[21] Expectations often run high when declining economic fortunes are responsible for the demise of autocratic regimes, and these expectations are usually disappointed when follow-on regimes have no more creative ways of financing reform than did their predecessors. Besides creating outright antipathy for new governments, economic restructuring quite often exacerbates class and ethnic conflicts in society, which in turn undermines the consolidation of democracy.

Indeed, the nature of African civil societies presents other impediments to democratization. In the classic "pluralist" model of Western democracy, civil associations, including professional groups, labor unions, voluntary associations, and other "interest groups," all make claims for particular needs on the state, which then mediates these claims in a way that benefits the common good. Moreover, societal institutions serve as a bulwark against excessive expansions of state power into the civil realm. Most notably, for instance, the press plays the role of watchdog over extra-constitutional suspensions of civil liberties. In many African countries, however, states have co-opted these institutions, rendering them subject to control by ruling authorities. Only a few African countries have maintained a free press, while labor unions and youth and women's groups were frequently created as, or converted to, official organs of the state. The domination of these groups by the state thus represents a severe constraint on the transition from authoritarianism. On the other hand, if the same groups are too strong in relation to the state, they can work to undermine the newly formed regimes that are constitutionally democratic. There is no denying that social organizations serving narrow constituencies, like unions that represent urban civil service workers, sometimes push newly democratic regimes into violent confrontations that end with a return to authoritarianism.

The relationship of democratization to other important components of civil society, such as class and ethnicity, is similarly complex. Generally, it must be said, African societies are marked by profound class oppression, albeit by an "organizational" bourgeoisie rather than a traditional Marxian bourgeoisie.[22] The distribution of income cross the economic spectrum has been far more skewed in African countries than in Western states, and the absence of a large middle class is universally regarded as an impairment to democratic rule. At the same time, evidence of class consciousness and class-wide political activity in Africa is far less evident than it has been in Europe or the United States. In this regard, the growth of class consciousness in Africa, to the extent that it leads to a redistribution of income, could create the conditions for democratic stability over the long term. But class consciousness can also lead to civil strife or challenges to elites that provoke more rigorously repressive measures by the state-controlling class, which of course defeats democratization in the near term.

On the whole, ethnic and ethno-regional consciousness in Africa has been stronger than class consciousness, the main civil wars of the continent (in Nigeria, Sudan, Zaire, Angola, and South Africa) having been fought chiefly along ethnic lines. Whether one views ethnic strife primarily as a product of manipulation by political entrepreneurs (the "instrumentalist" view), or as the inevitable result of competition among primordial groups whose members share common cultural symbols,[23] ethnic politics has been a constant in Africa since Europeans created the continent's artificial states a century ago. Even if the Western media takes Conradian delight in reporting the outrages of ethnic violence in Africa, there is no use denying the frequency of ethnic conflict, or viewing it strictly as a result of class divisions. While typically—and sensibly—arguing that economic contraction exacerbates ethnic tensions, sophisticated Marxist analysts acknowledge this point.[24] In fact, the weakening or removal of a number of authoritarian regimes, which had previously repressed ethnic-based opposition, has led to an outbreak of ethnic and ethno-regional strife in Africa. Recent events in Rwanda and Burundi are only the more visible manifestations of a recent wave of ethnic violence that has also affected Congo, Zaire, and many other African states after years of relative ethnic peace.

John F. Clark

Regarding political culture, a well-developed literature makes a strong case that the institution and maintenance of democracy depends largely on favorable attitudes toward democracy by elites and ordinary citizens. In one sense "democracy" is a state of mind; if people *believe* profoundly that democracy will work and are committed to a democratic form, then democracy *can* work regardless of other circumstances. Among elites serving the state, nondemocratic values, generated either by conviction or simple love of power, often prove insurmountable impediments to the removal of authoritarian regimes. The uncertain charms of democratic politics have rarely been more attractive to governing elites than the status and rent-generated wealth associated with holding high office. One should not delude oneself that all those who struggle against oppression are committed to liberty, since many opposition figures are no more democratic than those they oppose. As the cases of Zambia and Benin demonstrate, detention of political opponents is virtually a reflex to opposition for many African leaders, even those coming to power by election.

Among the masses, nondemocratic values—not to mention outright ignorance of the realities of democratic practice—are also an impediment to democracy. Mass political culture is mainly operative over the long term, affecting the consolidation and maintenance of democratic regimes more than their creation. Many regimes in Africa have begun their existence through elections or through popular pressures that have led leaders to promise elections and democratic constitutions. Yet in nearly as many instances, the general population has acquiesced in, if not favored, the end of democratic regimes, especially those that are perceived to be hopelessly corrupt. In Nigeria and Sudan for instance, the populations responded weakly to the seizure of power by high military officers in the mid-1980s because the civilian regimes were corrupt. In general, the masses often despise ruling authoritarians without having any real commitment to democratic principles. Finally, of course, the attitudes toward democracy of the masses and of the elite are mutually reflective and reinforcing; authoritarian leaders would not survive without some measure of popular support from an authoritarian-minded public, but these same leaders often promote the idea that multiparty politics is undesirable, unworkable, or "un-African."

According to one recent analysis, one can identify the roots of Africa's political cultures in three periods, the precolonial, the colonial, and the anticolonial (1945-1965),[25] to which one may add the period of independence. There is some validity in viewing certain features of African culture as subcontinent-wide,[26] and clearly distinguishable from those of, say, India, Indonesia, or Brazil. Even if one takes the view that "precolonial Africa consisted of many little traditions that did not . . . generate a great tradition,"[27] it remains true that the "great traditions" of other large world regions rendered them distinct from Africa as a whole. Moreover, all of Africa, arguably including Ethiopia and Liberia, carries the political legacy of the century-long direct confrontation with European colonialism. At the same time, the differences among the various indigenous political forms, patterns of colonial rule, and post-independence experiences are certainly great enough to have created different political cultures for African states and other distinguishable ethnic and religious groups.

One can trace both proto-democratic and authoritarian, even tyrannical, strains in the political forms of precolonial Africa. Many contemporary African elites, especially those hopeful to promote democracy on the continent, prefer to dwell on the popular or proto-democratic strains of precolonial political life,[28] and undoubtedly there was debate, consultation, well-developed legal systems, and checks on the abuse of power in many precolonial African societies.[29] Popular inclusion, the high value placed on public goods, and decentralization were other proto-democratic values prominent in many precolonial African societies.[30]

Popular Western accounts of precolonial Africa, by contrast, often seem to relish relating the gory details of some of precolonial Africa's most tyrannical regimes, like those of Shaka Zulu or Mutesa, king of Buganda.[31] Some Africans themselves are also anxious to debunk the "democratic myth" of African traditional societies.[32] Even in some of the cases in which traditional leaders consulted the people, as through the *kgotla* (assembly) in the Tswana culture, the public was not allowed to set the agenda, and those opposing the chief feared reprisals.[33] Nor did Islam bring much of a democratic tradition to those parts of Saharan, West, and East Africa where it has penetrated. Traditional Islam, like medieval Christianity, usually carried with it the largely antidemocratic values of paternalism, deference to authority, and reservation of political rights to believers. In the majority of Black African states, though, relatively unfettered kingship was the major source of political authority. Yet this heritage should not be an embarrassment to anyone since full democracy, including a universal franchise and reasonable protection of civil rights, was unknown *anywhere* in the world until the 20th century.[34]

Formal European colonialism in Africa, typically lasting some 70 years and being largely responsible for contemporary African political borders, did not obliterate existing political cultures, but did alter them profoundly. Inasmuch as political cultures pertain only to identifiable political communities, the advent of colonial states created new loci for the evolution of syncretic political cultures. These new cultures resulted from a mixture of both existing political attitudes and behaviors of diverse peoples incorporated into colonial states, and those absorbed from the practice of colonial rule. Of course, the main contribution of colonial rule was to reinforce the arbitrary and authoritarian aspects of political behavior in that its main object was to enable a more systematic and exhaustive exploitation of Africa's economic potential. This could hardly be accomplished without an authoritarian political structure, supported by a bureaucracy organized according to the principles of commercial efficiency. The denial of self-determination to Africans, like that of other races and peoples, could only be accomplished by the constant threat, and occasional exercise, of coercive means of rule. Doubtless, the political behavior of colonial authorities did not go unobserved by the new elites who were being trained for a role in administration themselves.

These rather conventional, if necessary, observations about the effects of colonial rule on political culture should not obscure the complexity of the overall effect of the penetration of European social, moral, and political thinking in Africa in the 20th century. For every Morton Stanley, liberally applying force as he slashed his way across the continent in order to organize Africans according to his rationalized concept of the world, there was a David Livingston sometimes preceding him, seeking to promote European values, and above all religion, in a gentler way. One legacy of this sort of European contact is that several generations of Africans, particularly in French and Belgian colonies, were educated in the religious schools promoted by colonial authorities. Accordingly, the religious component of the protest movements in Malawi or Zaire, or the fact that all of the Sovereign National Conferences were headed by Catholic archbishops, is an indirect consequence of this European heritage.

Likewise, with regard to education more generally, European values and outlooks were transmitted through these schools into the consciousness of African students. In the cases of British, French, and Belgian colonies lessons included—inevitably, if contradictorily, given the nature of colonial rule—the notion that democracy was a superior political form to kingship or authoritarianism. European powers took great pride in their own respective cultural heritages even if they did not practice what they preached. The comparisons between the Sovereign National Conferences and the Estates General of the French Revolution made during 1991 are evidence that some positive European values were transmitted to Africans. Thus, colonialism only added another layer of ambiguity to democratic values in African political cultures.

A final variable in the democratization equation is the "international factor," but, again, it is somewhat artificial to isolate external forces as a separate variable in determining outcomes in Africa's political campaigns. After all, Africa's political cultures, civil societies, and level of development are all to some extent a product of the continent's place in world history, and particularly, the world economy. It can hardly be an accident that the recent wave of democratization, which now seems to have peaked, ensued immediately after the collapse of Eastern Europe's Communist regimes.[35] Moreover, the World Bank certainly strengthened the prevailing *zeitgeist* of that fateful year with its call for improved "governance" in Africa. If internal frustrations alone were the only source of political tumult in Africa, the recent revolutions would have occurred in 1985, or even 1980.

Accordingly, the fate of African democracy also depends on the generosity of the international financial institutions and the developed countries generally. Of course, the near-term economic adjustments referred to previously derive largely from conditions imposed by the World Bank, which appears to be resolute in its determination to continue requiring structural adjustments in African economies in exchange for fiscal support and minor debt relief. A new study has just made the case that structural adjustment programs have only had modest result so far because African states have resisted so many of the requisite reforms.[36] Meanwhile, there is little evidence that the donor fatigue of the 1980s has lifted for individual developed countries, especially since the world recession lingers for Japan and Europe. In short, then, the external milieu provided a spiritual boost to would-be African democratizers in the immediate wake of the Soviet empire's collapse, but now the wealthy Western states are proving reluctant to ease the constraints on democratization with temporary subsidies for democratization.

The Case for Limited Democracy

In sum, democratization in Africa is in fact possible but is rendered extraordinarily difficult by its grave constraints. This analysis, however, only sharpens the question: What is the best course for the leaders of Africa's new postauthoritarian regimes to take? One option is that they may establish new authoritarian regimes, based either on the claim of the need for economic efficiency, or on the claim of the need for redistribution and revolution. Alternatively, they may try to make good on their asserted intentions to govern by the principles of democracy.

As briefly argued above, however, few are likely to take seriously the claims of benevolent authoritarianism today. The left-wing African authoritarian regimes of the past largely failed to deliver meaningful equality, while their right-wing counterparts failed to produce order and efficiency. In fact, the two varieties resembled each other far more than either would care to admit. Even if nondemocratic regimes had produced better results, it is morally doubtful whether the benefits would have been worth the costs, measured in terms of human rights abuses and suppressed human spirit. Moreover, the developed world is far less likely to accept the claims of the need for authoritarian rule today, since it has at last recognized such claims as cover under which nondemocratic rulers extract wealth from the societies whose interests they profess to serve. And, represented as they are by the IMF and World Bank, the developed countries are in a position to render unstable virtually any new regime in Africa. Finally, African populations themselves are far less likely to settle for authoritarian regimes than they were in the past, creating instant problems for any regime not acting on its promises of democratization.

Returning then to the idea that the opposition leaders who come to power should make good on their rhetoric, one is led to ask why full and unmitigated democracy should not at once be adopted. The answer is that African states and societies cannot, at this juncture, make the sudden leap from the coercive forms of control now commonly practiced to the complex and costly democratic forms of the Western world. The apparent paternalism of such an assertion makes it no less true. Consider, for instance, the prolonged rounds of litigation that are often required in the West to correct certain injustices in the behavior of police, employers, and merchants. African states certainly lack the resources to undertake large-scale judicial enquiries into social injustices, and African treasuries, bankrupt as they are, certainly cannot provide financial redress as Western courts often require. Indeed, to try would prove fatal to the new regimes. All of these constraints on democracy analyzed above will be apparent in Africa's new democracies. If, however, African citizens or Western governments withdraw all support for these regimes at the first sign of corruption, illegal detention, or menacing words directed at the press, none are likely to last long.

Accordingly, for democracy to work in the new African regimes, it will unfortunately have to be limited in a number of ways. In terms of social welfare, for instance, African states should probably recognize the limits of their capacities. To be sure, this situation is lamentable, but to argue that African states have failed unless they provide for people's overall welfare is to condemn them from the start, inasmuch as they simply lack the capacity to do so. This is not to say, of course, that African states should not try to marshall a reasonable amount of resources to mitigate the most grievous kinds of social deprivation. Most African states will, appropriately, try to provide some basic services to their citizens. Efforts to create and enforce social equality (as opposed to *political* equality), however, are infeasible and will send local capital out of the country while discouraging external capital investment. To try to deliver too much too soon only promises future rounds of political instability.

Similarly, even well-meaning elected leaders will be unable to improve the human rights situation immediately or dramatically. Not only politicians, but also policemen, prison guards, and army officers will have to accept the value of free and fair trials, security of the person, and freedom from torture. One cannot expect for a political culture that demands swift and harsh punishment for crimes, political and civil, to be changed by proclamation or edict.

If one considers the tremendously long period that it took for Western societies to make their democracies real, this view may offend less. After all, American "democracy" only approached some real approximation of popular rule after many decades of halting and difficult practice. It is striking that American "democracy" did not eliminate slavery until nearly 100 years into its evolution. Only a fraction of the British or American population could vote at the beginning of the 19th century, and the majority of citizens did not enjoy the franchise until well into the 20th century. What this suggests for Africa's new democracies is what one might call "democratic imcrementalism," which is in fact the course that Western democracies took. As much as this view smacks of late 1950s "developmentalism," none of the other, more transformational, models have so far offered Africa a better future.

Africa's new elected leaders themselves already recognize the limits of what they can deliver. It is striking, for instance, how little Zambia's Chiluba promised during his campaign for his country's presidency. He publicly and resolutely resolved to keep Zambia in compliance with the World Bank's harsh structural adjustment program and promised little in the way of immediate economic relief. Instead, he called on his people to work hard for better lives and merely promised to limit government interference in their ability to do so. Also, as noted above, Chiluba's regime briefly declared a state of emergency in 1993. Yet there is still hope for the Zambian experiment, despite its shortcomings, and the truest test will come with the next multiparty elections. Hopefully, Western leaders will continue to lend support to such democracies, flawed as they are. Then, perhaps, democratic practices will be entrenched, and broader social welfare policies can be attempted over time. In the meanwhile, limited democracy appears to be the best of a narrow range of options for Africa's transitional regimes.

NOTES

1. See John F. Clark, "The National Conference as an Instrument of Democratization in Francophone Africa," *Journal of Third World Studies*, XI, 1 (Spring 1994).

2. "Will More Countries Become Democratic?" *Political Science Quarterly*, 99 (Summer 1984).

3. See Huntington's deservedly famous *Political Order in Changing Societies* (New Haven, Conn.: Yale University Press, 1968).

4. *No Shortcuts to Progress: Africa Development Management in Perspective* (London: Heinemann, 1983).

5. Rodney M. Marsh, "Does Democracy Hinder Economic Development in the Latecomer Developing Nations?" *Comparative Social Research*, 2 (1979): 215-48.

6. Leonard Irving Markovitz, ed., *Studies in Power and Class in Africa* (New York: Oxford University Press, 1987), and Robert Fatton, *Predatory Rule: State and Civil Society in Africa* (Boulder, Colo.: Lynne Rienner, 1992).

7. Robert Fatton, "Liberal Democracy in Africa," *Political Science Quarterly*, 105, 3 (1990): 473; Fatton's specification of *liberal* democracy as inappropriate for Africa is indicative of his desire not to concede to the Western view that only multiparty, free market systems merit the label "democracy."

John F. Clark

8. *Democracy in Black Africa: Survival and Revival* (New York: Paragon, 1990), 6.

9. "Zambia: A Model for Democratic Change," *Current History*, 91, 565 (May 1992).

10. Adam Przeworski, "Problems in the Study of Transition to Democracy," in Guillermo O'Donnell, et al., *Transitions from Authoritarian Rule: Comparative Perspectives* (Baltimore: Johns Hopkins Univ. Press, 1986), 48; cf. the observation of Giuseppe DiPalma: "Political actors in a transition are not passive tools of history. If actors are aware of predicaments endemic to transitions and act in their own interests, then they *can* set in motion a process that, even under an unpromising start, may close (be it only in a few cases) with the adoption of appropriate democratic rules." *To Craft Democracies: An Essay on Democratic Transitions* (Berkeley: Univ. of California Press, 1990), 46.

11. Samuel Decalo, "The Process, Prospects and Constraints of Democratization in Africa," *Africa Affairs*, 91 (1992): 7-35.

12. "Paths toward Redemocratization: Theoretical and Comparative Considerations," in O'Donnell, et al., op. cit., 78-79.

13. Przeworski, op. cit., 61-62, and DiPalma, 44-75. Cf. J. Samuel Valenzuela, "Consolidation in Post-Transitional Settings," in Scott Mainwaring, et al., eds., *Issues in Democratic Consolidation: The New South American Democracies in Comparative Perspective* (Notre Dame: Univ. of Notre Dame Press, 1992), 84-87.

14. See DiPalma, loc. cit., and Richard Joseph, op. cit., 199-201.

15. See, for example, Seymour Martin Lipset, "Some Social Requisites of Democracy: Economic Development and Political Legitimacy," *American Political Science Review*, 53 (1959), and Larry Diamond, "Economic Development and Democracy Reconsidered," in Gary Marks and Larry Diamond, eds., *Reexamining Democracy: Essays in Honor of Seymour Martin Lipset* (Newbury Park, Calif.: 1992).

16. Conway W. Henderson, "Population Pressures and Political Repression," *Social Science Quarterly*, 74, 2 (June 1993): 330.

17. *The Theory of Social and Economic Organization* (New York: The Free Press, 1947), 347-57. Cf. the short discussion in Richard Sandbrook, *The Politics of Africa's Economic Stagnation* (Cambridge: Cambridge Univ. Press, 1985), 88-89 and the discussion of tributes, patronage, and prebends in Rene Lemarchand, "The State, the Parallel Economy, and the Changing Structure of Patronage Systems," in Rothchild and Chazan, *The Precarious Balance* (Boulder, Colo.: Westview, 1988), 151-54.

18. Crawford Young and Thomas Turner, *The Rise and Decline of the Zairian State* (Madison: Univ. of Wisconsin Press, 1985), 330-56.

19. Op. cit., 89; the classic argument for personal rule, and one of the seminal books on Africa of the 1980s, is that of Robert Jackson and Carl Rosberg, *Personal Rule in Black Africa* (Los Angeles: Univ. of California Press, 1982).

20. For one characteristically harsh assessment, see J. Barry Riddell, "Things Fall Apart Again: Structural Adjustment Programmes in Sub-Saharan Africa," *Journal of Modern African Studies*, 30, 1 (1992): 53-68.

21. Ibid. Also see John F. Clark, "Socio-Political Change in the Republic of the Congo: Political Dilemmas of Economic Reform," *Journal of Third World Studies*, X (Spring, 1993).

22. Irving Leonard Markovitz, *Power and Class in Africa: An Introduction to Change and Conflict in African Politics* (Englewood Cliffs, New Jersey: Prentice-Hall, 1977), 198-229. The "organizational bourgeoisie" is defined by their control over state offices that allow them to extract wealth from the economy rather than by their ownership of the means of production.

23. Perhaps the most representative example of the "instrumentalist" school is Aidan Southall, "The Illusion of Tribe," *Journal of Asian and African Studies*, 5 (Jan.-Apr. 1970). One classic example of the primordial approach may be found in Clifford Geertz, "The Integrative Revolution, Primordial Sentiments and Civil Politics in the New States," in Geertz, ed., *Old Societies and New States: The Quest for Modernity in Asia and Africa* (New York: Free Press, 1963).

24. For example, John S. Saul, himself a Marxist analyst, argues that "marxist scientists and African revolutionaries can only make progress when they take ethnicity . . . seriously as a real rather than ephemeral

and/or vaguely illegitimate variable." "The Dialectic of Race and Class," *Race and Class*, 20, no. 4 (1979): 371, cited in Chazan, et al., *Politics and Society in Contemporary Africa* (Boulder, Colo.: Lynne Rienner, 1988), 124.

25. Naomi Chazan, "Between Liberalism and Statism: African Political Cultures and Democracy," in Diamond, ed., *Political Culture and Democracy in Developing Countries* (Boulder, Colo.: Lynne Rienner, 1994), 69–76.

26. No less a figure than Julius Nyerere has claimed that "despite all the variations and some exceptions where the institutions of domestic of slavery existed, African family life was everywhere based on certain practices and attitudes which together mean basic equality, freedom, and unity." Cited in V. G. Simiyu, "The Democratic Myth in the African Traditional Societies," in Walter O. Oyugi, et al., eds., *Democratic Theory and Practice in Africa* (Portsmouth, N.H.: Heinemann, 1988).

27. Chazan, "Between Liberalism and Statism," 70.

28. See Sahr John Kpundeh, ed., *Democratization in Africa: African Views, African Voices, Summary of Three Workshops* (Washington, D.C.: National Academy Press, 1992), 9–10. Cf. the observation of Nyerere, note 32, *supra*.

29. For example, on the checks and balances in the political organization of the Yoruba (Nigeria), see Robert Smith, *Kingdoms of the Yoruba* (London: Methuen, 1976); on the importance of consultation among the Tswana (Botswana), see I. Schapera, *A Handbook of Tswana Law and Custom* (London: Frank Cass, 1970); and on the well-developed legal system of the Kuba (Zaire) see Jan Vansina, *The Children of Woot: A History of the Kuba Peoples* (Madison Univ. of Wisconsin Press, 1978), 145–52.

30. Chazan, "Between Liberalism and Statism," 70–71.

31. On the former, see David R. Morris, *The Washing of the Spears: A History of the Rise of the Zulu Nation Under Shaka and Its Fall in the Zulu War of 1879* (New York: Simon & Schuster, 1965), and on the latter, Alan Moorhead, *The White Nile* (1960, Middlesex, U.K.: Penguin, 1963), 58–66 and Thomas Packenham, *The Scramble for Africa, 1876–1912* (New York: Random House, 1991), 301–302.

Though the accuracy of these accounts may not be in question, they certainly feed the "heart of darkness" attitudes of common Western opinion about precolonial Africa.

32. Simiyu, loc. cit.

33. John D. Holm, "Botswana: A Paternalistic Democracy," in Larry Diamond, et al., *Democracy in Developing Countries: Africa*, vol. 2 (Boulder, Colo.: Lynne Rienner, 1988), 182.

34. And, one might add, since totalitarianism in some Western societies in the 20th century, especially Nazi Germany, reached depths of tyranny unknown anywhere in Africa.

35. Douglas Anglin, "Southern African Responses to Eastern European Developments," *Journal of Modern African Studies*, 28 (September 1990).

36. See World Bank, *Adjustment in Africa: Reforms, Results, and the Road Ahead* (New York: Oxford Univ. Press, 1994).

CHAPTER FOUR

Traditional Authorities and the Mozambican Transition to Democratic Governance*

HARRY G. WEST

NARRATOR: One of the greatest rewards of teaching is seeing the rise to fame of one's undergraduate students. In December of this year, Harry G. West will receive his doctorate at the University of Wisconsin in cultural anthropology. The intriguing title of his dissertation is "Sorcery of Construction and Sorcery of Ruin: Power and Local Discourse on the Mueda Plateau, Mozambique, 1922-1994."

He received his bachelor of arts degree with distinction at the University of Virginia with a senior honors thesis on revolution and development in Burkina Faso. He also received a General Course certificate at the London School of Economics and has been an affiliate of the Carter G. Woodson Institute for Afro-American and African Studies at the University of Virginia. Prior to that, he was a research assistant at the Land Tenure Center at the University of Wisconsin and held a series of fellowships, including the Charlotte W. Newcombe, Institute for the Study of World Politics, Gulbenkin, Wenner-Gren, U.S. Institute of Peace, Fulbright, and Foreign Language and Area Studies. On two occasions Harry West not only won a national award, but in one case he was number one in the nation—and this competition was broadly based in all fields. In

---

*Presented in a Forum at the Miller Center of Public Affairs on 25 April 1996.

another case he was number two. So he certainly has held his own in scholarly competitions.

His publication titles suggest a creative approach to the fundamental problems of Africa: "Development Communication and Popular Resistance in Africa: An Examination of the Struggle over Tradition and Modernity Through Media," "A Piece of Land in a Land of Peace?: State Farm Divestiture in Mozambique," and "Creative Destruction and Sorcery of Construction: Power, Hope and Suspicion in Post-War Mozambique."

Harry grew up in an academic family. His father taught at Penn State, so he has not only had a rewarding academic career but in early life grew up close to the scene of books and research. We are grateful that he could speak at the Miller Center.

MR. WEST: So many changes are occurring in Mozambique right now that it is quite overwhelming. It is a very exciting and confusing time for both the social scientist who is attempting to understand the changes that are taking place and for the people experiencing them. To provide context for my presentation, I will begin by providing a brief history of Mozambique.

Mozambique, like all of the former Portuguese colonies, is a bit unique in African history in that in the late 1950s and early 1960s when most of the other major European colonial powers were granting independence to their colonies, the Portuguese were preparing to stay for the long haul, convinced that their brand of colonialism was different. The Portuguese had no intention of giving up power. As a result, the nationalist movement in Mozambique made the decision to take up armed resistance.

The movement began in the late 1950s and was consolidated with the formation of the FRELIMO Party, the Front for the Liberation of Mozambique, in 1962. Between 1964 and 1974, FRELIMO waged a war for independence, beginning in the northern part of Mozambique and working their way south. This heritage of a war for independence, which is also shared by the other former Portuguese colonies in Africa—Angola and Guinea-Bissau—created a party whose experience in governance was gained over a ten-year period of exercising military authority in the rural areas.

Harry G. West

It also created a series of enemies for the FRELIMO Party, a series of social groups that FRELIMO referred to as "collaborators" with the colonial regime, or as "enemies of the revolution." Many of these individuals were people who fought in the Portuguese colonial army against the FRELIMO guerrilla army. In 1975 when independence was granted to Mozambique and FRELIMO came to power, many of these individuals fled the country, and some of them went into Rhodesia, which borders Mozambique to the west. In Rhodesia some entered into cooperation with the Rhodesian security forces, which were at the time fighting against Zimbabwean nationalist guerrillas in their own country. Mozambican recruits were used primarily to strike at Zimbabwean guerrilla bases inside Mozambique. When Zimbabwe gained independence in 1980 as Mozambique had five years earlier, once again these individuals were without a place, and so the apartheid regime in South Africa took them out of Rhodesia, trained them in South Africa, and reinserted them into Mozambique to destabilize their hostile neighbors. The group eventually would come to be known by the Portuguese acronym, RENAMO, the Mozambican National Resistance. Over the next 12 years, a civil war was fought in Mozambique in which this guerrilla army, RENAMO, fought against the FRELIMO government. By war's end, over a million people had died and over six million people (out of a population of approximately 15 million) had been displaced from their homes. Obviously, the impact was quite dramatic, and virtually no one in the country was left untouched by the violence of the war.

In 1992, however, with a treaty in Rome and the pledged support of the United Nations, the war came to an end. With the guidance of the international community, which at this point consisted of participants from both the Eastern bloc and the former Soviet Union as well as from Western European nations and the United States, elections were held, and the FRELIMO Party won over RENAMO.

Within the context of this transition after the war, people in Maputo were able to go back into the rural areas for the first time in nearly 15 years to see what had taken place there during the war. What they found was that most of the people in rural Mozambique had been placed in the middle of two warring armies whose politics were rather foreign and rather incomprehensible to them. Many of the traditional institutions in Mozambique (structured around chieftaincies at the local level) were battered and bruised but nonetheless somewhat functional.

Within the context of the elections that were held in 1994, both sides came to understand that these traditional institutions had an importance not only for the people in rural Mozambique but also for the parties that were attempting to attract electoral support. The relationship between these traditional authorities and the two parties, however, was very complex.

The FRELIMO Party had taken a rather antagonistic approach toward traditional institutions and traditional authorities since coming to power in 1975. FRELIMO viewed most chiefs as having been corrupted by cooperation with the colonial regime. In fact, when the Portuguese conquered Mozambique bit by bit, the way they did so was to arrive in a certain area and to "pacify" that area, as they referred to it, and to then demand that the people identify their chief. This chief was then forced to serve as an intermediary between the Portuguese colonial regime and the population in that area. The chief was forced to create a register of the people in his area and was forced to collect taxes from them. He was also forced to contribute individuals from the population who would provide labor on collective projects such as road construction or on colonial plantations. Over the approximately 100-year period in which the Portuguese colonial regime was functional, chiefs were placed in a situation where they either collaborated and were rewarded, or resisted and were punished.

When FRELIMO came to power in 1975, they determined that traditional institutions had to be eliminated, that they had become so corrupted by their participation in the colonial apparatus that they no longer had a place in independent Mozambique. FRELIMO held elections in the villages. Traditional authorities were not allowed to participate as candidates. Neither were they allowed to participate in any of the public proceedings in which communities would make decisions as to whom they wished to have as their representatives.

Consequently, when RENAMO began to spread across Mozambique in the period following independence, they encountered traditional authorities, who were rather upset with the FRELIMO government. They encountered people who had served a very important role within their societies, but had been marginalized since independence. In many instances, RENAMO immediately received support from these chiefs.

RENAMO's relationship with these figures was also rather complex. RENAMO's primary interest was not in governmental reform, whether at the national or local level. The history of the organization was founded in the experiences of individuals who had no position in independent Mozambique and whose objectives were largely determined by forces outside of the country—primarily, the apartheid regime in South Africa in the 1980s. RENAMO's interests in Mozambique were in gaining territory and in bringing populations under its control, which could then provide what it needed to reproduce itself as a guerrilla army—food, labor, porters (to carry military equipment across the border into Mozambique), and recruits for its army.

RENAMO's tactics were ruthless. The massacres they committed are well documented, and outside of any ideological discussion or debate, it is clear that RENAMO was not primarily interested in "liberating Mozambicans." Nonetheless, when it arrived in a rural area, it immediately contacted former chiefs, telling them that RENAMO was taking the area out of government control and that it wanted the chiefs to serve as its intermediary.

Initially, this approach attracted a great deal of support. There are several well-documented cases in the history of the civil war in which large populations defected en masse from government-held areas—picked up and moved 20 or 30 kilometers into RENAMO-held areas—and often these moves were orchestrated by chiefs in their respective areas. Once in a RENAMO-held area, these populations often found that life was hard; that they were being called upon to contribute large percentages of the crops that they cultivated and to contribute their children—boys and girls as young as seven or eight years of age—to participate in the war. It had not been "the better life" that they were promised by their chiefs.

When the peace treaty came in 1992, the situation was very complicated. Most people in the rural areas did not feel much of an affinity for either of the political parties. Most felt that they had been brutalized by one or the other, or both. Many also felt betrayed by traditional authorities, but at this particular moment in time, chiefs continued to play an important role. In the chaos that ensued as a result of the war, most people had sought guidance and leadership from traditional authorities. Their day-to-day problems continued to be resolved by traditional authorities. Chiefs continued to play an important role in the arrangement of marriages, in the distribution of land, and in the resolution of conflict both within families and between families and larger ethnic groups, as they did in the period prior to the colonial era. These individuals continued to play a role in the local ritual life of people, including various ceremonies blessing the harvest and ceremonies conducted every year at the beginning of the rainy season to ensure that the rains are good and steady.

In 1993 when the electoral campaign began, both of the political parties recognized that these traditional authorities with whom they had had rather complex relationships during the war could either make or break their political campaigns. Both parties headed off into the rural areas in their quests for the support of the chieftaincy.

At the same time, the international community was supporting what it referred to as democratization and political decentralization within the context of the peace process. Peace was linked to elections. The understanding was that the two warring sides in Mozambique would not come to terms unless and until they received a popular mandate and the people were able to make a determination as to what the respective representation of the two parties would be. As part of this, the international community advocated that democratization take into account the chieftaincy, traditional authorities. Everyone in Mozambique—from the United Nations to the World Bank to the United States Agency for International Development to NGOs such as Ox-Fam, CARE, and Save the Children—was talking about traditional authorities and their role in a democratized Mozambique.

This situation presented a number of complicated dilemmas because while it is true that traditional institutions have continued as a vehicle for politics at the local level, these institutions do not have the same definition of democracy that the international community has. Traditional institutions are not determined by election. In February, when I spoke to several chiefs in various regions in Mozambique about this issue, they said quite openly and quite frankly, "We're not interested in elections. We are chiefs because we have inherited our titles. We cannot be elected. We derive legitimacy from the fact that we have a direct link back to ancestors who were chiefs prior to us. This is not a question of elections, and to submit us to elections is to undermine the power of the chieftaincy."

At the same time, it cannot be forgotten that over the past century, the chieftaincy in Mozambique, like it or not, has been an institution that has been steeped in violence, cohesion, authoritarianism, and extraction of labor and economic resources from the populations that chiefs "represent." This is true in the precolonial period (where there were invasions of one ethnic group of another in which the invading groups immediately contacted the chiefs of the subjugated population and entered into an arrangement with them whereby they collected tribute) and in the colonial period (when the colonial administration pacified local populations with essentially the same arrangement). It is also true in both the periods of the war for independence (in which the FRELIMO organization entered into arrangements with local chiefs to garner support in terms of recruits, labor, and donations of food) and the civil war (in which RENAMO did the same). It is a history that repeats itself over and over again, one in which the chieftaincy always plays a role as mediator. The chieftaincy has always been caught in the middle of larger political and military institutions and between a population that it is said to "represent."

In the present day context, most people in rural Mozambique are quite confused as to what democracy means and what role traditional authorities might play in it. "Civil society," as much of the literature in political science would refer to it, is extremely weak in Mozambique. There are very few voluntary or spontaneous social and political organizations in Mozambique. Given the decades of war, there has neither been the time nor the political space for these kinds of institutions to be created and to sustain themselves. Therefore, local politics is expressed primarily through kinship-based organization, namely, chieftaincies.

There are various levels within the chieftaincy. They are nested political structures based upon highly variable lineage structures in various parts of Mozambique, essentially constructed of heads of family, heads of large extended families, then, in some areas, heads of lineages and heads of larger ethnic groups that may number in the tens or hundreds of thousands of people.

There is a new constitution in Mozambique that protects individual rights, freedom of the press, freedom of religion, and freedom of political expression. With a constitution designed to protect basic human rights, bringing the chiefs back to play their former role—and by former role it is not clearly understood which former role and to which period one is referring—is highly problematic when one understands that chieftaincies and the particular figures of authority within them have historically depended upon collaboration with larger, and normally violent, institutions to enforce their decisions, and that their exercise of power has been flavored with their ability to extract tribute and uncompensated labor.

The question then becomes what to do. I am not going to pretend to have the answer to that question today. Mozambique has had far too many oversimplified answers in the past couple of decades. People at the local level are now seeking to find ways in which local communities are able to determine for themselves not only who their representatives are, but also what kinds of roles they will play. In other words, if chiefs are not selected through an election process, then there needs to be a way for local populations to determine the legitimacy of one or another claimant to the position of chief and control the individual who exercises that authority. At the same time, local populations need to be able to determine the relationship between the chieftaincy and local government. Constitutional reform is a part of that process, as is legal reform. What is also needed, however, is an understanding by people at all levels in government that the language of democracy spoken in Mozambique will be very different from the models being imported—Western models that are based on the participation of "civil society," elections, and such things.

I would like to describe briefly the focus of my dissertation because it is an interesting example of what I have been discussing.

Although it presents more questions than answers, nonetheless it is rather revealing with regard to the present situation.

My research was conducted in the northern part of Mozambique in the district in which the FRELIMO guerrilla army based itself during the war of independence. It is the district in which FRELIMO defined its relationship with the chieftaincy in the course of its attempts to garner support from local populations. It is a district that since 1964 has had 30 years of experience with FRELIMO's orchestrated maneuvers against the institutions of the chieftaincy. In this district, the chieftaincy has nearly disappeared, at least at the level of traditional authorities that had been brought into formal cooperation with the Portuguese colonial regime.

Nonetheless, populations in this area recognize traditional authorities at a lower level. I previously discussed the nested levels of traditional authority in Mozambique—the heads of family, the heads of lineage, and the heads of larger political institutions that encompass entire ethnic groups. In this particular case, people have focused their interests on a lower level in the chieftaincy closer to the family level, underneath the level of authorities that were recognized by the Portuguese colonial administration and underneath the level of authorities that were openly attacked by the FRELIMO government after independence. That is one way in which they have dealt with the situation. Today, despite the fact that the government has institutions to oversee decisions regarding distribution and titling of land and the resolution of conflict, questions of marriage and divorce and questions requiring public gatherings are resolved by these heads of family. They continue to go to these heads of families when there is a crisis in the village or even in the district.

In my dissertation I am researching local understandings of how power functions. I have found in this particular district that people understand politics in part through a language of sorcery. Political conflict is understood as conflict between sorcerers. When problems arise, it is because someone has committed an act of sorcery. Sorcery can cause a child in the village to fall ill and die. It can cause the local water supply system to become dysfunctional—cause the pump to break. Sorcery can cause the rains not to come. At the same time, locally, people understand the responsible exercise of political authority as one in which the leader is able to recognize, or "see," these acts of sorcery and put an end to them. Local leaders are understood as sorcerers who are both more powerful and more benevolent than the other sorcerers who are creating political and social problems within the village.

In the precolonial period, this is how people understood power. In the colonial period, people continued to understand power in this way because the Portuguese administration did not attempt to insert itself at the level of the village. When FRELIMO attempted to displace local authorities, local populations interpreted this as a claim on the part of FRELIMO and its government representatives to be more powerful sorcerers than the chiefs. So locally, people treat representatives of the government as they would treat local chiefs—with the same expectations, with the same restrictions, and with many of the same understandings of the way in which their power functions.

It is all rather confusing when political parties at a certain level are participating in democratization as understood in Western terms, but the populations give it meaning according to other terms. Democratic reform in Mozambique is necessary because the war could not have been resolved at upper levels without elections. The political parties and the armies that they controlled would not have come to the table and would not have given up their arms had there not been a promise of elections. But as the elections are pushed out on the local populations (and now there is talk of elections at the local level for positions from district administrator all the way down to president of the village), local populations find the confusion they create threatening. If people are to understand what is going on in Mozambique—or for that matter, if they are to understand the different historical contexts that have given rise to current U.N. formulas and models for resolving the varied conflicts taking place in the world and to have any success in ending them—they need to understand how people at the local level are understanding and experiencing the changes that are being forced upon them and how they are trying to control, steer, and give sense to it all on their own terms.

LYN GRAYBILL: Can you comment on the election results? Were you surprised that RENAMO did as well as it did? The popular view is that they had no real support; it was totally illegitimate and totally fueled by South Africa, outside agents. Is that surprising?

MR. WEST: In one sense it is very surprising because on one level populations in most areas of the country felt that the legitimacy of RENAMO was almost nonexistent; their agenda was not clearly defined in political or ideological terms. In another sense, however, the election results were not surprising, given the way people experienced the election process. In 1994, about six months before the elections, I was able to travel the entire length of the country by road and to spend time in every province talking to people about elections. I often asked people whom they intended to vote for. They would immediately return my question with the question of who I thought would win. They made their decisions based on the answers others and I gave them. Frequently, people would phrase the question in terms of "who is the *real* chief?" What most people wanted to know was who had more power. Once people understood who was the power to be reckoned with, they wanted to be able to fall in line behind it.

The election results were a checkerboard. Areas that were held by RENAMO voted for RENAMO. Areas held by FRELIMO voted for FRELIMO. Almost without exception, the people had bitter complaints against the power that held their district. Their understanding was that elections are a form of recognition. Most people were afraid that if their district or their village was seen as having voted against the power to be, they would be in trouble. There were many threats of house burnings, assassinations, and so forth. Thus, in that sense, it was not surprising at all. But RENAMO cannot claim the electoral results as a popular mandate.

QUESTION: In the course of this long conflict, where did the combatants obtain their arms?

MR. WEST: In the war for independence, arms were coming primarily from Eastern bloc countries and China.

TRADITIONAL AUTHORITIES AND THE MOZAMBICAN TRANSITION

QUESTION: Did they pay for them, or were the arms contributed?

MR. WEST: They were contributing the arms. China contributed military trainers as well as arms. Interestingly enough, FRELIMO was always quite successful in straddling divides and was receiving a great deal of financial support—though not support in arms—from the Nordic countries, Italy, and many private organizations in the United States, Great Britain, and West Germany throughout the period of the war for independence.

RENAMO was originally a part of the Rhodesian security forces (after the unilateral declaration of independence and during the white minority regime of Ian Smith). Afterwards they were receiving most of their support in both arms and equipment, as well as in financial and technical support, from South Africa. They had support from private organizations (primarily in West Germany and the United States), but this support was being funneled through South Africa until the later part of the war when schisms developed between the various sources of support.

QUESTION: So there was never any shortage of armaments?

MR. WEST: Never. It was estimated that there were two million AKMs in the country when the peace accord was signed, and the United Nations was attempting to collect all of them. They probably collected about half of them. Approximately two-thirds of the remaining arms appear to have been sold on the black market and have fed into what has become an enormous crime ring in southern Africa that crosses international boundaries. This situation is creating headaches for the South African regime and for Mozambique, Zimbabwe, Zambia, and Malawi.

QUESTION: What is the population of Mozambique?

MR. WEST: Mozambique's population is approximately 15 or 16 million in what is a fairly large country geographically. The population density is therefore rather low. With regard to the urban rural divide, when the civil war began, about two million people lived in the cities—about a million in the capital city and another million or a million-and-a-half in the other cities. By the end of the war, probably five million people were living in the cities. There was a process whereby people in the villages moved into the district seats. People in the district seats moved into the provincial capitals; people in the provincial capitals moved to the capital city; and people in the capital city left the country. That process is now taking place in reverse. People refer to it as leapfrogging.

QUESTION: Surely the United Nations has some anthropologists on their staff to aid in policy implementation.

MR. WEST: Yes, the United Nations did have a number of anthropologists on staff, including some who specialized in refugee resettlement and others who were experts on de-mining. In a country where there were an estimated two million mines, these anthropologists were able to contribute to programs designed to inform people about the dangers of mines and to teach them ways to avoid those dangers, as well as other related problems.

Relatively speaking, the U.N. operation in Mozambique was quite large in both personnel and funding. Having failed recently in Angola and in the process of failing in Somalia, Bosnia, and virtually everywhere else, the United Nations needed a success. The presence of so many U.N. people, however, was overwhelming to the population of Mozambique.

QUESTION: What is the current state of Mozambique's economy? Also, what has happened to the educational system?

MR. WEST: RENAMO's primary agenda within Mozambique was the destruction of infrastructure—the destruction of roads and transport capability—and at the village level, the destruction of anything that indicated the presence of FRELIMO. The two greatest signifiers of FRELIMO's presence in a village were elementary schools and health clinics. Virtually the entire educational structure outside of provincial capitals was destroyed as a result. Health clinics were literally smashed—systematically destroyed. Everything that they could not cart off, they destroyed. It was a classic tale of the horror of destruction. As a result, the economy is in complete shambles. The rural areas are very detached from the urban centers. Marketing and trade was paralyzed by the war.

Because of the peace treaty and because of developments in South Africa, a large number of people are returning to Mozambique—many of them former Portuguese colonials and many of them South Africans who no longer feel secure and are abandoning South Africa and moving to Mozambique. This is the reverse of what they did 10 or 15 years ago.

A great deal of investment is occurring right now, with much of it highly speculative and most of it not legal. In many cases the same plot of land has been sold by the government to four or five different investors, with government officials in many cases taking kickbacks in the process. Land conflicts are a terrible problem, as are conflicts over property. The tremendous amount of change occurring is dizzying for people, not to mention not necessarily good.

QUESTION: Have the Portuguese left any worthwhile legacy in Mozambique?

MR. WEST: Unfortunately, they have left very little. They never planned to leave, so when they did leave, they left very little by way of training and very little by way of human infrastructure. They also sabotaged much of the infrastructure they left behind. The district in which I worked was a plateau area without water sources, and the Portuguese had built a diesel pumping system to bring water up from the lowlands. When they left, they filled the tubes with concrete. A hotel in Maputo provides a similar, but more famous, illustration of what the Portuguese did before leaving. They were in the process of building a 20-story hotel on the beach—a beautiful hotel in a beautiful location. Maputo was quite a tourist attraction in colonial times for South African and Rhodesian tourists. They were about halfway finished in 1975 when they had to pull out, and in parting, they filled the elevator shaft with concrete so that it would not be possible to recuperate the building. As a result, it is now a 20-story concrete monument to the end of the colonial era.

QUESTION: Didn't Portugal as a strong Catholic nation leave any Catholics who could do some good in Mozambique?

MR. WEST: In the religious breakdown of the country, large numbers of individuals do identify themselves as Catholic. The Portuguese did construct a number of missions in the country and permitted a number of Protestant sects as well to set up missions in the southern part of the country. Those religions coexist with religious beliefs founded within local cosmologies.

QUESTION: How do you think the situation will be settled?

MR. WEST: I wish I had a clue as to how these issues will be resolved. What I do not see occurring is a replication of the models one might apply from the outside. I do not see the reproduction of a Western model of a liberalized economy, or one of a multiparty democratic electoral political system. That is not to say, however, that those will not be immensely important components of the system that eventually evolves. What I find striking in my experience—I have done research for about four years in Mozambique, so it is a limited period of time—is that people in Mozambique show a tremendous capability to deal with changes that are thrust upon them and to make the effects of those changes their own. They show a tremendous capability to borrow and adapt and retool the things that arrive on the horizon—everything from religious beliefs to economic practices to political structures and institutions. The end point of these current changes will likely be something uniquely Mozambican, but at the same time related to larger global processes.

QUESTION: Given your many interests, why did you and Ms. Graybill choose to concentrate your studies on Africa?

MS. GRAYBILL: I have been asked that question before, and I do not have a good answer. I became really interested in South Africa while taking a course on the politics of South Africa at the University of Virginia, and I became hooked on the subject. Robert Fatton, a professor who teaches classes on African politics at the

University of Virginia, is wonderful. His classes on Africa are not very popular, however, because most students are not studying Africa or African politics. The lack of interest illustrates the marginalization of the continent. People are not interested in it anymore, which is a shame. Fortunately, some people are still doing research on Africa. There are many possibilities there. Certainly South Africa is a bright spot on the continent.

MR. WEST: I have Mr. Thompson to blame in part for my interest. When I first began my studies, I was interested in pursuing a medical career, but I was very interested in international organizations like the World Health Organization. I began to take classes on the side to gain a better understanding of international politics. I found the international relations classes that I took with Mr. Thompson and others here much more interesting than chemistry, biology, calculus, and so forth. After about two years, I decided that I would rather spend time studying politics and international development than medicine.

I did fall into Africa in some of the same ways. I spent a year studying in London as an undergraduate, and when it came time for me to make a trip to examine questions of politics as they related to the developing world, Africa was the closest place for me to go. My experience there was very interesting. When I went to Burkina Faso, a country with many of the same experiences as Mozambique, I found the contradictions of socialist ideology very interesting—also a model taken from outside of Africa. I learned a little about local political understandings and practices, as well as how people attempted to make sense of two worldviews coming together—the contradictions and conflicts as well as the potential for cross-fertilization. Most of what I am doing now is just further inquiry into these same questions.

NARRATOR: We have thoroughly enjoyed hearing Harry West's presentation and observing his professional growth in the field he has chosen. He is a credit to the University of Virginia and the Miller Center, and we thank him for his discussion today.

CHAPTER FIVE

Mobutu Sese Seko of Zaire as a Nondemocratic Presidential Leader*

JOHN F. CLARK

NARRATOR: One of the objectives of the Miller Center staff is to make ourselves obsolete, and we have tried to do that through the quality of the younger scholars who have worked at the Miller Center. John Clark is one of them. He is currently assistant professor of international relations at Florida International University in Miami teaching both undergraduate and graduate courses. He graduated *magna cum laude* from Georgia Southern with a major in political science. While an undergraduate, he studied French at Caen and again at the University of Laval (Quebec) as a graduate student. He has received a number of fellowships—Earhart, Eisenhower, Dorman, Bell—and as a graduate student served on the staff of the National Model United Nations. He also worked at the Miller Center for three-and-one-half years while at the University of Virginia.

John wrote his master's thesis on "Realism in the Reagan Doctrine" and his dissertation on "Superpower Intervention in Several Conflicts of Sub-Saharan Africa." He is currently completing a book on reform in Francophone Africa. Some of us, including Mr. Inis Claude, are very proud that John Clark is here today to give us his impressions of Mobutu Sese Seko and Zaire.

---

*Presented in a Forum at the Miller Center of Public Affairs on 30 June 1994.

MR. CLARK: Thank you, Mr. Thompson. I have just returned from Africa, where I spent three weeks in Zaire and one in Zimbabwe. While in Zaire, I interviewed some 15 prominent political figures, including the chief opposition leader, whose name is Etienne Tshisekedi. Among the others whom I interviewed was Mobutu's chief of staff, Vendauwe Te Pemako, so I had a tremendous opportunity to gain understanding from these people who have dealt with Mobutu. Mobutu is a figure of historical significance who has been the president of Zaire since 1965 when he seized power in a coup d'etat.

I. Is It Useful To Study Mobutu As A "Presidential" Ruler?

Perhaps this presentation requires some justification: Is it appropriate or useful to discuss Mobutu Sese Seko, who is widely regarded as a dictator or even a tyrant, in a research institute on the American presidency? A case can be made that this topic *is* appropriate, both because of the nature of Mobutu's rule and because of the need for comparative thinking about the American presidency.

First, Mobutu can claim with some reason to be a presidential ruler. At the risk of imbuing Zaire's ruler with undue legitimacy, one has to admit that he has made some efforts—albeit mostly cosmetic and rhetorical—to rule in the name of the people. Although he is an authoritarian ruler, Mobutu has never tried to declare himself emperor, after the fashion of Jean-Bedel Bokassa (of the Central African Republic), or president-for-life, like Hastings Banda (from Malawi). Rather, he has always insisted on having elections, however fraudulent, to try to legitimate his rule. Although he is a military man, Mobutu prefers to emphasize his title as "president" over that of "marshall," and he generally wears civilian rather than military dress.

Mobutu's creation of a political party, the Popular Movement of the Revolution (MPR), also reflects his desire for legitimacy. Perhaps for pragmatic reasons, he has not sought to rule through terror alone. Finally, Mobutu makes some concessions to the rule of law. Like the old Soviet leaders, Mobutu may be repressive, but he likes to have the paperwork in order; you may be arrested, but if so, at least until recently, there was generally an order for your detention signed by proper authorities. This has certainly not always been the case; many people have been illegally detained in Zaire, but breaches of the rule of law have occurred in Western democracies as well.

Second, it is useful and appropriate to examine non-American presidential rulers for comparative purposes. If nothing else, studying Mobutu may put the excesses of Nixon or Reagan or Clinton in some perspective. Not that people should excuse the indiscretions or crimes of these leaders, but they do seem far less serious when compared with those of some Third World dictators. Hillary Clinton's $100,000 made on a suspicious cattle futures deal pales in comparison to the billions that have disappeared from Zaire's treasury. The self-restraint and relative honesty of our own rulers are put in better perspective by comparing their comportment with that of Mobutu. Perhaps this recognition will make people less cynical about American politics. Moreover, Americans can see how their own institutions have worked to limit executive abuses and how the wisdom and restraint of American leaders have made democracy possible.

II. Mobutu's Background

In examining Mobutu's rule, it helps to begin with his personal background. Mobutu Sese Seko, formerly Joseph-Desiré Mobutu, was born in the town of Lisala in October 1930 in the former colony of Belgian Congo. Lisala is in the northern part of the region of Equateur near the Zaire (Congo) River and is quite remote from the main urban centers. His "ancestral village" is Gbadolité, which he has now turned into a major town in Zaire, complete with an international airport and a palace.

Mobutu's father, who died in 1938, was a cook and earned some money working for various Belgian employers. By all accounts, Mobutu's family was very poor, even desperately poor, after his father's death, which may explain his current obsession with money. Mobutu apparently loved his mother, after whom the central hospital in Kinshasa, Mama Yemo, is now named. He grew up speaking both his tribal language and Lingala, a trade language of Zaire and Congo, and learned French at a young age. Despite his poverty, Mobutu managed to complete primary school and then went on to a missionary school in Mbandaka (a city in southern Equateur). Mobutu claims that he is a devout Catholic and brags of his meetings with Pope John Paul II.

According to Mobutu, he got into trouble with his Catholic teachers when he went to Kinshasa for a few days in December 1949. Many Zairians say that he was caught in the act of petty theft. In any case, he was expelled from school and sent into the *Force Publique* in 1950. Mobutu then went to the military base at Luluabourg (now Kananga) in the region of Kasai. Although he never finished his formal studies, Mobutu received a diploma as an accounting secretary in 1952. Mobutu received some rudimentary journalistic training in the army, and he wrote some articles for a newspaper called *L'Avenir Colonial Belge*. It is difficult to determine what he actually wrote because the articles were unsigned, but most people whom I met laughed when I asked if Mobutu was a skilled writer. In 1958-59 Mobutu was sent to Belgium, where he took a few short courses on writing at the Office of Information and Public Relations for Belgium's colonies. Congolese people were not allowed to become officers in the colonial period, so Mobutu only rose to the rank of sergeant in the army.

Mobutu was in Brussels during the famous roundtable conference of January-February 1960, at which time the Belgians abruptly agreed to grant Congo independence six months later. Patrice Lumumba, who was Congo's first leader after independence, was released from jail to attend the conference. Mobutu claims that he was sympathetic to Lumumba at this early moment and was a member of Lumumba's Congolese National Movement Party (MNC). Mobutu was also a Congolese delegate at the economic roundtable in April and May 1960. Mobutu did in fact agree with Lumumba on one key issue: that Congo should have a centralized government, not a federation. Contrary to his later claims, however, Mobutu had no local constituency in Congo at this time and had virtually no role in achieving independence for Congo.

John F. Clark

After independence for Congo and the beginning of the mutinies soon thereafter, Lumumba dismissed the Belgian officers from the National Congolese Army (ANC) and began promoting the Congolese noncommissioned officers. Mobutu became a colonel, effectively the second in command of the ANC as chief of staff to General Victor Lundula. Apparently, Lundula had little organizational skill or political savvy, however, and Mobutu soon became the most important Congolese military figure.

During the early months of the First Republic, a series of political crises broke out in the Congo. First was the mutiny of the army, during which some Europeans were assaulted; second was the intervention of the Belgian army troops, which exacerbated the situation; third, the region of Katanga seceded under the leadership of Moise Tshombe; and finally, there was the intervention of the United Nations forces, which lasted until 1963, after having defeated Tshombe's secession. Unilateral interventions by both superpowers and other actors also occurred in Zaire during this time.

To focus on 1960 for a moment, the tensions created by the uncertainties of the U.N. mission to Congo caused a split between President Kasavubu and Prime Minister Lumumba, and each announced the dismissal of the other. It was during this chaotic environment that Mobutu first appeared on the Zairian political scene. Specifically, his action at the time was to announce the "neutralization" of both politicians and to appoint a neutral, technocratic government, which only lasted for some weeks. As the conflict evolved between the pro-Western Kasavubu, who was president, and the radical Patrice Lumumba, who was prime minister, Mobutu generally favored the former. According to one source, some of Lumumba's supporters even tried to assassinate Mobutu. Mobutu's generally conservative outlook and disapproval of Lumumba's behavior turned Mobutu against the prime minister. Around the same time, the CIA became interested in Mobutu, particularly in cultivating him as an alternative to Lumumba, who was greatly feared and despised in Washington as a potential Communist, and Kasavubu, who was regarded as lacking in vigor. According to Africanist orthodoxy, the CIA operatives in the Congo made contact with Mobutu at this early stage and bribed him into cooperating with their plans. Although Mobutu himself denies any responsibility, saying that he was simply following Kasavubu's orders, Mobutu was responsible for Lumumba's arrest in January 1961, after which Lumumba was sent to Shaba, where he was murdered by Tshombe's men, probably with CIA encouragement, though not direct involvement.

According to the same Africanist orthodoxy, Mobutu was important behind the scenes during the subsequent years under the regimes of Prime Ministers Joseph Ileo and Cyrille Adoula (Kasavubu remained president). It is impossible to discern his precise role, however. Between 1961 and 1963, U.S. support for these regimes became quite firm, and relatively substantial aid began flowing to the Congolese army. A series of rebellions continued during these years, led by a former Lumumba lieutenant, Antoine Gizenga and by a charismatic Maoist in Bandundu (Kwilu) named Pierre Mulélé. As the effective leader of the army, Mobutu was involved in suppressing these movements with American aid. Mobutu and the Congolese army also had a minor role in ending the secession in Katanga in December 1962.

While Kennedy was president of the United States, American diplomats worked hard to make democracy work in the Congo, despite the incredible difficulties. Through 1963, it is unlikely that the United States would have approved of a Mobutu coup. After Kennedy's death and Johnson's ascension, however, American policy became more vigorously anti-Communist, rather than pro-democracy. During the 1964 Stanleyville crisis, for instance, U.S. intervention was the most overt and unilateral that it had been to that point. This may have given the green light to Mobutu.

The actual set of events that provoked Mobutu's seizure of power in Congo was yet another political crisis that began in February 1965 after Congo's first independence-era elections. The outcome of these elections was unclear, but Tshombe, who had briefly succeeded Adoula as premier, thought that he should be again named prime minister. President Kasavubu, however, refused Tshombe and appointed someone else, who was not confirmed by the Parliament. This led to a long political feud, which finally ended on 24 November 1965 when Mobutu seized power in the name of a military high command.

John F. Clark

After a year and a half of completely arbitrary rule, Mobutu began to put in place the new institutions of state. In 1967 a new single party for the country, the MPR, was created to unify the country and legitimate Mobutu's rule. Also in that year, a new constitution, largely written by the current head of Mobutu's opposition, Etienne Tshisekedi, was adopted by the people. Mobutu's direct control over the state was further strengthened by a revised constitution in 1974. At the same time, "Mobutuism," a vague doctrine based on the traditional patrimonial rule of the chief of state, was made the official ideology of the state. This was the beginning of Mobutu's cult of personality that he has tried to foster.

In discussing the Second Republic period as a whole, one is best advised to follow the lead of Crawford Young, who is one of the ablest Africanists ever produced in the United States and whom the Rockefeller Foundation chose as their field director in Africa. Young, with his collaborator Thomas Turner, wrote a major work on Zaire under Mobutu in the 1980s. According to this account, Mobutu enjoyed some legitimate popularity and success as a leader and state-builder from 1967 to about 1973. During this time, Zaire enjoyed relative prosperity and some recovery from the civil war. In the late 1960s, people were so exhausted by civil war that they were simply happy to see a return of order, even if it meant repression. The same period was marked by relatively high world prices for copper, which has consistently been Zaire's largest revenue earner. As a result, the country made some modest development gains and began to rebuild its infrastructure. Zaire even enjoyed a stable currency during these years.

After peaking at some $860 million in 1974, copper revenues declined by 50 percent the following year and failed to recover to a similar level throughout the 1970s and 1980s. Meanwhile, the Zairian population was burgconing. At the same time, Zaire was slowly building up a more substantial international debt. From the second half of the 1970s throughout the 1980s, the Zairian state was in steady decline. The state became more and more corrupt and inefficient, and Mobutu did nothing to save it. Beginning in 1973, Zaire began taking over foreign economic interests under a program that Mobutu called "Zairianization." Essentially, Mobutu seized foreign assets and turned them over to his supporters as a reward for political loyalty—a classic example of African patron-client relations. These new owners, however, lacked the ability to manage their new enterprises, and domestic production declined dramatically in the 1970s. Many of the new owners simply wanted to become rich, not manage economic enterprises. As the economy declined, Mobutu had to increase his repression accordingly to prevent the population from revolting against him.

The country continued to decline throughout the 1980s: Most of the infrastructure deteriorated (Zaire only has a fraction of the roads left that it had in 1960, at independence); the debt continued to rise; and literacy rates stagnated, then declined. Meanwhile, a number of massive development projects, including the Inga-Shaba electric power scheme, went sour. During this time, the population continued to grow, and as a result, the standard of living for most Zairians in the 1980s was lower than it had been at independence in 1960.

Zaire's political stagnation led to the emergence of a rather vigorous opposition in the 1980s. The current head of the opposition, Tshisekedi, first broke with Mobutu in 1980 when he led a group of disaffected parliamentarians into opposition and exile. Mobutu responded with detention, assaults, and efforts to co-opt these politicians with money. Tshisekedi and others suffered internal exile and physical abuse while detained, and some had their houses burned or attacked. Beginning in 1989, heartened by the collapse of Eastern European totalitarian regimes, the Zairian opposition became more and more active, initiating a number of public protests and demonstrations. Under this mounting pressure, Mobutu made a speech in April 1990 promising to allow the beginning of a multiparty system in Zaire.

Since 1990, the country has been on the path of transition, but no one can say where the transition will lead. The written press has been freed, though the government still controls the electronic media. Moreover, at the end of 1990, legislation legalizing political parties was passed, and an enormous number of parties have now emerged. The original focus of the opposition was to hold a "Sovereign National Conference" beginning in August 1991, which they forced Mobutu to allow. The conference lasted until September 1992, having been suspended for extended periods. At the end of the conference, Tshisekedi was named prime minister, against Mobutu's wishes. Tshisekedi's job was to lead a transitional government and organize elections. Inevitably, Mobutu clashed with Tshisekedi, particularly over access to money, and announced his dismissal and the appointment of a new prime minister, Faustin Birindwa. Politics had come full circle in Zaire after more than 30 years—again, the country had two competing governments.

During 1993, there was a long, continual stalemate: Tshisekedi had his *de jure* government in place, and Birindwa ran a *de facto* government. Neither side would budge, and the economy continued a dizzying decline. Finally, in December 1993, a compromise was reached whereby a new Parliament would be formed, including both pro-Mobutu and anti-Mobutu forces. Nominally, the opposition members hold the majority, but the meaning of "opposition" is unclear. There are really two oppositions: the hard-core opposition led by Tshisekedi and a nominal opposition that has only emerged since 1990. This latter pseudo-opposition is organized outside the platform known as the Union Sacrée, which groups together the real opposition. The main element of the pseudo-opposition is the Union des Democrates Independents, derogatorily referred to as the Union des Dinosaurs Impunis. Their leader, Kengo wa Dondo, was just recently named the new prime minister. The Western press refers to him as the leader of the "moderate opposition," but he stole millions as Mobutu's last Second Republic prime minister.

III. The Secrets of Mobutu's Success

The strength of the opposition has now been broken, and Mobutu is now paving the way for fraudulent elections to maintain his power and legitimate his rule. The opposition appears to have peaked in 1992 and is now hopelessly divided and unsure of itself; only Tshisekedi remains firm. Therefore, it is now possible that Mobutu will be in power for several more years. The French have already accepted this and with characteristic cynicism have re-embraced Mobutu. Given Mobutu's success in staying in power and winning friends abroad, if not in helping his people and building the state, what else contributes to his strong power?

One has to acknowledge the importance of his various security agencies. There is the National Documentation Agency (AND) and the National Service for Intelligence and Protection (SNIP), which engage in surveillance of Mobutu's enemies and, when necessary, in detention as well. Their activities are well documented in Michael Schatzberg's book, *The Dialectics of Oppression in Zaire* (1988). Lately, these agencies have fallen on hard times: Now that opposition to Mobutu is open and public, these agencies cannot possibly keep track of the hundreds of thousands of public protestors. They do, however, still exist and do still engage in selected harassment of Mobutu's enemies. On 13 June 1994, when Kengo was named prime minister, Tshisekedi himself was briefly detained by these police. SNIP still operates, and people still fear it.

There is also the Zairian Armed Forces (FAZ) and the various elite elements within it. The regular army itself is now so poorly paid and trained that it is more of a threat to Mobutu than support. Without pay or food, the regular army lives by extorting money from the common citizens of Zaire and by trying to extort money from foreigners. Mobutu's kleptocractic behavior now extends to the common soldiers. Zaire has no regular police or *gendarmerie*, so the soldiers act as police. Mobutu relies on his elite Special Presidential Division (DSP) to put down popular revolts and to keep the regular army in line. The DSP has been trained by the Israelis and South Africans, and it is well disciplined. Certain paratroop units and the Civil Guard are also relatively more reliable than the regular army.

At this point, I will address the issue of human rights in Zaire. Mobutu's security police and his armed forces have never hesitated to commit grievous crimes against the Zairian people. In Kinshasa, one is constantly harassed by the soldiers. After he was exiled, Nguz a Karl-I-Bond described in excruciating detail the tortures he suffered while in detention. Tshisekedi was also brutalized while in detention. Mobutu often does not intend for these kinds of things to happen, but he does not exercise full control over his police or the army. Mobutu has not engaged in random terror against his people, as did Stalin or the Argentines during the "dirty war" of the late 1970s. Although anyone engaging in dissent invites the force of the state to come crashing down on him, ordinary citizens have not been randomly arrested or killed in Zaire. They have, however, been systematically exploited, economically and politically.

Mobutu and Money in Zaire

The great source of power for Mobutu is his control over the financial resources of the state. Many knowledgeable analysts have estimated Mobutu's personal wealth at over $5 billion, all secure in Swiss bank accounts and European *châteaux*. I became convinced during my recent trip that Mobutu does not have nearly that much, but no one really knows. When I asked people why Mobutu wanted so desperately to keep power, they indicated that he needed a continuing income to support his lifestyle. There is no doubt that Mobutu has stolen $5 billion or more, but he has also spent a great deal of it as well. Apparently, much of his day is spent listening to petitioners and giving them money. Especially since the "transition" has begun, he has spent millions co-opting people. There is no doubt that Mobutu is very wealthy. Mobutu genuinely does not perceive the difference between public and private money. As president, he sees nothing wrong with calling the governor of the *Banque du Zaire* and demanding a few million dollars. After all, he thinks the people expect an African president to live well.

As a result of this behavior, however, the level of development in Zaire has lagged far below what one would expect and in many ways is below what it was in 1960. Major cities such as Kikwit or Mbuji Mayi, which have hundreds of thousands of people, lack electricity. No radio or television reaches these people; for them, the Zairian government virtually does not exist. Roads have crumbled into dust. In such conditions people can survive only by turning to the informal economy. Mobutu's development record is absolutely abysmal. Most of the large development projects, like the Inga-Shaba electric-power generating project, have turned out to be disasters, mostly because of the failure of the Zairian state to provide the necessary infrastructure and security.

Mobutu has used Zaire's national wealth to buy influence for himself and to co-opt politicians into supporting him. As a result, little money is left for investment. It is not true, as many on the

Left believe, that multinational corporations and Western investors have made a great deal of money in Zaire; most of them have actually lost money and have pulled out. In fact, I toured a burned-out General Motors assembly plant in Kinshasa during my recent visit, which was looted in 1991 and 1993.

Mobutu and Ethnicity: the Paradox

Another secret of Mobutu's success is his careful manipulation of Zaire's fractious ethnic forces. This is a paradox; on one hand, he has publicly disavowed ethnic politics and has sought wide ethnic representation in the cabinet, in the MPR, and in the Parliament. On the other hand, he has sought to divide his enemies along ethnic lines when it suited his purposes, as during the national conference. Specifically, nearly everyone in Zaire believes that Mobutu was behind the recent ethnic tensions in Shaba between the "indigenous" Shabans and the Kasaians. By appointing and co-opting Nguz, an important Shaban figure, Mobutu successfully split the opposition, both at the level of the leaders and the masses. (Tshisekedi is a Kasaian.)

Furthermore, Mobutu has also quietly relied on his own Ngbandi friends from Equateur to hold key positions in the security forces. For instance, his security chief, Gbanda, is an Ngbandi, as are his chief of staff, Vendauwe Te Pemako, the heads of the DSP (Nzimbi), the SNIP (Mudima), and the Civil Guard (Baramoto). Allegedly, the bulk of the DSP soldiers themselves are also from Mobutu's tribe. Even the recently appointed prime minister, Kengo wa Dondo, grew up in Mobutu's area, though his father is a Pole. When I asked Chief of Staff Vendauwe about this ethnic favoritism, he explained that in times of trouble, one always relies on one's family. He also pointed out that President Clinton is a "tribalist" too, insofar as much of his staff is from Arkansas.

Manipulation of Nationalist Feelings and Symbols

Mobutu has also used Zairianization and the manipulation of national symbols with some success. The most obvious step he took was changing the place names and personal names in the country in the early 1970s. For example, "Congo" became "Zaire," and "Leopoldville" became "Kinshasa." Individuals were obliged to stop using their Christian or European names and had to adopt authentic African names. Mobutu chose "Sese Seko." Some people have recently reverted to using their Christian names to spite Mobutu. Mobutu also outlawed ties and introduced a style of clothing called *Abacos*, a shortened version of the French *A bas le costume!* (Down with the business suit!). He also forbade women to wear pants, insisting on skirts or traditional dress. Despite his reputation as being a lackey of the West, Mobutu took many steps to defy Western habits. These changes may be mere window dressing, but they have had a certain appeal. Mobutu has also used the memory of Patrice Lumumba, embracing him as an authentic Zairian hero. There is a large, though incomplete, monument to Lumumba on the outskirts of Kinshasa. Certainly the nationalization of foreign firms has been popular with the Zairian people, particularly with those who benefited directly. The old *Union Minière du Haut Katanga* was another symbol of foreign domination, and Mobutu replaced it with Gecamines.

Foreign Policies: Another Paradox

Another hallmark of Mobutu's rule has been his manipulation of the United States and other Western powers. He has successfully portrayed himself in the West as an anti-Communist and as the sole bulwark against chaos or civil war in Zaire. Africanist orthodoxy argues that the United States put Mobutu in power in 1965 and has maintained him ever since. This view somewhat overstates the case, however. Although the United States certainly did support Mobutu, he also has a support base in the army, in the political class, in his home province, and in certain rural areas.

During the 1970s, Mobutu became infatuated with China. The *Abaco* style of dress suspiciously resembles the Mao jackets of old. The title of address, *"Citoyen,"* is Jacobin in its political symbolism, not Western-democratic. In short, Mobutu has not respected American-style political values, and he maintained excellent relations with foreign leaders of various political persuasions. In the mid-1970s, Mobutu accused the United States of supporting a coup against him, and he forced the recall of the American ambassador. Under Carter, U.S.-Zaire relations were also cool. President Bush, despite his closeness with Mobutu, eventually appointed Melissa Wells, an outspoken critic of Mobutu, as ambassador.

Mobutu tried to ingratiate himself with other African leaders through his attempted mediation of conflicts, such as in Chad and Angola. There is a myth in the United States that Mobutu is skilled at negotiation, but I know of no conflicts that he actually resolved. In fact, his efforts to mediate the Angola civil war may have made it worse. Nevertheless, it must be said that Mobutu has been grudgingly accepted by all but the most radical African leaders. Most of them are dictators themselves, of course.

A few items of Machiavellian miscellany merit mention. Another key to Mobutu's enduring role has been his reliance on traditional rulers, who tend to respect whomever is in power and enjoy being acknowledged by them. Mobutu maintains a surprisingly high degree of support in rural areas because of the chiefs. Similarly, Mobutu relies on the common people's belief in magic and fetishes. Perhaps this is not unlike a Western leader carrying the Bible, but it goes beyond that. Common people believe that Mobutu has magic, and he promotes this belief.

Like so many authoritarians who have been in power for a long time, Mobutu has apparently developed some bizarre personal indulgences. For instance, many people, including some of his supporters, say he has the habit of sleeping with the wives of his political opponents. Such behavior is as much about power as it is about sex: It is a way of humiliating people and taking away their self-respect.

During the recent transition, Mobutu employed virtually all of these techniques to divide, co-opt, and weaken the opposition. For instance, it is widely believed that he was behind the 1992-93 ethnic cleansing in the Shaba province, which left thousands dead and hundreds of thousands homeless (Berkeley). This was a way of reducing support for his chief opponent, Tshisekedi.

Mobutu has also successfully co-opted a number of prominent politicians by offering them important posts, including the prime ministership. Those co-opted include Nguz, Birindwa, Kamitatu, and Kengo wa Dondo. Mobutu has also allowed the opposition's own natural ambition to work against them. Every bright young person in Zaire dreams of becoming a minister, and Mobutu has been able to dazzle many of his opponents with the prospect of a lucrative government post.

Evaluation

One has to acknowledge Mobutu's skills as a politician. It is no mean feat to rule such a big and fractious country for 30 years. He understands much about common people and his former external supporters. Nevertheless, Mobutu relies far too much on force in carrying out state-building. Both Weber and Machiavelli, two notable realists, believed democracy could be a useful instrument of state-building. They recognized that popular participation rallies people behind state aims. Mobutu, however, has suppressed democratic aspirations. He might be forgiven some of his excesses if he had developed the economy, as Houphouët-Boigny did in Côte d'Ivoire. About the only positive thing one could say of Mobutu is that he has kept the state intact and prevented a Rwanda-style tragedy. Others could have done the same, however, and Mobutu does not deserve any particular credit. In fact, he may now be laying the groundwork for future ethnic conflict.

The Mobutu experience allows us to appreciate our own system and to recognize that the longer one stays in power, the more corrupt one becomes. As mentioned earlier, the flaws of our own statespersons appear less egregious by comparison. Apparently, Lord Acton was right to say that absolute power corrupts absolutely. If Mobutu had retired in 1975, he might be remembered much more fondly. Instead, he is destined to be remembered as a notorious dictator who held on until the bitter end.

QUESTION: From your travels in the area, could you assess how strong or vocal Tshisekedi's popular support was?

MR. CLARK: Tshisekedi's popular support is very deep and very broad. My host in Zaire has a small cellular phone business in Kinshasa, and whenever people would come into his office I would ask them, "If you had a chance to vote for president between

Tshisekedi and Mobutu, for whom would you vote?" Virtually all of the people with some level of political sophistication said they support Tshisekedi. The only people who were undecided were people who had no education and refused to even think about politics. Tshisekedi also has a great deal of support in his home region of Kasai, which is where they mine diamonds.

QUESTION: Do any segments of the military support Tshisekedi?

MR. CLARK: Yes. The distinction between the regular army and Mobutu's elite forces is important. Although they do not voice their opinions, a great many ordinary soldiers are quite supportive of Tshisekedi. One exception is in Shaba, where there is a longstanding, bitter dispute between some ethnic groups, especially the Lunda and Luba-Shaba peoples and the Luba from Kasai. As a result, many people in the Shaba province do not like Etienne Tshisekedi. Nguz a Karl-I-Bond, an infamous leader from Shaba, fostered considerable resentment against Tshisekedi. Nguz was in the opposition for a while, but he was co-opted by Mobutu. Incidentally, Nguz recently had a heart attack and was taken to South Africa for treatment.

Zaire's hospitals are another example of the deteriorating infrastructure. I did not visit the main hospital, Mama Yemo Hospital, but I visited one of the private hospitals, which was supposed to be much cleaner and better supplied. What I saw was shocking by our Western sensibilities. The hospital was dirty and completely lacking in equipment and medicine. [One private hospital was run by a Connecticut doctor, and although it had a better reputation than some in Zaire, it was shocking.]

QUESTION: What is the present relationship between Shaba and the rest of the country?

MR. CLARK: That question is on everyone's mind in Zaire because of the history of secession. Many people doubt that Katanga (or Shaba) province will try to secede again, and Nguz's illness also reduces that likelihood. The governor of Shaba has indicated a few times that if Tshisekedi became the president of the country, Shaba would secede. Many people suggest, however, that even though the governor might announce secession, there is not sufficient support among the Shaban people to actually do it.

QUESTION: The Soviets set up Lumumba University in Moscow after Lumumba's murder. Do its graduates, who were quite active in the early 1960s, have any influence on the contemporary government?

MR. CLARK: Students are among the most vocal opposition in Zaire, but I have never run into anyone in Zaire who was trained at Patrice Lumumba University. I do not think Mobutu let too many Zairian students attend that university, because he was hostile to the Soviet Union. When I was in Congo-Brazzaville four years ago, however, I encountered many people who were trained at that university and who used Marxist-Leninist rhetoric. They referred to me as a "Western imperialist" and asked why the World Bank takes food out of the mouths of hungry Congolese children. Many students from Angola were also trained at Patrice Lumumba University.

QUESTION: Do any of the provinces that threaten secession have enough resources to survive as independent countries, or is Zaire better off as a unified country despite its problems?

MR. CLARK: The answer is "yes" to both questions. Zaire's copper wealth is located in the Shaba province, and recognition of that fact influenced Tshombe's effort to have Shaba secede in 1960. It would have been a very wealthy small state, while the rest of Zaire would have been correspondingly impoverished. Therefore, it is much better for most people who live outside of Shaba for Zaire to stay unified. At the same time, it might be better for the Shabans if they did secede, because they would be comparatively wealthy. A similar situation encouraged Biafra's secession in 1966, which sparked the Nigerian civil war. Biafra had much of the oil wealth of Nigeria, where oil is the country's main resource.

Resources definitely encourage ethno-regionalism in Zaire. For example, the diamond wealth of Zaire is located in Kasai, which is Tshisekedi's home province. Recently, he threatened to call for a strike among the diamond workers if Mobutu did not appoint him prime minister. Gecamines, which runs the copper mines, has almost completely ceased to function, and as a result, Mobutu does not have that source of money any more. Therefore, he has been increasingly reliant on the diamond income, which gives Tshisekedi a certain leverage over him. If Tshisekedi persuaded the miners to shut down or sabotage the diamond mines, that would undermine Mobutu. The location of wealth in the country is very important.

NARRATOR: We have very much enjoyed having John Clark back at the Miller Center for a discussion on President Mobutu of Zaire and wish him well as he continues to study this very important area. We are proud of his accomplishments.

John F. Clark

BIBLIOGRAPHY

Andriamirado, Sennen. "Les Barons de Mobutu." *Jeune Afrique*. No. 1631 (9-15 April 1992): 50-55.

Africa Watch. "Zaire: Inciting Hatred." Vol. 5, No. 10 (June 1993).

_____. "Zaire: Two Years Without Transition." Vol. 4, No. 9 (July 1992).

Berkeley, Bill. "An African Horror Story." *The Atlantic Monthly*. Vol. 272, No. 2 (August 1993), 20-28.

Boyle, Patrick. "Beyond Self-Protection to Prophecy: The Catholic Church and Political Change in Zaire," *Africa Today*. Vol. 39, No. 3 (1992), 49-66.

Braeckman, Colette. *Le dinosaure*. Paris: Fayard, 1992.

Busaki-Onken, Cyprien. "Vers la Republique Federale du Zaire (Congo)." *Nouvelle Société*. No. 1 (November 1991), 26-31.

Buana, Kabue. *Citoyen Président*. Paris: Editions L'Harmattan, 1978.

Callaghy, Thomas. *The State-Society Struggle: Zaire in Comparative Perspective*. New York: Columbia University Press, 1984.

Clark, John F. "Ethno-regionalism as an Impediment to Democratization in Zaire," in Harvey Glickman (ed.), *Ethnicity and Democratization in Africa* (Atlanta: ASA Press, forthcoming).

_____. "The United Nations' Mission to Congo, 1960-65: Lessons for the Post-Cold War World," *The Journal of Political Science*, 13 (1994).

Chomé, Jules. *L'ascension de Mobutu*. Brussels: Editions Complexe, 1974.

Dungia, Emmanuel. *Mobutu et L'Argent du Zaire: Révélations d'un diplomate, ex-agent des Services Secrets*. Paris: Harmattan, 1992.

Elliot, Jeffrey and Mervyn Dymally (eds). *Voices of Zaire: Rhetoric or Reality*. Washington: Washington Institute Press, 1990.

Faes, Géraldine. "L'implosion." *Jeune Afrique*. No. 1700 (5–11 August 1993): 21–23.

Hoskyns, Catherine. *The Congo Since Independence: January 1960–December 1961*. London: Oxford Univ. Press, 1965.

Jackson, Robert and Carl Rosberg. *Personal Rule in Black Africa: Prince, Autocrat, Prophet, Tyrant*. Berkeley: Univ. of Calif. Press, 1982.

Kamitatu-Massamba, Cléophas. *La grande mystification du Congo-Kinshasa: Les crimes de Mobutu*. Paris: Maspero, 1971.

Lemarchand, René. *Political Awakening in the Belgian Congo*. Berkeley, Calif: Univ. of California Press, 1964.

_____. "Mobutu and the National Conference: The Arts of Political Survival." Typescript, August 1992.

MacGaffey, Janet. "Initiatives From Below: Zaire's Other Path to Social and Economic Restructuring." In Goran Hyden and Michael Bratton (eds.), *Governance and Politics in Africa*, Boulder, Colo.: Lynne Rienner, 1992.

Ndjoli, Ernest. "Comment le Nord a mis le Sud à genoux." *Mambenga* (Zairian Weekly), 29 November–6 December 1991, 8.

Nguz a Karl-I-Bond. *Mobutu: Ou l'incarnation du mal zairois*. London: Rex Collins, 1982.

O'Brien, Connor Cruise. *To Katanga and Back: A U.N. Case History*. New York: Grosset & Dunlap, 1962.

Remilleux, Jean-Louis. *Mobutu: Dignity for Africa. Interviews with Jean-Louis Remilleux*. Paris: Albin Michel, 1989.

Schatzberg, Michael. *The Dialectics of Oppression in Zaire*. Bloomington, Ind.: Indiana Univ. Press, 1988.

_____. "Fidélité au Guide: The J.M.P.R. in Zairian Schools." *Journal of Modern African Studies*, 16 (1978), 417–31.

_____. *Mobutu or Chaos* (Lanham, Md.: University Press of America, 1991).

Somerville, Keith. "The Failure of Democratic Reform in Angola and Zaire," *Survival*, Vol. 35, No. 3 (Autumn 1993), 51–77.

Soudan, Francois. "Les Chances du Premier ministre bis." *Jeune Afrique*. No. 1682 (1–7 April 1993).

Turner, Thomas. "The Case of Zaire: Is Mobutu a Corporatist?" in Julius Nyang'oro and Timothy M. Shaw (eds.), *Corporatism in Africa: Comparative Analysis and Practice*. Boulder, Colo.: Westview, 1989.

Weiss, Herbert. *Political Protest in the Congo: the Parti Solidaire Africain During the Struggle for Independence*. Princeton, N.J.: Princeton Univ. Press, 1967.

Weissman, Stephen R. *American Foreign Policy in the Congo, 1960–1964*, Ithaca: Cornell Univ. Press, 1974.

Williame, Jean-Claude. *Patrimonialism and Political Change in the Congo*. Stanford, Calif.: Stanford Univ. Press, 1972.

Young, Crawford. *Politics in the Congo: Decolonization and Independence*, Princeton, N.J.: Princeton Univ. Press, 1965.

_____. *The Politics of Cultural Pluralism*. Madison: Univ. of Wisconsin Press, 1976.

Young, Crawford and Thomas Turner. *The Rise and Decline of the Zairian State*. Madison: Univ. of Wisconsin Press, 1985.

CHAPTER SIX

The Nigerian Press Under the Military: Persecution, Resilience, and Political Crisis (1983-1993)*

ADEYINKA ADEYEMI

To criticize Nigeria is to criticize God.[1]
Alex Akinyele,
Nigeria's Minister of
Information and Culture

Background

Nigeria is pre-eminently Africa's press giant. With about one fifth of Africa's population,[2] and a size more than double that of California, Nigeria is one of only five countries in Africa (of 48 listed by UNESCO)[3] that had more than ten newspapers in 1990. Of these five, Nigeria maintains a clear lead. In 1990, Nigeria had 31 daily newspapers, followed by South Africa (22 daily newspapers), Egypt (14 newspapers), Morocco (13 newspapers), and Algeria (10 newspapers). By the first months of 1993, there were 66 major newspapers, 60 "regularly published" magazines, 50 state-

---

*Reprinted with the permission of The Joan Shorenstein Center on the Press, Politics and Public Policy, John F. Kennedy School of Government, Harvard University. Copyright © 1995, Presidents and Fellows of Harvard College.

owned television stations, and 40 state-owned radio stations.[4] Nigeria also has the highest newspaper growth rate in Africa[5] and arguably the freest and probably the most resilient on the African continent.

For a clearer understanding of the state of the press in Nigeria, it is important to keep in mind the geographical distribution of the mass media, especially the print media, vis-à-vis Nigeria's ethno-political configuration.

There are 250 ethnic groups in Nigeria of which three, Hausa/Fulani of the north, Yoruba of the southwest, and Ibo of the southeast, make up 65 percent of the population. The principal languages are English (the official language), Hausa, Yoruba, and Ibo. Hundreds of dialects and variations of the main languages, however, are spoken throughout Nigeria.

About half of Nigeria is Muslim and predominantly in the north while the south is predominantly 40 percent Christian and 10 percent animists/atheists. An interesting aspect of the Nigerian press is that more than 95 percent of all news publications in Nigeria are published in the south. Of the 49 publications cited by Agbaje, for instance, only four are/were published in the north, one in the middle belt, and the rest in the southern cities of Lagos, Owerri, Enugu, Ibadan, Calabar, Port Harcourt, Akure, and Benin.[6]

Since independence in 1960, Nigeria has had eight military coups d'etat and two civilian regimes.[7] A third attempt at democracy was truncated by the military government of Ibrahim Babangida, an action that was the precursor to the political crisis that this study examines.

Over the years, regardless of the nature of government, the Nigerian press traditionally takes seriously the guarantees of free expression in all four constitutions to date. Section 24(1) of the 1960 Independence Constitution states that:

> Every person shall be entitled to freedom of expression, including freedom to hold opinions and to receive and impart ideas and information *without interference.*

This guarantee is replicated in the 1963 Republican Constitution as section 25, in the 1979 Constitution as section 36(1), and as section 38(1) in the 1989 Constitution. The guarantee was by no means absolute. According to section 24(2) of the 1960 Constitution, for instance, press freedom could be limited in the interest of public safety, defense, and health. Similarly, the 1989 Constitution states that the right to freedom of expression and the press shall not:

> invalidate any law that is reasonably justifiable in a democratic society (a) for the purpose of preventing the disclosure of information received in confidence, maintaining the authority and independence of courts or regulating telephony, wireless broadcasting, television or the exhibition of cinematograph films or (b) imposing restrictions upon persons holding office under the government of the Federation or of a State or of a Local Government, members of the Armed forces of the Federation or members of the Nigeria Police Force or other government security services established by law.[8]

These provisions have been repeatedly stretched and tested in the Nigerian courts. Between 1960 and 1987, for instance, more than 100 libel cases were decided by the courts, many decided against the press.[9] For instance, in the case of *Lateef Jakande v. Concord Press of Nigeria*, the Court ordered the *National Concord*, a Nigerian newspaper to pay 25,000 naira to former governor of Lagos, Lateef Jakande, for a libelous story captioned "Jakande's 900 Plots."[10] In other instances, the courts held that the confidentiality of a reporter's source of information was not absolute[11] and upheld directives by the management of a television station that prohibited its reporters from covering fraud stories that allegedly implicated the former head of state, General Olusegun Obasanjo.[12]

Therefore, it would seem that there are ample provisions in Nigerian law to protect ordinary citizens and government from the excesses of the press.[13] Yet it is this same "need to protect" that serves as the rationale for the military's imposition of antipress laws. Consequently, the position of this study is that this rationale is flawed, dishonest, and a contrivance. It is this rationale that produces the two key elements focused on in this study—persecution and resilience, the dynamics of which, in turn, produces a peculiar government/press relationship not fully explained, and, indeed, unexplainable by many existing academic models of press/government relations.

Theoretical Framework

The press/government relationship in Nigeria does not fit any of the models formulated by Fred Siebert, Theodore Peterson, and Wilbur Schramm.[14] It is not *authoritarian* because the Nigerian press is not required by law or necessarily expected to favor government or support its program and agenda. It is not *social-centralist* because the press is not an arm of the Nigerian government and has no *a priori* commitment to government propaganda as obtained, for instance, in the former Soviet Union, China, and Cuba. This is so, even in spite of the fact that the Federal Ministry of Information, along with its subsidiaries in the 30 states (including the federal capital territory, Abuja) fund and "oversee" the operation of Nigeria's only wire service, the News Agency of Nigeria, the Nigerian Television Authority, the Federal Radio Corporation of Nigeria, and the Voice of Nigeria, Nigeria's equivalent of VOA and BBC. Government has considerable influence in these agencies (for instance, the minister of information appoints, and can remove, the board members of the agencies). Such influence does not apply, *a priori*, to the majority of the print press, which remains private.

Nigerian government officials, and indeed Nigerian journalists, like to pride themselves on having the freest press in Africa. But calling the press/government relationship in Nigeria *libertarian* would be insulting the almost total freedom of the American press. As William Hachten said, the libertarian model must be considered irrelevant to most African countries because:

> The Western model of the newspaper as a profit-making enterprise, independent of government and supplying the public with reliable and objective news and public information is seldom found, although many African journalists aspire to such a press. Economic and social factors—poverty, illiteracy, economic

structure, linguistic and ethnic diversity—have combined to inhibit such media development.[15]

The *social-responsibility* model arose out of the realization that a laissez faire approach to media control could neither guarantee the freedom of the press nor its responsibility to the society to report truthfully and fairly.[16] Therefore, while this model does not oppose press freedom per se, it does not emphasize it. Instead, "it stresses responsibility."[17] This is because, according to this model, the obligation of the press to be "socially responsible" is equally as important as press freedom. Indeed, unless the press was willing to embrace this obligation, "government might go into the communications business to properly inform the citizens."[18] It was this need to "properly inform" that caused government to impose regulations to guide the broadcast media in the United States.[19] This is the vital difference in the case of Nigeria where the aim of control is not fair reporting, but political consolidation. For instance, the control of the electronic media, in particular the radio, is predicated upon its efficacy as an instrument in the military's struggle for succession to political power.[20] The need to control the radio for political and hegemonic purposes became more pronounced shortly after the 22 April 1990 failed military coup when government barred all civilians, except workers on duty, from the vicinity of the Federal Radio Corporation (FRCN) building in Lagos after dusk.[21]

Not even is William Rugh's attempt to classify the Arab press in Africa sufficiently applicable to the Nigerian situation.[22]

Therefore, there appears to be a need for a new theoretical model that will fit the Nigerian situation: a government/press relationship hinging on mutual suspicion, hatred, and distrust, characterized by power disequilibrium and resilience.

In a 1975 address to the Royal African Society in London, Babatunde Jose, one-time chairman of *Daily Times*, Nigeria's largest newspaper, said, "Many African journalists still believe that a good press is one that is in a constant state of war with the government; that a 'progressive' journalist is one who writes anti-government articles every day and a leading journalist is one who is in and out of prison for sedition."[23]

I suggest that an automatic battle line is drawn between government and the press where a government is inept and corrupt and the mass of people is impoverished. In such a milieu, true and responsible reportage becomes seditious and pro-masses (pro-democracy) journalism becomes antigovernment. Although Jose's remark serves to portray African journalists as fatalistic glory-seekers, it underscores the nature of the government/press relationship in an emerging democracy like Nigeria and reveals, *a fortiori*, the difficulty in understanding this relationship through a recourse to classical theories. I suggest that a new model, hegemony, provides a better understanding.

I

Hegemony as a Model of the Press/Government Relationship in Nigeria

The process of domination of the Nigerian press by the military can be immediate (as was the case under Buhari) or gradual (as was the case under Babangida). But whether it is immediate or gradual, the process reveals two principal features of hegemony as a model of press/government relations. The first is a *big tree/small axe configuration.* Typically, because it has the use of the instruments of force without the obligation of statutory accountability to the people (through the legislature, for instance), the military government is what I refer to as the big tree. It uses force to cower, control, and dominate the press in line with its calculated objectives, often explained as public interest. Of course, what the ruling elites describe as the public interest is not necessarily what is in the interest of the public.[24]

In the clearest indication of this fact, a former minister of information of Nigeria, Alex Akinyele, once said that a report by William Keeling of the *Financial Times* of London on improper government use of oil revenue could "sabotage the security" of Nigeria. In the said report, Keeling wrote about how the military had spent about $3 billion of the $5 billion windfall that Nigeria received from higher oil export earnings during the Gulf crisis.[25] Keeling was deported from Nigeria, an action that Akinyele differentiated from censorship. He said of reporters like Keeling: "Let them write what they want to write. But if anybody does anything that is against the national interest, that person will have to answer questions."[26] The "small axe" is the press: It remains sharp, vibrant, and resilient.

The second feature of hegemony is a *series of peaks and plateaus* indicating the periods when government's persecution of the press is at a high and when it stabilizes, usually due to internal and/or external pressures on government.

As a theoretical model of government/press relationship, hegemony describes a limited short-term toleration, even wooing, of the press for the calculated purpose of consolidating political power and constructing legitimacy. Once legitimacy has been attained and power consolidated, the relationship sours between the press and government, and public policy becomes an avenue for dominating, intimidating, and punishing antagonistic groups, even as it rewards friendly pro-establishment ones (in Nigeria, rewards come in the form of patronage in advertising, import license for printing materials, public office appointments, etc.).

I have no desire here whatsoever to dabble into the Gramscian controversy about hegemony.[27] Rather, I prefer to adopt his rather commonsense meaning of a social group dominating *"antagonistic groups, which it tends to 'liquidate,' or to subjugate by armed force."*[28] (Emphasis mine)

For the purpose of this study, successive military regimes in Nigeria will constitute "social class" and the press "antagonistic group." It is the dynamics of this interrelationship that produces government persecution (which I define as official antipress actions) and press resilience (which I define as the degree to which the press performs its functions in the face of persecution) that characterized Nigeria's political crisis in the period under review.

This study is divided into seven sections. In the next section, I advance two viewpoints of press freedom in Nigeria within the theoretical model of hegemony. Then, in the next four sections, I examine hegemonic elements in the three military regimes in power in Nigeria during the period: General Muhammadu Buhari

(1983-85), General Ibrahim Babangida (1985-93) and General Sanni Abacha (17 November 1993-?) with particular reference to the extent to which the first two soldiers put antipress laws to use and what the press is likely to look like under the third. I lay emphasis on "direct actions" (military tribunals, decrees, control of the judiciary, promulgation of retroactive laws, etc.) and "indirect actions" (manipulation, coercion, self-censorship, and "settlement").[29]

In particular, I address the following questions: How did the press act and react in response to the military's persecution? How did the international press react to the Nigerian crisis, especially after June 12? What role did the U.S. congressional subcommittee of the House of Representatives and the State Department play in terms of policy and to what extent did reportage shape policy?

In section seven, I conclude by suggesting some practical steps through which an appreciable measure of press freedom and respect for human rights can be achieved in Nigeria.

I have chosen the time period (1983-1993) for only one reason: This has been a period of intense encounters of the press with two military heads of state of drastically different approaches and tendencies—Buhari, who, *ab initio*, declared his intention to be ruthless with the press and during whose tenure the infamous Decree 4 was promulgated and tested, and Babangida, during whose tenure the press became more persecuted, even though he proscribed Decree 4 and declared, *ab initio*, his commitment to a free press.

II

The Dialectics of Press Freedom in Nigeria

In Nigeria, the issue of press freedom is frequently a clash of two viewpoints: the *national development* and the *theoretical*. The national development viewpoint is the domain of, generally speaking, the privileged class who benefits from the status quo. It places emphasis on a perceived symbiotic relationship between press freedom and good governance, but it does so in a manner that suggests that both notions are mutually antithetical.

The theoretical view is principally held by Nigerian journalists and pro-democracy enthusiasts (who do not profit from the status quo) who ardently argue that speech and the press ought to be free from government's hegemonic interference and controls. It stipulates that such freedom is fundamental to good governance and that any transition to democracy (which is the constant promise of successive military regimes in Nigeria) that does not include the right to free speech and press freedom is injurious to democracy. This positive view of the symbiosis derives directly from the spirit of the First Amendment to the Bill of Rights of the United States Constitution, after which the Nigerian Constitution of 1979 (reviewed 1989) was modeled. The First Amendment categorically stipulates that

> Congress *shall make no law* respecting an establishment of religion, or prohibiting the free exercise thereof; or abridging the freedom of speech, or of the press; or the right of the people peaceably to assemble, and petition the government for a redress of grievances.[30]

III

Hegemonic Elements in General Muhammadu Buhari's Regime (1983-1985)

The 41-year-old Army general, Muhammadu Buhari, who toppled[31] Nigeria's second republic represents, in a classical sense, a national development notion of press freedom. Press/government relationship under him was a study in hegemony. His coup d'etat of 31 December 1983 was a welcome relief for Nigerians[32] who had become disillusioned with a double-digit inflation rate, increasing crime, and unabated corruption by public officials. In one demonstration of the typical corruption that characterized the second republic (under President Shehu Shagari, 1979-1983), military men found about $4 million in cash in the home of the ousted governor of Kano State, Alhaji Bakin Zuwo.³³ For Buhari, the deplorable economic situation of Nigeria and falling living standards, which resulted in frustration with the "extravagance of many politicians with private jets, elegant cars, and palatial residences"³⁴ made the construction of legitimacy a *fait accompli*. The press was therefore not critical in Buhari's quest for legitimacy. In one of his earliest interviews, he told journalists that he would not tolerate the press. Years later, out of office, he still bragged about his antipress resolve: "Yes, I told (slain editor of *Newswatch*) Dele Giwa that I would tamper with the press freedom and I fulfilled my promise, didn't I?"³⁵ He would harbor no respect for the rule of law, and he would be generally hostile.³⁶

As soon as he settled in, Buhari promulgated Decree No. 1, which suspended the 1979 Constitution.³⁷ This decree suspended, *inter alia*, the National Assembly, the State Houses of Assembly, the executive powers of the president and the governors, all political parties, and political activities. The decree also abrogated, outright, the Electoral Commission, the Economic Council, the National Population Commission, and the National Security Council established under section 140 of the 1979 Constitution. It abrogated the Code of Conduct Bureau, the appellate jurisdiction of the Supreme Court, and the Court of Appeal on the validity of elections of candidates, on rights to peaceful assembly, and association as it affects political parties, among others.³⁸

Then, Buhari announced that "corrupt" officials would be thrown in jail without indulging in the "nonsense of litigation."³⁹ Accordingly, he promulgated Decree 2, the "State Security (Detention of Persons) Decree of 1984," which allowed the military to detain indefinitely and without trial any person suspected of being involved in "acts prejudicial to state security or [who] has contributed to economic adversity." Under the cover of this decree, Buhari's government announced on 20 January 1984 that 600 politicians had been detained and 300 held for questioning, while another 71, including former Vice President Alex Ekwueme, were kept at the Kirikiri maximum prison. Although the decree was signed by Buhari on 9 February 1984, it was "deemed to have come into force on 31st December 1983"⁴⁰ in direct violation of Section

4, subsection 9, of the 1979 Constitution, which forbids retroactive laws.

In particular, the decree also suspended[41] portions of Chapter IV of the 1979 Constitution, the section dealing with fundamental rights of every Nigerian. Along with guarantees of personal liberty, the right to freedom of the press, the right to peaceful assembly and association, right to freedom of movement and from discrimination, Section 33(4) of the Constitution promises that

> Whenever any person is charged with a criminal offence, he shall unless the charge is withdrawn be entitled to a fair hearing within a reasonable time by a court or tribunal.

However, S4(1) of Decree 2 took care of that situation. It declares: "No suit or other legal proceedings shall lie against any person for anything done or intended to be done in pursuance of this Decree."

This set the stage for government/press relations under Buhari. In his first press briefing, his deputy, Brigadier Tunde Idiagbon, the chief of staff, accused some newspapers of printing "half-truths and falsehoods which are capable of creating confusion and causing dissension in the society." He warned that the military would "not tolerate instigation and innuendo calculated to create dissension among our people."[42]

In the same tone, Buhari told the *Financial Times* of London that he believed a vigorous press was "a weakness" to Nigeria. There is ample evidence to show that Buhari's overall hostility to the press was rooted in his encounter with the press years before he became head of state, an encounter that brought his character, honesty, and probity to question in a country where Buhari was considered "an island of probity in a sea of corruption"[43] and shaped government/press relations between 1983-1985.

Between 1976 and 1978, Buhari was the commissioner for petroleum resources in the administration of General Olusegun Obasanjo when Nigerian newspapers began to carry a report by the former governor of Central Bank, Clement Isong, about a missing 2.8 billion naira (about $3 billion at the time) from the national treasury, a charge that implicated Buhari. The allegation was first reported by the *New Nigerian*, a newspaper then owned by the governments of the northern states of Nigeria.

Buhari's persistent position was that in printing that allegation, the press became an accomplice in deceiving and misinforming Nigerians. He believed that his reputation as a tough, honest, and highly disciplined soldier was roundly tarnished by reporters who did not consider the virtual impossibility of taking out such a large sum of money from the treasury. As he said years after he had been toppled, "You'll find that it was not possible to take 2.8 billion naira out from Nigeria at that time . . . there is no banking system that can allow you to take 2.8 billion naira just like that, no matter the amount you have. This is because the money is not just there."[44]

He then invoked the classical "national development" argument when a reporter suggested that a respected prominent journalist had reported that the amount was paid into a particular public account. Said he: "You Nigerians, *especially you journalists, you have to help this country*. In fact there are some things that you shouldn't publish."[45] (Emphasis mine)

He went on:

> I was disappointed with the press. I was disappointed because . . . some things are not supposed to be published. For example if some illiterate brought to you something very sensational and unbelievable, you must have the integrity to resist it if it is against national interest. . . . If we were going to do any meaningful work, the situation of things in Nigeria in 1984 demanded that the press be dealt with.[46]

But Buhari's policy in 1984 revealed that he was neither concerned with the veracity of a story nor the right of the public to know. On 29 March 1984, he signed Decree 4 into law. It was payback time to Nigerian journalists.

The decree, titled "Public Officers (Protection Against False Accusation) Decree," became the singular most significant barrier to free speech and freedom of the press in Nigeria. Section 1(1) of the decree warns that

Any person who publishes in *any* form, whether written or otherwise, any message, rumor, report or statement . . . which is false in any material particular *or* which brings or is calculated to bring the Federal Military Government or the Government of a State or a public officer to ridicule or disrepute shall be guilty of an offence under this decree. (Emphasis mine)

By the provision of this section, free speech and opinions became encumbered and any report, even if true, that embarrassed any public official became an offense punishable by up to two years imprisonment without the option of a fine and, in the case of a corporate body, a fine of not less than 10,000 naira.[47] The decree placed the burden of proof on the journalist charged with the offense "notwithstanding anything to the contrary in any enactment or rule of law."[48]

It empowered government to prohibit the circulation of any newspaper it considers "detrimental to the interest" of Nigeria,[49] confiscate the equipment of the newspaper, radio, or television,[50] and unless they can prove that the offense was committed "without his consent," the decree found guilty "every person who at the time of the commission of the offense was a proprietor, publisher, general manager, editor, secretary" in an offending corporate body.[51]

Offenders were to be tried by a government-appointed tribunal consisting of a High Court judge as chairman and three members of the armed forces not below the rank of major. The tribunal's verdict could not be appealed[52] and the validity of any direction, notice, or order it gave could not be inquired into in any court of law.[53]

The Guardian, a newspaper that prides itself as the flagship of Nigerian journalistic excellence, gave the government an opportunity to put the decree to a test. On 31 March 1984, two days after the decree came into existence, the paper's senior diplomatic correspondent, Tunde Thompson, quoting "reliable sources," printed a report headed "11 Foreign Missions to be Closed." The next day, again quoting "reliable sources," the paper came out with another report headed "Eight Military Chiefs Tipped as Ambassadors." Then on 8 April, another Thompson report headed "More Names for Ambassadorial Posts" was accompanied with a rider "Haruna to replace Hannaniya." Until *The Guardian* came up with stories, the military government and its External Affairs Ministry had been under the illusion that their deliberations had been confidential. It became necessary for them to identify who had been speaking to the press.

In his memoirs,[54] Thompson said that his original report to the assistant news editor, Nduka Irabor, did not specify who was replacing whom, but that the editor's own sources had disclosed that some western countries did not want serving military men as ambassadors to their countries, and in particular that one Major General Hannaniya was to be replaced by a retired Major General I. B. M. Haruna. He said that he could not verify Irabor's addition to the original story but had no reason to doubt the news editor's sources.

That front page lead of 8 April in *The Guardian* soon landed the two journalists in detention for about three months before the first hearing was held. While in detention, vigorous attempts were made to make the journalists disclose their sources. Yet in *Tony Momoh v. Senate of the National Assembly and 2 Ors (1981)*, the court had held that it was a violation of a reporter's fundamental rights to be forced to disclose his sources and that the press may have the obligation to keep certain information confidential.[55] Although not under any illusion that a judicial precedent could matter to a regime that had suspended some portions of the constitution dealing with human rights, the journalists still refused to disclose their sources.

During the ensuing trial by a High Court judge and three military men, a prosecution witness, and a permanent secretary in the Ministry of External Affairs, Ambassador George Dove-Edwin testified that 10 of the 11 missions[56] reported by *The Guardian* as being considered for closure were right and that eight military officials indeed were being considered for ambassadorial posting. But he said "there was no time Major General Haruna was considered to replace Major General Hannaniya as High Commissioner to the United Kingdom"[57] and that indeed, "it was Major General Hannaniya and not Haruna who was appointed ambassador."[58]

It was on the grounds of that error, which at best should have been warranted a correction or a retraction by *The Guardian*, that the two journalists were sentenced to one year in jail and their newspaper to a 50,000 naira (about $35,000) fine, payable within 24 hours. On the first anniversary of *The Guardian*, and ironically, the anniversary of United States independence—4 July 1984—the two victims of a government's inherent hatred for journalists were carted to jail where they spent the next year. *The Guardian* paid its fine.

It should not be assumed that the press was the only target of the Buhari administration. Indeed, it went further to attack and alienate almost every segment of the society, especially the middle class: politicians, the universities, the unions, students, and even the judiciary, the same groups that welcomed and supported it.

Having banned all political parties, the University Teachers' Union, the National Association of Nigerian Students, the Buhari regime warned Nigerians not to hold any meetings or demonstrate against the government. Calling all such meetings "nefarious acts"[59] that would not go unpunished, the administration said that it was aware that "members of some banned political parties have been holding secret meetings in different parts of the country."[60] The administration then launched what remains the most large scale and drastic war against corruption in Nigeria.[61] For the sole purpose of rendering worthless money stolen by officials of the last regime, the administration introduced a new currency, imposed a wage freeze, laid off thousands of deadwood civil servants and reduced spending by 15 percent,[62] actions that resulted in the reduction of Nigeria's foreign exchange deficits to 180 million naira in 1984 from three billion naira in 1983[63] but failed to satisfy the yearnings of Nigerians who "looked forward to a quick improvement in their standard of living."[64] Little surprise, then, that in a country where "people don't like to be dictated to,"[65] prolonged economic hardship in the face of laws that prohibited free expression, free association, and free press[66] soon led to open press criticism that the government was putting too much energy into investigating the corruption of the last civilian regime at the expense of economic and social reconstruction. In a view that was typical of the press criticism, the executive editor of *The Guardian*, Stanley Macebuh, said: "At the moment, we're looking at a clear movement toward authoritarian dictatorship. It's a trend that disturbs a lot of people, not least those who welcomed the change of government."[67]

It was therefore not totally unexpected that another military coup was imminent. It came on 27 August 1985, headed by Buhari's Army chief of staff, General Ibrahim Babangida. Babangida's regime, which lasted until 26 August 1993, provided another classic case of hegemonic tendencies in government/press relations. Under him, the Nigeria press went through some of its most tragic experiences, yet no one saw it coming.

IV

Hegemonic Elements in General Babangida's Regime (1985–1993)

The palace coup that brought Babangida to power was more a direct result of intense intra-military cleavages than a real commitment to saving Nigerians from the economic morass of the Buhari era.[68] From the start it was obvious to Nigerians that Babangida and his co-plotters were more motivated by their own personal frustrations with President Buhari rather than a real commitment to arresting Nigeria's downward economic slide. In his maiden address to Nigerians on 27 August 1985, Babangida accused Buhari of disregarding "the principles of discussions, consultation, and cooperation which should have guided the decision-making process of the Supreme Military Council." He said that Buhari "was too rigid and uncompromising in his attitudes to issues of national significance" and that his assistant, Major General Idiagbon, "arrogated to himself absolute knowledge of problems and solutions, and acted in accordance with what was convenient to him, using the machinery of government as his tool."

In pursuit of legitimacy, therefore, Babangida knew that he had to present to a largely economically victimized people a palatable entree. His tactic was to reverse every single policy that had alienated the past regime from the people. Accordingly, Babangida committed himself to human rights. In a jab at the Buhari regime's policy of indiscriminate detention of politicians, Babangida declared: "We must never allow ourselves to lose our sense of natural justice. The innocent cannot suffer the crimes of the guilty."[69] Then he released about 100 political detainees from the Buhari era[70] and freed a press that had been hitherto gagged. Babangida declared:

> As we do not intend to lead a country where individuals are under the fear of expressing themselves, the Public Officers Protection Against False Accusation Decree No. 4 is hereby repealed. And, finally, those who have been in detention under this decree are hereby unconditionally released. The responsibility of the media to disseminate information shall be exercised without undue hindrance.[71]

Babangida's maiden address sparked in Nigerians a renewed sense of freedom, a positive perception of the regime, and rekindled liberalism in a subdued and encumbered press. As I will show in this study, however, having successfully constructed legitimacy on the platform of human rights and press freedom, Babangida began to exhibit age-old hostility to the press and disregard for human rights in a corruption-ridden administration.

There are two distinct features of press/government relations under the Babangida regime. For one, Babangida seemed to have an implicit faith in the inherent greed of man and his corruptibility, an attitude that was reflected in a simple premise: to consolidate power, co-opt the opposition. In this way, potential opposition of the Babangida regime became accomplices. As Agbaje puts it, "The military regimes, especially that of Babangida, appear to have perfected incorporationist strategies in the service of a corruption-propelled authoritarianism."[72] Perhaps a most ardent believer in James Madison's "if men were angels, no government would be necessary" credo, Babangida vigorously co-opted powerful and influential segments of the Nigerian society into his administration. These included the press, the judiciary, the intelligentsia, military officers (who are predisposed to carrying out military coups), musicians (who have tremendous mass appeal), and social critics. This strategy, more than anything else, sustained his regime for the next eight years and effectively diluted potential antagonism to it. As former head of state, General Olusegun Obasanjo observed:

> Most of those who can, with some respect and credibility, speak out against the ills of the present, have become victim of the practice that has come to be called "settlement." Choosing a moment when they are most vulnerable, the government steps in with generous assistance . . . From this point on, their silence is assured.[73]

A few examples will suffice. Apart from "clandestine meetings" between government, security agents, and chief executives of newspapers,[74] the administration targeted journalists who were perceived to have been wronged by the previous regime. Duro Onabule, the editor of the *National Concord*, was tipped as chief press secretary to the president, and Nduka Irabor, the assistant news editor of *The Guardian* and one of the casualties of Decree 4, was appointed the press secretary to the vice president. The dynamism, camaraderie, and professionalism of these otherwise fine journalists soon fizzled out as they got absorbed in government and became accomplices in its antipress machinations.[75]

Moreover, there was a systematic attempt by government to lure the various trade unions through thinly veiled monetary "donations." The Nigeria Union of Journalists, the Nigeria Bar Association, the Professional Musicians Association of Nigeria, among others, each reportedly received 10 million naira from the presidency. In particular, the echelons of the Bar Association were targeted for the post of the attorney general and minister of justice. Accordingly, two of the last three presidents of the Bar Association, Prince Bola Ajibola (later, a judge of the World Court) and Clement Akpamgbo, became the minister of justice and subsequently drafted most of the draconian decrees of the period.[76]

Then, using public funds, Babangida bought nearly 3,000 Peugeot 504 sedans and gave them as gifts to military officers.[77] Furthermore, the administration targeted Nigeria's most famous social critic, Tai Solarin, who had been detained for 17 months during Buhari's regime for writing articles critical of the military, and made him the chairman of People's Bank, a credit program for small-scale entrepreneurs. Babangida's choice of Solarin, a school teacher, totally inexperienced in banking or any type of business, was seen as "an effort to silence one of his most vociferous critics."[78] It worked. As the chairman of Nigeria's Civil Liberties Organization, Olisa Agbakoba said, "One has seen a change in Solarin's public utterances since he joined the government. He's been compromised."[79]

Incorporationism paid some dividends also with the press. Newspapers began to focus on the president's "humane" nature, and even while he was cracking down on dissent, banning unions, closing 30 universities, detaining journalists, seizing magazines, and shuffling his cabinets arbitrarily, newspaper cartoonists "sketch the President as a soccer star . . . weaving unscathed through his nation's problems"[80] and editorial writers nicknamed him "Maradona," after the Argentine soccer star adroit at dribbles. Babangida became loved for his famed unpredictability. As I have argued elsewhere, elevating such a character flaw to the level of admiration had serious economic and political consequences for Nigeria.[81]

But not all sections of the press fell for the president's charm and his administration's corporatism. The regime found, in particular, *Newswatch*,[82] *Tell*,[83] and *The News*[84] too hot to handle. Started in 1984 by four of Nigeria's best journalists, *Newswatch*'s forte was incisive investigative stories that did not spare the government. Its U.S.-trained editor, Dele Giwa, was detained for one week in 1983 for publishing what the police called "classified material." His death on 19 October 1986 by a parcel bomb was one of the three major developments that soured press/government relations under Babangida.

On that Sunday morning, a thick envelope was delivered by a messenger to Dele Giwa while he was having breakfast at home in the company of a colleague. "Lettering on the package said it was 'from the office of the C-in-C' (commander in chief) and that it was to be opened only by Giwa."[85] Believing the mail was from the president, Giwa opened it. It was a mail bomb. It exploded in his lap, severing his thighs and killing him one hour later.

Two days before his death, on 17 October 1986, Dele Giwa had been summoned by the deputy director of the State Security

Services (SSS), Colonel A. K. Togun and accused of various "antigovernment" activities as well as attempting to import arms to foment insurrection against the military government. In a letter to his lawyer, government foe Gani Fawehinmi, Giwa said the allegations by the SSS put him in a "state of shock" and begged the lawyer to help clear his name.[86] He also told Ray Ekpu, his colleague at *Newswatch*: "If they can think this of me, then my life is not safe."[87]

The day before the mail bomb was brought to Giwa's residence, the director of Military Intelligence, Colonel Halilu Akilu, telephoned Giwa's wife and asked: "Where is the place you stay? What is the address?"[88] The day after Giwa was killed, Akilu denied any connection in the bombing. Although the government seemed implicated in the whole incident, no real attempts were made at thorough investigation. Indeed, the minister of information, Tony Momoh, who had earlier pledged a government probe of the incident, soon capitulated and said that the matter was one for police investigation and that "a special probe would serve no useful purpose."[89] And although the Nigerian police did not have the technical expertise to analyze how the bomb was built, no attempts were made to get outside expertise.[90] Giwa's lawyer, Fawehinmi, tried unsuccessfully[91] to bring the two government agents—Akilu and Togun—to court, an action that even *Newswatch* directors dissociated themselves from, apparently for fear of government recriminations.[92] Eight years later, the death remains unsolved. But it would also not go away.

On 6 April 1993, government security officials picked up the publisher of *Newbreed* magazine, Chris Okolie, and four of his journalists in connection with alleged publication of "false information about some eminent Nigerians including President Ibrahim Babangida and Dr. Nnamdi Azikwe."[93] According to *Newbreed* counsel, Nnaemeka Amachina, Okolie had written the director of military intelligence, Akilu, about a taped confession by an ex-soldier who claimed to have a hand in the murder of Dele Giwa, and implicated senior military officials in the murder. Okolie had sent a copy of the tape to Akilu and requested an interview with the soldier. In return, security forces visited Okolie, arrested him, and demanded the tape and other materials given him by the ex-soldier.

The ex-soldier in question is Edmund Onyeama. In an interview with *Tell*,[94] Onyeama said that he and six other military intelligence officers had been ordered by Akilu to execute the plan to murder Giwa. He said that after the editor had been killed, Akilu "called us and told us to be happy because we were involved in a successful operation. He said it was the head of state who approved that he should be killed."[95] Revelations and/or allegations such as this will eventually force the government into a full-fledged investigation once the military hands over power to an elected government.

The second event that soured government/press relations under Babangida was the so-called IMF debate, which began a few weeks after he seized power. An important element in his populist strategy, the debate was to get national consensus on whether to accept a $2.4 billion loan from the International Monetary Fund together with very painful conditionalities that included devaluation of the naira,[96] retrenchment, and removal of the petroleum subsidy. While government-sponsored advertisements favored the loan, the press countered by reporting the growing public opposition to the loan, tagging it "a tentacle of capitalism" and questioning its whole essence.[97] There was even opposition from at least one Christian denomination.

During a Sunday service at First Baptist Church at Lagos, the sermonist, Bishop Festus Segun, looked directly at President Babangida, who was in the congregation, and waxing emotional, said: "Those in a position to take the decision on the loan should note that we already have debt burdens."[98] The barrage of opposition to the loan was so strong in the press that President Babangida soon declared, "If the country is determined to do without it, fine."[99]

When Babangida, however, eventually adopted all of the IMF conditionalities (devaluing the naira and causing by default double-digit inflationary trends, removal of oil subsidy, and reduction of the civil service) that Nigerians had feared would worsen their standard of living, it was an affront to his avowed populism, an indication of a disconnect with Nigerians and a rude awakening to a press that had deluded itself about the president's responsiveness to the will of the people. The structural adjustment programs that came with the loan resulted in prolonged suffering, spiraling unemployment, inflation, higher cost of living, and lower standard of living for Nigerians. In Nigeria, when a government policy results in such hardship for the citizens, the press traditionally sides against the government and on the side of the people.

The third development in the downward slide of the government/press relationship was the political crisis, which came to a head in June 1993 after President Babangida annulled a presidential election that more than 100 international observers adjudged to be the freest and fairest Nigeria ever had. That election, between a Kano (northern) businessman, Bashir Tofa, and a Lagos (southern) businessman, Moshood Abiola, was believed to have been won by the southerner. Its annulment sparked violent protests by Nigerians that claimed dozens of lives and pitted the press against the government.

Between January and September 1993, more journalists were jailed and more publications were closed down by the government in this period than any other (more than 60 journalists and 44 publications). The press exhibited the highest degree of resilience, manifested in the birth of underground publishing.

The stage for press/government confrontation was probably set in about 1989 when it became clear that Babangida was not going to keep to his promise to hand over power to an elected president in 1990 because according to him, he did not want to "rush the process." This excuse did not jive with a press that was witness to all of the arbitrariness characteristic of the whole process (disqualification of 13 political parties that applied for registration, banning dozens of politicians; government created the two political parties to which all Nigerians were expected to belong; government wrote the party manifestoes and promulgated decree 13, which put the National Electoral Commission beyond the reach of the law). Later, in order to allow for "proper coordination," Babangida, again, said that he was changing the hand-over date to 1 October 1992. Then he changed it to 2 January 1993, and then to 27 August 1993. Apart from continually changing the dates, he amended the transition program 38 times.[100] Confounding the apparent unwillingness to vacate power was the sudden emergence on the political landscape of various organizations, like the Committee of Elder Statesmen, the Association for Better Nigeria, and so forth, and anonymous people campaigning for Babangida to stay on four more years.[101]

As the last promised date—27 August—drew near, Nigerians began to see more clearly indications of their president's insincerity. Stating that the government was manipulating the transition process, former head of state General Obasanjo gave voice to a national feeling: "Until Babangida goes, I don't believe he will go . . . I believe that Babangida is playing games. I believe that the great impediment we have against democracy in (Nigeria) today is Babangida himself."[102] In a similar vein, Odumegwu Ojukwu, who led the Biafra secession attempt by easterners during the civil war of 1967-70, said in March 1993: "If you want to hand over to a civil government, you don't need many years for it . . . All you need for a transition can be achieved in, say, three months if you are really serious."[103]

Things got more interesting. In April, Babangida's greatest nemesis, former head of state Olusegun Obasanjo, told the nation that Babangida's administration was "deficit in honesty, deficit in honor, deficit in truth. The only thing it has in surplus is saying something and doing something else,"[104] and Tai Solarin, Babangida's appointee to the People's Bank who had resigned under a cloud of fraud by his subordinates, said, "We have gotten to a point where we have to get our guns and gunpowder ready. If Babangida does not go, I will not sit idly."[105]

The constant barrage of press reports assailing the president's sincerity was so eroding the residual hopes of Nigerians in the man and his word that on 9 May 1993, the press secretary to the president, Duro Onabule, took out paid advertisements in several Nigerian newspapers assuring Nigerians that his boss would truly hand over power on 27 August 1993. "Finally," Onabule's ad read, "members of the public and organs of the mass media are hereby warned that henceforth, *its respect for the right to freedom of expression notwithstanding*, the government will deal severely with violations of the relevant decrees on the transition program. Members of the press may wish to note that *the propagation of views that can lead to the derailment of the transition program, constitutes an offence under the relevant decrees."* One of the decrees Onabule was referring to was the so-called Death decree—the *Treason and Treasonable Offence Decree of 1993.*

Signed into law on 4 May 1993, barely a month before the presidential election, the decrees expanded the meaning of treason. The attorney general, Clement Akpamgbo, while briefing the press said that it was now treasonable "to say or publish" anything capable of disrupting the fabric of the country or any part of it would be guilty of treason and, on conviction, shall face the death penalty.

The press instantly lashed out at government. The chairman of the editorial board of *The Guardian*, Olatunji Dare, said that the decree was barbaric. "It trivializes life. It is barbaric especially at a time when civilized countries the world over are stopping death sentences, we are here penalizing people for expressing their opinions." He said the Nigerian press was far too vibrant for this latest government attempt. Said Dare: "Decree 4 (under which Dare's men at *The Guardian* were jailed) did not kill the press. Rather, it brought out the best in journalism and I believe this will do the same. We shall be relentless in doing what we have to do to ensure a democratic future."[106] Chris Okolie, publisher and editor-in-chief of *Newbreed*, called the decrees the handiwork of a "drowning man" that will not achieve its purpose because "people like me will still talk."[107]

And indeed, people were still talking, and the press got more critical. In New York, former head of state Olusegun Obasanjo said that the decrees were not worth anyone's serious attention.[108]

It was in this climate of severe press criticism and government repression that the presidential election was held on 12 June 1993. But desperate attempts were made to stop the election by the Association for Better Nigeria (ABN). On 9 June, ABN filed a suit asking a High Court in Abuja for an interlocutory order to postpone the presidential election.[109] Many people, including officials at the United States Embassy in Lagos, saw materialization of a long-time fear on the horizon.

In a bold move that set the stage for subsequent U.S. policy, the director of the U.S. Information Service in Lagos, Mike

O'Brien, issued a terse statement warning that any attempt to postpone the election would be unacceptable to the United States. He was immediately ordered to leave Nigeria within 72 hours for interfering in Nigeria's internal affairs, a mere symbolic action since Mr. O'Brien had already been scheduled to leave Nigeria for the United Kingdom on a higher posting anyway. Britain joined the United States in sending a similar signal. Probably because of the strong signals and the determination of Nigerians united behind a resilient press and because the electoral commission relied on its protection under Decree 13, the election took place on 12 June. The next day, the results began to trickle in from Abuja, the headquarters of the electoral commission. In New York, faxed copies of the returns from 14 states that the electoral commission had officially released were circulating freely among Nigerians. General Obasanjo said that within 48 hours, he had obtained a copy of the initial returns, which indicated that the SDP candidate, Moshood Abiola, was not only winning, he had won in the key northern states of Kano (the home of his opponent), Jigawa, Borno, and Kaduna.[110] It was the first time a southerner would win key states in the north.[111] And there was a clear possibility that Nigeria was set to have its first southern president, once the remaining results were released. But it was also clear that many supporters of the ABN, which successfully got a court order to stop the election in the first place, were not going to give up. What followed brought the Nigerian judiciary into a political mess as court rulings began to reflect more and more a north-south divide.

On 15 June, three days after the election, Chief Judge Dahiru Saleh of Abuja, the Federal Capital Territory, ordered the NEC to suspend further release of election results pending the resolution of the ABN suit. Although it had ignored an earlier court order, the electoral commission chose to honor this latest one. Days later, in the south, a Lagos High Court judge, Justice Olugbani, gave the electoral commission 24 hours to release the remaining results. Olugbani said: "Even if heaven falls, NEC should declare the results and name the winner, irrespective of any court order or injunction that may be issued against the election."[112] That order by Justice Olugbani was ignored without repercussion.

It was clear to all Nigerians that in accordance with the revised electoral laws, unless the election results were declared before 20 June 1993, the whole exercise could be legally nullified. Since the NEC did not seem prepared to release the results, the Campaign for Democracy, a not-for-profit human rights organization, which already had the full results in its custody, did it for NEC on 18 June.[113] That move was not legal in any way, but it put the results in the laps of all Nigerians. Within hours, the results were being faxed to Nigerians abroad; photocopies were being sold at bus terminals and open markets in Lagos and other major cities, and days later, many news magazines not only began to print them, they began to carry cover stories that revealed, to the embarrassment of the government, a deep-rooted insincerity in the president and the supposed reluctance of the northern elite to accept defeat in a fair election, which resulted in a victory for a southern candidate.

The suits and counter-suits for the official release of the election results and the pronouncement of the winner continued up until 23 June 1993, when in an unsigned statement from the State House the military government said it was annulling the election "in order to rescue the judiciary from intra-wrangling" and "protect our legal system and the judiciary from being ridiculed and politicized both nationally and internationally." The statement also said that the government had suspended the electoral commission and repealed the decrees—the Transition to Civil Rule (Political Program) (Amendment) (No. 3) Decree 52 of 1992 and the Presidential Election (Basic Constitutional and Transitional Provision) Decree 13 of 1993—that empowered it. The statement said: "All acts or omissions done or purported to have been done or to be done by any person, authority, etc., under the decrees are hereby declared invalid." It also said that "all acts or omission done or purported to be done (by the electoral commission) are hereby nullified."

That action immediately opened a floodgate of outrage and condemnation internationally. Thirteen major American newspapers wrote critical editorial opinions not less than 26 times[114] (between June and September alone), the House of Representatives subcommittee on African Affairs held a special hearing on the

Nigerian situation and the United States, along with Britain and France, took a hard line against the Nigerian military. The United States and Britain immediately condemned the annulment. While Britain said it would reassess its ties with Nigeria in protest, the U.S. State Department warned that "a failure by the military to hand over power to civilians in August as originally planned would have serious implications for U.S./Nigerian relations."[115] The department said that the United States remained concerned about the continuing repression of the press and democratic forces and that "all aspects of our bilateral relations, including our $22.8 million in bilateral assistance are currently under review."[116]

In Washington, D.C., a strongly worded memorandum signed by 39 members of the Congressional Black Caucus and addressed to Secretary of State Warren Christopher said that the annulment "must not be allowed to stand." Stating that the issue of the annulment required "attention at the highest level," the Caucus warned that a retreat from democracy in Nigeria could spell trouble for the entire West African subregion.

Nigerians in the United States who have a reputation for group disunity, found a common need to maintain the momentum for democracy. Dozens of protest marches were carried out in New York, Washington, Atlanta, Los Angeles, among others, where hundreds of demonstrators urged the United States to stand by their 12 June election and institute sanctions against the military government. The American press towed the same line.

In typical editorials, the *Christian Science Monitor*[117] called for freezing Nigeria's assets and visas for the military rulers, while the *San Francisco Chronicle* said that the "U.S., Britain, and other Western well-wishers would be doing Nigeria a significant favor by cutting diplomatic ties to the military regime."[118] The *Washington Post* challenged the Clinton administration to begin its avowed support for "the movement to freedom in Africa" in Nigeria while the *Atlanta Constitution* urged the administration to dispatch General Colin Powell, chairman of the Joint Chiefs of Staff, to Nigeria to "persuade General Babangida that armed forces must subordinate themselves to civilian control sooner than later and that the people's choice, Mr. Abiola, should be president."[119]

The policy adopted by the U.S. State Department reflected most of the opinions of the major media. That policy was to steadfastly put pressure on President Babangida to respect the wishes of Nigerians or face sterner measures from the United States and its allies. Nigeria's ambassador, Zubair Kazaure, according to reliable sources at the Nigerian embassy in Washington and the consulate-general in New York, repeatedly told aides how irritating he found incessant threats by department officials on the issue of the 12 June election.

On 20 July 1993, Ambassador Kazaure was once again invited to the State Department and told that the United States was "reviewing—with the presumption of denial—applications for the commercial export of defense articles bound for Nigeria; restricting the remaining Nigerian military attachés access to the U.S. government and asking five Nigerian military officers studying in the United States under the auspices of the International Military Education and Training program to depart the United States."[120] He was also told that additional measures were in the offing unless the civilian government elected on 12 June was in place by 27 August 1993. Then, action moved to the Congress of the United States.

On 4 August 1993, the House congressional subcommittee on Africa held a special hearing on "Nigeria: Which Way Forward."[121] Assistant Secretary of State George Moose told the subcommittee that the future policy of the United States must be to remove the risk to Nigeria's national integrity that the political crisis posed by making sure the military left. "If the military understands its interest will suffer if it tries to retain power, it may be possible to strengthen those in Nigeria seeking to persuade the military leadership to turn power over to duly-elected civilians."[122] Other testimonies by Dr. Richard Joseph of the Carter Center at Emory University; deputy assistant secretary of defense for African affairs, James Woods; and Holly Burkhalter of Human Rights Watch all had a common thread of recommendation: The United States should prepare for the long haul; it should continue to stand by the 12 June election, and it should continue to impose (and threaten further) sanctions.[123]

Many factors served to further concretize a U.S. policy that rested on the recognition of the 12 June election:[124] the congressional hearing; incessant critical newspaper editorials in the United States; Abiola's trip to France, England, and the United States to shore up support for his election; Abiola's meetings with Vice President Gore, Chief of Staff Thomas McLarty, Senator Simon, and Representatives Hamilton and Johnston; and the various work strikes and demonstrations in Nigeria in support of a return to democracy.

But a shift was noticeable towards the end of August. A recalcitrant President Babangida, after Abiola's SDP refused to take part in a fresh election, handed over power to a handpicked interim government headed by the former chairman of the United African Company (UAC), Ernest Shonekan, on 26 August.[125]

The State Department increasingly became less strident regarding its stand on the 12 June election, especially in the first weeks of August. Indeed, its policy shifted from threats of sanctions to the demand for inclusion of Abiola in the resolution of the political crisis. The tame, subdued, tone of a State Department release on 2 September 1993 points to this shift. The release said: "Now that Nigeria's military regime ostensibly has transferred power to civilians, Nigerians have the right to expect an unhindered civilian government." The department also began to stress, rather needlessly, that U.S. support had always been for the process, and not individuals, a rather disingenuous rationale since its earlier support for the 12 June verdict was also, by extension, a support for the individual who won and the 14 million Nigerians who voted for a president. That shift in policy was completed when Walter Carrington, the new U.S. ambassador to Nigeria, was confirmed by Congress.[126]

V

The Press Under the Interim Government

Although this study is on the Nigerian military, it is necessary to cast a cursory look on press/government relations under the interim government of Ernest Shonekan, a Babangida creation that remained highly unpopular and was consumed in its pursuit of legitimacy.

Like Babangida, his predecessor, Shonekan, professed his support for free speech and press freedom and released many of the journalists who had been detained under Babangida. "The interim national government has no interest in hounding the press or any group of citizens for that matter,"[127] he declared. He said that his government understood and accepted "the constructive and enabling role a free press could play in our national aspiration for enduring democracy."[128]

But even as he courted the press, Shonekan defended the antipress actions of the military before him. He told the delegation that the military proscribed some publications "to protect the larger interest of the federation from reckless sensationalism, licentious dissemination of falsehood, and unrestrained abuse of public servants by the press to the neglect of constructive evaluation of policies."[129] To shed his image as a military stooge, he removed many of the appointees of the Babangida regime and deployed the very powerful director of military intelligence, Akilu, who had been implicated in the murder of Dele Giwa.

Stating that a fresh presidential election would be held in February 1994, Shonekan waged a short-lived war against official corruption. He appointed a new Central Bank governor who ordered the investigation of more than 20 commercial banks while his oil minister, Don Etiebet, began an anticorruption crusade at the Nigerian National Petroleum Corporation.

In his Independence day address on 1 October 1993 to commemorate Nigeria's 33rd anniversary, Shonekan promised that a commission of inquiry would be set up to investigate the circumstances leading to the annulment of the presidential election. He spoke of Nigeria's immense economic problems, "a history of one political crisis after another and of economic opportunities lost."[130]

In a declaration that was music to journalists' ears, Shonekan said that he would soon ask the National Assembly to repeal four decrees made under Babangida that impeded speech and threatened press freedom: the Detention of Persons Decree 2, Treasonable

Offenses Decree 29, Offensive Publications (Proscription) Decree, and the Newspaper (proscription and prohibition from circulation) Decree 48. He did not get to do that before he was forced out of office on 17 November 1993 by his minister of defense, General Sanni Abacha.

Three factors, all occurring in November, facilitated that ninth military coup in Nigeria. First was Shonekan's 700 percent increase in fuel prices, an action that undermined his already low popularity, sparked mass resentment, and caused the 2.3 member-strong Nigerian Labor Congress to call out its members on strike.

Second was the landmark decision of 10 November by the High Court in Lagos ruling the Shonekan government unlawful. The decision came as a result of a suit filed by Abiola urging the court to find that former president Babangida had no power to nominate a president for Nigeria. Abiola's argument rested on a simple technicality: Babangida stepped aside as president on 26 August while Decree 61, which established the interim government, came into being on 27 August. No law in Nigeria, not even military decrees, empowered a former president to handpick his successor.

Third, there was the unease that the Shonekan government caused by its anticorruption crusade among senior military officials who had profited from the corrupt Babangida regime. The enormity of the corruption was contained in a confidential 60-page report, *Final Report of the Budget Monitoring Committee*, commissioned by Shonekan while he was the head of the transition council. Submitted to Shonekan on 24 August, the report says in the first half of 1993 that oil sales worth "a total sum of $1.537 billion was paid into various dedicated accounts" and that the monitoring committee was unable "to have access to detailed information on the operation of these accounts."[131] It expresses concern about "non-payment of revenue of 1.1 billion naira expected from the sale of domestic crude oil lifted and refined by NNPC for local consumption," the high cost of warehousing procured weapons abroad, and the accumulation of huge debts by the Ministry of Defense, which Nigeria was not in a financial position to honor.[132]

Quoting Western diplomats who had access to the report, *The Financial Times* said that army generals frustrated the committee's effort to make government spending more transparent and ensure an independent audit of the NNPC. It also said that the Nigerian army had purchased substantial weaponry, "much of it unnecessary or inappropriate while failing to maintain existing ones" and that "commissions" to middle men ranged from 20 to 40 percent of the contracts.[133]

Faced, therefore, with low popularity and a military that "feared exposure of the corruption that pervades the political system,"[134] the military takeover of the Shonekan government presented little surprise.

VI

Hegemonic Elements in General Sanni Abacha's Regime (1993-?)

As soon as General Abacha took control of the government, he created a Provisional Ruling Council and declared himself the head of state. His subsequent actions suggested a hegemonic pattern in the mold of Babangida.

Abacha lifted the ban imposed on some newspapers under Babangida but warned journalists to be careful what they report and write. At the same time, he dissolved all political institutions—the national assembly, the electoral commission, and the political parties—and banned political activities. Then he met with union leaders and succeeded in getting them to call off the strike after cutting the 700 percent fuel price increase by half. To those who might be willing to test his government, Abacha said he would be "firm, humane and decisive."[135]

Then in classic Babangida style, he embarked on a grand program of incorporatism. He met with Abiola[136] and appointed his running mate, Baba Gana Kingibe as minister of external affairs. He also picked one of the most vocal adversaries of military rule, Dr. Olu Onagoruwa, as his minister of justice and attorney general and Alex Ibru, the publisher of *The Guardian*, which suffered under Buhari, as minister of internal affairs. Then, picking from a pool of known competent as well as inept ex-convicts, Abacha swore in a 32-

member cabinet on 27 November. The cabinet included former World Bank economist Kalu Idika Kalu (minister of finance); the former governor of Lagos and publisher of *Lagos News*, Lateef Jakande, who was detained under Babangida (minister of works and housing);[137] Samuel Ogbemudia (minister of labor and productivity);[138] Solomon Lar (minister of police affairs),[139] and so forth.

Counting on the assured silencing of the opposition through incorporatism, the Abacha regime may have bought itself some time. But his image as a weak[140] soldier abroad, the association of the military with corruption in Nigeria, and a hostile largely uncooptable private press will be significant elements in monitoring press/government relations in the future under Abacha.

While he seems to have succeeded in carrying the west along,[141] the first signs of opposition in Nigeria began to appear within two weeks of the Abacha takeover. Nobel prize winner, Wole Soyinka, called on the international community to completely isolate the "regime of infamy." He said: "This is going to be the worst and most brutal regime that Nigeria ever had. This regime is prepared to kill, torture, and make opponents disappear."[142]

The Nigerian press soon began echoing that sentiment. *Newswatch* said Abacha's coup was a result of his "lust for power," *The Guardian* newspaper, whose publisher became Abacha's minister of internal affairs, called it "unwarranted," while *The Vanguard* warned that the Abacha regime would be economically devastating to Nigerians.[143] The official government reaction to the negative press reports has been one of tolerance. This pattern will remain until the new regime fully legitimizes itself and consolidates political power. Thereafter, conforming to the hegemonic model, the Abacha regime can be expected to embark on its own antipress actions—putting journalists in jail, impeding free speech, and curtailing free expression.

VII

Conclusion

It is still too early to fully understand press/government relations under Abacha and to what extent those relations would impact on public policy. However, because he was party to most decisions made under Babangida as a cabinet member (and these must include antipress and antihuman rights acts), we can safely assume a similarity of approach, a hegemonic pattern of press/government relations, tolerating some free speech as he constructs legitimacy, and turning against opposition once this has been accomplished.

An American-type free press is not attainable in Nigeria in the foreseeable future until the country adopts, sustains, and perfects a solid democratic culture, an independent judiciary, and a respectable apolitical military that is eager and willing to serve under an elected commander in chief.

On the domestic front, the vibrant Nigerian press can be trusted to continue to steer Nigeria toward these goals. Technological advances in communication, the growing popularity of pro-democracy forces (lawyers, human rights monitors, and so forth), the increasing interest of the world media in Nigeria will continue to draw attention to autocratic maneuvers and work against them.

The Nigerian military will continue to be sensitive to political dynamics in Washington, London, and Paris, among other Western countries, as evidenced in the reported millions of dollars spent on lobbying efforts in these countries and the resonance in Abuja and Lagos of statements, actions, and policies emanating from the west. Therefore, on the inter-national front, editors of influential media organizations should "write editorial comments in support of journalists who are still being persecuted and harassed."[144] Indeed, such reports along with domestic dynamics in Nigeria (protests, strikes, press conferences by respected elder statesmen, and so forth) are responsible for the "plateaus" that form an element of the theoretical framework I presented in section one of this paper. The experience in Nigeria is that press persecution by the military reduces (or "plateaus") the more international attention focuses on the country's human rights abuses. Furthermore, countries like the United States that trade substantially with Nigeria should expand their "national interest" definition to incorporate democracy and respect for human rights and act decisively on the side of democracy at all times.[145]

APPENDIX

Press Persecution Under Babangida 1990-1993[146]

1990:

- The deputy editor of *The Vanguard* arrested on 24 April.
- The *Punch* newspaper closed on 29 April.
- *The Vanguard* and *Champion* newspapers closed on 9 June after reports that suggested that an international market was closed by the military governor of Lagos, Rajio Rasaki, out of ethnic bias against Ibos.
- Three journalists of *Champion* were detained on 12 June.
- *Lagos News, Lagos Evening News, Sunday News* closed 1 May and editor and publisher and former governor of Lagos, Lateef Jakande, was detained because of a "negative and critical" editorial on the 27 April 1990 coup attempt.
- *Newbreed* closed 8 June for publishing a letter from one of the alleged coup plotters.

Source: *Africa Watch Reports*

1991:

- Editor and news editor of *Lagos News* detained.
- Thirteen journalists of *Lagos News* were detained, including the publisher and former governor of Lagos, Lateef Jakande, on 14 March. Jakande became minister of works and housing two years later.
- Four reporters of *Guardian Express* were detained on 29 May.

- The military governor of Lagos closed *The Guardian, The Guardian on Sunday, African Guardian, Guardian Express, Lagos Life,* and *Guardian Financial Weekly* on 29 May.
- *Financial Times* correspondent, William Keeling, deported from Nigeria on 29 June.

Sources: *African Watch 1991 Reports* and Nigerian newspapers.

1992:

- Thirteen publications were closed at various times in 1992.
- Ten thousand copies of *Quality* magazine were seized.
- Six journalists were unlawfully arrested and detained.
- Three journalists were wrongfully suspended.
- Seven journalists faced punitive redeployment.
- Five journalists were forced to resign at the *African Concord* after they refused to apologize to government for stories carried.
- Four Press Centers were sealed up by government forces on four occasions.
- One journalist had acid thrown in his face by people suspected to be acting in behalf of a state governor.
- One journalist was ejected from her house illegally by police.
- Ten journalists were beaten by government forces.

Source: *Report by the Biennial Delegates Conference of the Nigeria Union of Journalists,* May 1992

1993:

- Sixteen media houses (*The Reporter, The News, Tell, Daily Sketch, Sunday Sketch, Newsday, The Observer*, Ogun State Broadcasting Corporation, and eight publications of the Concord Group) were closed down by government.
- 140,000 copies of *The News* and *Tell* were seized by government.
- The whole editorial board of *The News* was declared wanted by government.
- Eight journalists (four from *Tell*, two from *Newsday*, one from *Satellite*, and one from *The News*) were detained.
- The wife of Dapo Olorunyomi, deputy editor in chief of *The News*, and his three-month-old child were detained in lieu of the journalist on 29 June. They were released after the child became ill.
- Decree 48 was issued on 16 August to proscribe *Concord* group of publications.

Source: *Africa Watch 1993 Reports; The Punch* (Lagos), 20 May 1993

Adeyinka Adeyemi

NOTES

1. Cited in *World Press Review*, February 1992, 13.

2. There seems to be no agreement on the actual population of Nigeria. While official Nigerian government figures put it at 88.5 million (May 1992), the Central Intelligence Agency's *The World Factbook* (July 1992, 253) puts it at 126 million with an annual growth rate of 3 percent; UNESCO estimates it as 109 million (*Statistical Yearbook 1992*) while Roger East (ed.) *World Fact File* (New York, 1990, 386) puts it at 106 million. This study will use an approximate median of 100 million.

3. *Statistical Yearbook 1992* (UNESCO).

4. These figures were extracted from "This is Nigeria," material prepared by the *Nigerian Information Service*, Consulate-General of Nigeria, New York, for the press during the October 1993 visit of the interim head of state, Chief Ernest Shonekan, to the United States.

5. In 1984, there were 14 daily newspapers; in 1985 through 1986, there were 19; and in 1988 through 1990, there were 31. In most other countries of Africa, including South Africa, no newspaper growth was registered. Indeed, there was a decrease in many instances. See *Statistical Yearbook* 1983/84; 1987 (United Nations) and *Statistical Yearbook 1992* (UNESCO).

6. Adigun Agbaje, *The Nigerian Press, Hegemony and the Social Construction of Legitimacy* (New York: Edwin Mellen Press, 1992), 319–321.

7. Successful military coups were carried out in January 1966, July 1966, July 1975, December 1983, and August 1985. Aborted coups were carried out in February 1976 and April 1991. The only democratic governments in Nigeria were in 1960–66 under Prime Minister Tafawa Balewa and 1979–83 under President Shehu Shagari.

8. Section 38(3); also section 36(3) in the 1979 Constitution.

9. See Gani Fawehinmi, *Nigerian Law of Libel and the Press* (London: Eastern Press, 1987).

10. LD/803/80 of 30 July 1982. For full text of judgment, see Fawehinmi, ibid., C156–C166.

11. In *Senate v. Tony Momoh* (1983) *4 Nigerian Constitutional Law Reports* 269, the Court of Appeals held that the press cannot constitute itself into the fourth arm of government; that the publisher of a newspaper had no special immunity from the application of general laws, and that in some cases, the press can be ordered to disclose its sources. See Fawehinmi, ibid., C101–C155.

12. *Oyewole and Ors v. Nigerian Television Authority* (1980) 2 OYSHC 413. In judgment, the Court awarded 150 naira (at the time, about $200) costs to the television authority against its reporters.

13. For instance, there are federal laws against "seditious publications" (*Criminal Code*, Chapter 42, sections 50–52, *Laws of the Federation of Nigeria 1958*); against leakages of classified materials (*Official Secrets Act, No. 29 of 1962; Official Secrets (Amendment) Act No. 30 of 1962*; against publication of false news with intent to cause fear and alarm (*Section 59 of the Criminal Code cap 42, laws of the Federation 1958*); against publication of obscene matters (*Obscene Publication Act No. 51 of 1961*) and laws protecting children from "harmful" publications (*Children and Young Persons (Harmful Publications) Act No. 52 of 1961*).

14. According to Fred Siebert, Theodore Peterson, and Wilbur Schramm, in *Four Theories of the Press* (University of Illinois Press, 1956), most relationships fit the social-centralist, authoritarian, libertarian, and social-libertarian models.

15. William Hachten, *Muffled Drums* (Ames: Iowa State University Press, 1971), 272.

16. William Rugh, *The Arab Press: News Media and the Political Process in the Arab World* (Syracuse, N.Y.: Syracuse University Press, 1987).

17. John Merill, *Global Journalism: A Survey of the World's Media* (Longman, 1983), 26.

18. Ibid., 26.

19. For more on this, see T. Barton Carter, Marc Franklin, and Jay Wright, *The First Amendment and the Fifth Estate: Regulation of Electronic Mass Media* (New York: The Foundation Press, 1986).

20. All military coups but one in Nigeria—seven successful and two aborted ones—were carried out on the radio. Typically, armed soldiers take over the Federal Radio Corporation station in Ikoyi, Lagos (which transmits nationally), force an announcer to break transmission, slot in some martial music, and soon after, someone announces he is taking over the government. The latest military coup of 17 November 1993 by General Sanni Abacha, a prominent figure in the 1983 coup and defense minister, entailed forcing the interim head of state, Chief Ernest Shonekan, to resign. It should be stressed that in 1993, the military government in Nigeria granted licenses to 14 private television stations to operate. Radio remains government-controlled.

21. Oblivious to this regulation, as a fresh visitor from the United States, this writer was once arrested by armed soldiers on Awolowo Road, Ikoyi, a good distance from the radio station, physically assaulted, and accused of wanting to "overthrow government."

22. William Rugh, *The Arab Press*, speaks of *mobilizing*, a subset of the authoritarian system in which government mobilizes the media to concentrate on development issues; *loyalist*, in which the media is entirely loyal to the government; and *diverse*, a system in which public and private press co-exist. This last categorization, under which Nigeria seems to fall, is entirely too generic and fails to convey the essential unique elements of Nigerian press/government relationship.

23. Cited in Frank Barton, *The Press of Africa: Persecution and Perseverance* (Macmillan, 1979).

24. For an analysis of the nexus between public needs and public goods as well as the connection between the public and the public interest, see Frederick Schauer, "First Amendment Theory" in *California Law Review*, Vol. 74, No. 3, May 1986.

25. Quoting donor agencies, Keeling said that the Babangida regime embarked on "extra-budgetary expenditure," spending up to $500 million to intervene in Liberia, $150 million to host the 1991 summit of the Organization of African Unity (OAU) (building facilities and buying Mercedes stretch limousines to transport heads of state), an amount "that exceeded the level of contributions made to OAU (in

1990) by member countries," awarding a contract for 150 Vickers military tanks and starting the construction of an aluminum plant at a cost of 60–100 percent higher than similar plants elsewhere in the world. See *The Financial Times*, 27 June 1991, 10.

26. Cited in *World Press Review*, February 1992, 13.

27. The contradictions of the Gramscian notion are well known. For instance, on one ground, he tends to argue that hegemony does not involve the use for force or coercion by the state, but on the other hand, he says the exercise of hegemony is characterized "by the combination of force and consent." See Antonio Gramsci, *Selections from the Prison Notebooks* edited and translated by Q. Hoare and G. N. Smith (London: Lawrence and Wishart, 1971), 80. For other treatments of hegemony and its contradistinctions with concepts such as legitimacy, supremacy, class, and counter-hegemony see Adigun Agbaje, *The Nigerian Press, Hegemony and the Social Construction of Legitimacy (1960–1983)* (The Edwin Mellen Press, 1992), 1–18; and Toyin Falola and Julius Ihonvbere, *The Rise and Fall of Nigeria's Second Republic, 1979–84* (London: Zed Books, 1985).

28. Gramsci, *Selections from the Prison Notebooks*, 58.

29. According to former head of state, General Olusegun Obasanjo, "settlement" has become Nigeriaspeak for the way the Ibrahim Babangida regime silenced dissent and cowered/controlled the press. See Olusegun Obasanjo, "Our Desperate Ways," in *Newswatch* magazine, Lagos, Nigeria, 23 November 1992.

30. There is no exact parallel to this provision in the Nigerian Constitution. While the First Amendment categorically states that Congress *shall not* make laws that impede free speech, Section 10(1) of the 1989 Nigerian Constitution states that "The National Assembly may, subject to the provisions of this section, *alter any of the provisions of this Constitution.*"

31. It should be stressed that according to the Constitution of Nigeria all military coup d'etat are treasonable acts. Section 1(2) of the 1979 Constitution states: "The Federal Republic of Nigeria shall not be governed, nor shall any person or group of persons take control of the Government of Nigeria or any part thereof except in accordance with the provisions of this Constitution."

32. See "Angry Nigerians shed few tears over coup," in *The Christian Science Monitor*, 10 January 1984, 7 and "Nigerian Merchants Welcome Coup," in the *New York Times*, 8 January 1984, 3.

33. See *The Christian Science Monitor*, 26 January 1984, 9.

34. *The Christian Science Monitor*, 10 January 1984, 7.

35. Interview with *The News*, 5 July 1993.

36. Previous attempts to explain the typical hostility of the Nigerian military have placed mountains of blame on the colonial experience (See, for instance, T. N. Tamuno, *The Evolution of the Nigerian State: The Southern Phase, 1898–1914*, London: Longman, 1972) and "shamelessness" (See Arthur Nwankwo, *The Military Option to Democracy*, Enugu: Fourth Dimension, 1987). Instant legitimacy and Buhari's own personal past grudge with the Nigerian press offer better explanation for his hostility.

37. Decree No. 1—Constitution (Suspension and Modification) Decree 1984.

38. For an analysis of the effects of Decree 1, see Niki Tobi, *Legal Impact of the Constitution (Suspension and Modification) Decree, 1984 on the Constitution of Nigeria, 1979* (Calabar, Nigeria: Centaur Press, 1985).

39. *New York Times*, 7 January 1984, 23.

40. Section 5(1) of Decree.

41. The Constitution of Nigeria does not provide for the suspension of any of its provisions unless by the National Assembly and in accordance with section 10, subsections 2 and 3. In particular, subsection 3 states that Chapter IV of the constitution, dealing with fundamental human rights, shall not be altered unless such a proposal is approved by the votes of not less than four-fifths majority of all members of the Senate and the House of Representatives and approved by resolution of the Houses of Assembly of not less than two-thirds of all States.

42. *Washington Post*, 21 January 1984, A18.

43. Cited in the *Christian Science Monitor*, 16 January 1984, 7.

44. Interview with *The News* (Lagos, Nigeria), 5 July 1993, 17.

45. Ibid.
46. Ibid., 18.
47. Section 8(1). In 1984, 10,000 naira equalled about $9,000.
48. Section 3(1).
49. Section 2(1).
50. Section 8(3).
51. Section 8(2).
52. Section 8(4).
53. Section 9.
54. Thompson, Tunde, *Fractured Jail Sentence* (Enugu, Nigeria: Fourth Dimension Publishers, 1988).
55. *4 Nigerian Constitutional Law Reports 269*, 1983. For text of judgment, see Fawehinmi, C101–C155.
56. The foreign missions mentioned by *The Guardian* are: Athens, Ankara, Beirut, Brazzaville, Hong Kong, Liverpool, Hamburg, Bata, Rio de Janeiro, Doula, and Buea. The prosecution witness said that all but Buea were correct.
57. Quoted in Thompson, 82.
58. Justice O. Ayinde, Judgment in *Federal Republic of Nigeria v. Tunde Thompson, Nduka Irabor, Guardian Newspapers Ltd.*, POPT/L/1/84 of 4 July 1984, C518.
59. *New York Times*, 29 April 1984, 5.
60. Ibid.
61. A 30-year-old truck driver, Vincent Agulannah, was sentenced to death for storing about 5,000 gallons of gasoline; an American, Marie McBroom, was detained without charge for nearly ten months and tried for conspiracy to export or illegally exporting about one million barrels of crude oil and 20,000 metric tons of fuel, charges that could bring her before a firing squad; hundreds of politicians were detained for months without charge; a Spanish sea captain, Jose Luis Pecina,

was sentenced to death along with two Nigerians for illegally exporting two million barrels of gasoline (the sentences were later commuted to 25 years' imprisonment); more than 500 officials of former President Shehu Shagari were tried by military tribunals for economic offenses; former governor of Plateau State, Solomon Lar, was sentenced to 22 years for misappropriating the equivalent of $24 million. See the *New York Times*, 26 June 1984, 5; *New York Times*, 28 January 1985, 4; *Los Angeles Times*, 14 April 1985, 9; and *Chicago Tribune*, 21 March 1985, 5.

62. *New York Times*, 8 May 1984, 30.

63. See *Annual Register: A Record of World Events 1984* (Detroit: Gale Research Corporation, 1984).

64. *New York Times*, 1 May 1984, 11.

65. See David Winder, "Nigeria Tries to Bounce Back to Influence in Midst of Chaos," in the *Christian Science Monitor*, 29 February 1984, 16.

66. The 1984 *International Press Institute* annual report cited Nigeria as one country where "one of the most striking turnabouts in press freedom" happened where government "severely restricted what was once the freest press in Black Africa."

67. Cited in the *New York Times*, 1 May 1984, 11.

68. For more on intra-military and inter-military cleavages in Nigerian politics, see Arthur Nwankwo, *The Military Option to Democracy* (Fourth Dimension Publisher, 1987), 146–176.

69. Maiden address to Nigerians on 27 August 1985.

70. *New York Times*, 4 September 1985, 10.

71. Ibid.

72. Adigun Agbaje, *The Nigerian Press, Hegemony and the Social Construction of Legitimacy* (Edwin Mellen Press, 1992), 265.

73. Olusegun Obasanjo, "Our Desperate Ways," an address to the meeting of National Council of States attended by President Babangida, in *Newswatch*, 23 November 1992, 36–37. "Settlement" as stressed in

footnote 27 is Nigeriaspeak for all compensatory attempts by government and any other privileged persons to influence the outcome of events in a manner that favors that government or person(s). It is similar to what is called "bribe" or "kickback" in some societies.

74. *The Newbreed* (October 1990 [Lagos, Nigeria]) reported that at one such meeting in July 1990, government officials gave material inducements to media chiefs in exchange for press loyalty and kid-glove reportage.

75. Irabor once fired a Nigerian Television Authority editor who had the effrontery to demand a signed statement in place of a news item that Irabor was dictating over the phone. In a chat soon after the episode, Irabor told this writer that editors at the television had broadcast news given in that fashion in the past without question. Irabor was the one who distributed unsigned statements which state that the 12 June presidential election had been annulled and threatened the imposition of state of emergency in states where trouble erupted in the wake of that annulment. Until he was co-opted by government, Irabor was one of Nigeria's most respected journalists. As the editor of *Guardian Express* (on which this writer did *Express Circuit by Yakoli El-Fanta*, weekly columns that were critical of the harsh government of Buhari), Irabor exhibited excellent journalistic qualities, protecting the identity of his writers, championing the cause of free speech.

76. The only president of the Nigerian Bar Association in the period under review who did not become minister of justice was Alao Aka-Basorun, an ardent critic of the administration's human rights abuse. He was also reported to have campaigned against the taking of monetary donations from government. His passport was seized on 16 August 1990. He later escaped from Nigeria to England. See *Africa Watch*, Vol. 2, No. 30, 20 September 1990.

77. The government said that the recipients of these cars deserved the gestures. For more, see the *New York Times*, 2 December 1993.

78. See "Nigeria Enlists the Nettlesome Man in Short Pants," *New York Times*, 29 December 1989, 4.

79. Ibid.

80. *New York Times*, 11 August 1988, 6.

81. See "The Babangida Flaw," Stranded by Choice by Yinka Adeyemi in *Nigeria Homenews*, 13–19 September 1990 (London).

82. *Newswatch* itself was shamelessly patronizing to Babangida in the first five months of his regime. Babangida was on the magazine's cover four times, the first three in the first three months. He was also the subject of three favorable editorials in the magazine. Indeed, the editor's opinion columns "criticized anyone ... who attempted to make life unpleasant for Babangida." See Dele Olojede and Onukaba Adinoyi-Ojo, 162.

83. *Tell* was founded about 1991 by a splinter group of *Newswatch* journalists led by Nosa Igiebor. Having established itself as a serious alternative to *Newswatch*, some of whose directors had started to patronize the military (director Alex Akinyele became the minister of information; Deputy Editor-in-Chief Dan Agbese got appointed to the Board of the Nigerian Television Authority), *Tell* suffered tremendous blows in the hands of the military in 1993 for publishing stories uncomplimentary of the Babangida regime, beginning from a 15-page interview with former head of state, General Olusegun Obasanjo, who described President Babangida as a fraud (See *Tell*, 19 April 1993: Lagos, Nigeria). The following issue carried a cover "Go, IBB, Go," a call on General Ibrahim B. Babangida to follow through with his hand-over plan, while in May 1993 the magazine carried another cover, "Transition Against Handover," a story that highlighted 21 traps against the transition program. Security officials seized 70,000 copies of that edition. *Tell* later got a court injunction restraining government security forces from sealing off its offices. See "The Siege on *Tell*," *African Concord* (Lagos, Nigeria), 17 May 1993, 3.

84. *The News* was founded in 1993 by a group of *African Concord* journalists who resigned in protest after publisher Moshood Abiola (who later ran for president and was believed to have won before his election was annulled by President Babangida, his self-admitted friend) ordered them to apologize to the military government over some stories carried in *African Concord* that had caused a government siege on the magazine.

85. *Washington Post*, 17 March 1987, A19.

86. For full text of letter, see Dele Olojede and Onukaba Adinoyi-Ojo, *Born to Run: The Story of Dele Giwa* (Spectrum: 1986), 191–192.

87. Ibid., 173.

88. Ibid., 177.

89. Ibid., 182.

90. *Washington Post*, 17 March 1987, A19.

91. Chief Gani Fawehinmi has filed at least 32 cases and made 315 court appearances on the Dele Giwa issue. See *West African News* (New York), 8 November 1993, a story culled from *Tell* magazine (Lagos, Nigeria).

92. *Newswatch* did not, however, escape government recrimination. Less than one year after the murder of its founding editor, the magazine was proscribed by the Babangida regime for allegedly publishing "classified and confidential matters in its Volume 5, No. 15 issue of *April 13, 1987*." The decree that proscribed *Newswatch*, "Newswatch (Proscription and Prohibition from Circulation) Decree 6 of 1987," was signed by the president on 6 April 1987, but it purported to punish an infraction committed on 13 April 1987, indicating retroactivity. To give the action the force of the constitution, the preamble to the decree cites section 36(3) of the 1979 Constitution, the section dealing with the legal grounds of press control. See footnote 8, p. 4.

93. See "Echoes of Dele Giwa," *Newswatch* (Lagos, Nigeria), 26 April 1993, 33. While in the 4 April 1993 edition of *Newbreed* it was alleged that some eminent Nigerians, including President Babangida, First Republic President Nnamdi Azikiwe, former President Shehu Shagari, were members of a secret cult, *Newbreed* staffers believed that this had nothing to do with the real reason they were arrested. They believed that the real reason had to do with the magazine's possession of a taped confession of Dele Giwa's murderer.

94. Culled by *West African News* (New York), 8 November 1993, 10–11.

95. Ibid.

96. The official exchange rate of the naira in 1985 was one naira to $1.08, but on the black market, four naira were being sold for $1. In 1993, the official exchange rate fluctuates around $1 to 20 naira, but the parallel (black) market is $1 to up to 40 naira.

97. Editorials in the *Daily Star* said: "IMF Loan: A Tentacle of Capitalism" and the *Sunday Herald* asked "IMF: What For?" See the *Chicago Tribune*, 10 October 1985, 26.

98. *Chicago Tribune*, 10 October 1985, 26.

99. *New York Times*, 8 October 1985, 8.

100. *The News* (Lagos, Nigeria), 28 June 1993, 23.

101. See "Pro-military Ads Cloud Nigeria's Political Future," *New York Times*, 1 May 1993.

102. Interview with *Deutsche Welle* (Voice of Germany), 16 January 1993. Quoted in *The Guardian* (Lagos, Nigeria), 18 January 1993, 1.

103. Quoted in *Tell*, 5 July 1993, 13 (Lagos, Nigeria).

104. Interview with *Tell*, 26 April 1993 (Lagos, Nigeria).

105. Interview with *The News*, 10 May 1993 (Lagos, Nigeria).

106. Interview with *Tell*, 24 May 1993 (Lagos, Nigeria), 31.

107. *Tell*, ibid.

108. General Obasanjo at a dinner in his honor at the writer's residence on 22 June 1993 at which he addressed about 20 Nigerian community leaders.

109. Delivering judgment in a suspicious suit filed by Abimbola Davis on behalf of ABN, Justice Bassey Ikpeme, fresh on the bench, ruled that the election should not hold, despite Decree 13 of 1993, which puts the National Electoral Commission (NEC) beyond the reach of the courts, and Decree 19 of 1987 (amended by Decree 52 of 1992), which provides that NEC cannot be sued. In a shocking press conference on 16 July 1993, Davis, who was ABN's director of organization, confessed that ABN's plan was actually to derail the transition and have Babangida in power for four more years and that the attorney general, Brigadier General Halilu Akilu, head of the State Security Service who was implicated in Dele Giwa's mail bomb death, Judge Ikpeme and Babangida knew of the plan in advance. For full and unedited text of Davis's statement, see "Coup Against the Civilians: My Role, My

Regrets," in *The African Guardian*, 26 July 1993, 22–23 (Lagos, Nigeria).

110. Obasanjo during the reception at the writer's residence, ibid.

111. See "Man of History" cover story, *The News*, 21 June 1993, A1–A8.

112. Quoted in *The African Guardian*, 28 June 1993, 23.

113. According to the returns published by the organization, which were not controverted by government or NEC, of a total of 14.3 million votes cast, the Social Democratic Party (SDP) and Abiola got 58.36 percent and National Republican Convention (NRC) got 41.64 percent.

114. Based on a Nexis/Lexis search: *Christian Science Monitor* (25 June, 9 July), *New York Times* (1, 14, 15 July; 17 August), *San Francisco Chronicle* (25 June), *Boston Globe* (24 June, 18 July, 29 August), *St. Louis Post Dispatch* (9 July, 11 September), *Houston Chronicle* (25 June), *Washington Post* (2, 6, 21, 24 July; 28 August), *Chicago Tribune* (29 June, 18 August), *Cleveland Plain Dealer* (10 July), *Sacramento Bee* (3 July), *Atlantic Journal Constitution* (19 July), *Hartford Courant* (10 July), and *Orlando Sentinel* (22 August, 4 September).

115. U.S. State Department, Office of the Spokesman, 23 June 1993.

116. Ibid.

117. *Christian Science Monitor*, 25 June 1993, 18.

118. *San Francisco Chronicle*, 24 June 1993, A22.

119. *Atlanta Journal Constitution*, 19 July 1993, 6.

120. Press Statement, *U.S. Department of State*, Office of the Spokesman, 22 July 1993.

121. The witnesses at the hearing, which this writer also attended, were: James Woods, deputy assistant secretary of defense for African affairs; George Moose, assistant secretary of state for African affairs; Andrew Young, former U.S. ambassador to the United Nations; Dr. Richard Joseph of the Carter Center; Holly Burkhalter of Human Rights Watch; and Gregory Copley, the witness-in-chief of General Babangida.

122. See "Testimony of Asst. Secretary of State, George F. Moose" before the Subcommittee on Africa of the House Foreign Relations Committee on Nigeria's Political Crisis. 4 August 1993, 5.

123. It is important to stress that not all of the testimonies reflected these recommendations. In particular, the principal witness for the Nigerian military government, Gregory Copley, editor-in-chief of *Defense & Foreign Affairs* in London, painted rosy, even fallacious, pictures of Nigeria. He said that Nigeria was the freest country in Africa; that its judiciary was one of the most independent; that Babangida was sincere; that the presidential election was corrupted by the supposed winner; that the election did not represent the will of the Nigerian people; that the Nigerian press was corrupt, and that the press in Nigeria did not represent the majority because the largest circulating newspaper, *The Daily Times*, was read by only 60,000 in a country of 100 million. For full text, see Gregory Copley, *Testimony Before the Subcommittee on Africa*, 4 August 1993, 1–15.

124. In Nigeria, a decree was to be promulgated that made it a felony to refer to the 12 June election.

125. Chief Ernest Shonekan is a civilian and close ally of President Babangida, a successful businessman, and chairman of Babangida's transition.

126. At a September 1993 reception in his honor in Boston, this writer asked Ambassador Carrington why the United States was making its ambassador present credentials to an illegitimate and unelected government imposed by a military government that the United States pressured out of office. Carrington said he and the State Department were deeply worried by the possible implications of his posting to Nigeria.

127. Shonekan, while addressing a three-man delegation of the Nigerian Press Council that visited him on 14 October 1993. (See *News Agency of Nigeria* dispatch, Abuja, 15 October 1993). The "Nigerian Press Council" was established by General Babangida's administration by decree in 1992. It replaced the "Nigerian Media Council," which was established by Decree 59 of 1988. The chairman of the 17-member Press Council shall be appointed by the president, commander in chief after due consideration of suggestions by the Nigerian Press Organization (section 2 of decree). Also, the representatives of the

Nigerian Union of Journalists, the Nigerian Guild of Editors and the Newspaper Publishers Association of Nigeria "shall be appointed by the minister [of information] after an election by or on the nomination of the union, association or other body concerned" (section 3). The other members are appointed by the minister. The Council's functions are, *inter alia*, to enquire into complaints about press, research into contemporary press development, foster high professional standards, review developments likely to restrict the supply of information of public interest, and ensure the protection of rights and privileges of journalists in the lawful performance of their professional duties. The Council was unable to protect journalists under Babangida. See *Press Council, At Last*, Media Review, January 1993 (Lagos, Nigeria, 12–18).

128. Shonekan, to Nigerian Press Council delegation, ibid.

129. Ibid.

130. See *West African News* (New York), 11 October 1993, 3.

131. *Financial Times* (London), 22 November 1993, 14.

132. Ibid.

133. Ibid.

134. Ibid.

135. *News Agency of Nigeria* dispatch (datelined Lagos), 19 November 1993.

136. Abiola, who had been vehemently opposed to the interim government, kept a low profile after Abacha's coup. He met with Abacha on 20 November 1993 for 90 minutes. (See the *New York Times*, 25 November 1993, A10.) On 25 November, he criticized the return of the military, but in a reversal of his stand on Babangida, he said that "he was not calling on his supporters to rise up against it" (see *Reuters* dispatch (datelined Lagos), 25 November 1993).

137. Known as "Action Governor," Jakande was widely acclaimed as one of Nigeria's most efficient governors during the second republic.

138. Samuel Ogbemudia was made the military governor of the former midwest state after the Nigerian federal troops took over Benin City during the civil war on 20 September 1967. By 1975, he had acquired a farming estate at Nsukwa, the Palm Royal Hotel, four houses, a

piece of land (plot 855) on pricey and prestigious Victoria Island, Lagos; and farms in eight villages in the former midwest state (now Edo and Delta states). See Billy Dudley, *An Introduction to Nigerian Government and Politics* (Indiana University Press: 1982, 318).

139. Under the Buhari regime, Solomon Lar, former governor of Plateau State, was sentenced to 22 years in jail for misappropriating the equivalent of $24 million.

140. See "Nigeria's rapacious generals," editorial in the *Boston Globe*, 23 November 1993, 14.

141. In a spineless statement, the only one in the first two weeks, the United States said that "further measures" to frustrate democracy would result in a confrontation with the international community and that a "demonstrated commitment to an early return to civil rule" would determine Western measures against the military. This seems to suggest that only additional measures, not the military coup *per se*, and Abacha's failure to show that he would not sit tight in power, could inspire the West to act. In a similar move, Britain and its European Union partners, after their meeting in Luxembourg on 22 November, to consider sanctions against the Abacha administration, decided not to cancel all arms trade contracts because such may increase unemployment (See the *Financial Times*, London, 25 November 1993).

142. See the *New York Times*, 25 November 1993, A10.

143. All cited in the *New York Times*, ibid.

144. Attributed to Peter Galliner, director of the International Press Institute. See "Stop Harassing Journalists," *Weekend Concord* (Lagos, Nigeria), 22 May 1993, 18.

145. It is suggested that the lukewarm U.S. reaction to the military in Nigeria is explained by the fact that Nigeria is the second largest supplier of oil to the United States and its sixth importer of wheat. Until Washington was able to convince former President Babangida to lift the ban on U.S. wheat imports, the United States lost about $162 million annually. Oil and wheat were important elements of American national interest in Nigeria.

146. Statistics before 1990 were either scanty or unreliable.

CHAPTER SEVEN

The Supreme Court of Zimbabwe*

ANTHONY R. GUBBAY

NARRATOR: It is our pleasure to welcome the Honorable Chief Justice Anthony Roy Gubbay of Zimbabwe. He received his bachelor's degree from the University of Witwatersrand in South Africa and his master of arts and master of laws degrees from Cambridge University. He has held various positions—senior counsel, president of the Matabeleland and Midlands Valuations Boards, and national president of the Special Court for Income Tax Appeals, the Fiscal Court, and the Patents Tribunal. In 1977 he was sworn in as a judge of the High Court, and he was appointed as acting judge of the Supreme Court in 1983. After serving as acting chief justice on five occasions from 1984 to 1990, he was appointed chief justice of the Supreme Court on 3 August 1990. Two years later he received an honorary fellowship at Jesus College at Cambridge. He is a member of the Permanent Court of Arbitration and the recipient of an honorary doctorate from the University of Essex. He is also president of the Oxford and Cambridge Society of Zimbabwe.

CHIEF JUSTICE GUBBAY: Before discussing the Zimbabwean legal system, I will provide some general background about the country, focusing, in the main, upon events since 1980.

Zimbabwe is situated in south central Africa. It is bordered on the south by South Africa, on the north by Zambia, on the east

---

Presented in a Forum at the Miller Center of Public Affairs on 3 April 1996.

by Mozambique, and on the west by Botswana. It is a landlocked country. Our population is between 11 and 11.5 million. At the present time, there are about 100,000 white Zimbabweans, which is less than 1 percent of the population. There is also a small Asian community, as well as a small sector of what we call colored persons—people of mixed races; each of these groups numbers about 3,000 to 4,000.

Zimbabwe's main source of export revenue is the mining sector, which accounts for about 45 percent of its total foreign exchange earnings. This includes gold, silver, platinum, diamond, emerald, chrome, and coal mining. Zimbabwe also depends heavily on tobacco exports and has a very good beef industry whose products are sold on the European Common Market. In other words, the country is dependent on its agricultural and extractive export industries.

Zimbabwe's main city is its capital, Harare, with a population of about a million people. Twenty-five miles away is a high-density area known as Chitungwiza, where many indigenous people live. About a million of them come into Harare every day to work. Harare is quite unlike most Third World capitals. It is an attractive city with high-rise buildings, excellent hotels and restaurants, good quality services, and some beautiful residences. Those of us who are privileged enough to afford this luxurious lifestyle have everything we need.

Since 1992 the economy has opened up considerably. Chronic shortages of foreign exchange are a thing of the past, and an abundance of imported goods are now available in the shops. There are no shortages at all. The cost of living is high for Zimbabwean people, however, and so is the inflation rate. Our currency is devaluing continuously against hard currencies. The present rate of exchange is almost 15 Zimbabwean dollars to one English pound and nine Zimbabwean dollars to one U.S. dollar. This creates a problem for Zimbabweans who travel abroad and those who need to import manufactured goods and equipment. The general pattern in Africa seems to be that once the local currencies begin to fall, they continue on a downward trend and never recover.

In the early years of independence, beginning on 18 April 1980, the policy of the government was socialist and hostile to foreign investment. Many Zimbabwean people did not want foreigners making money and then removing their profits from the country. Because foreign investment was discouraged, the country did not develop as it should have.

Over the last five years, however, government policies have changed. An economic structural adjustment program has brought in much more foreign investment. People of Zimbabwe now realize that if the country is to make progress, foreign companies must be afforded the opportunity to make investments and repatriate profits. Within the last two years, there has been enormous investment in platinum mining from an Australian company, which has provided employment for between 3,000 and 4,000 indigenous people. New roads, schools, and houses have been built. A continuation of this economic strategy is absolutely necessary for the country's prosperity.

Zimbabwe's unemployment rate runs at about 30 percent. The only effective way to deal with this problem, in my view, is to open the economy further and encourage foreigners to invest in the country. Unfortunately, there is now substantial competition from South Africa, Namibia, and Botswana. Competition with Namibia has intensified since that country obtained its independence in 1989. Namibia's policies were always more pragmatic than those of Zimbabwe. South Africa is now very attractive to foreign investors, and it is a country with a very sophisticated infrastructure. One can hardly think of South Africa as part of the Third World.

Zimbabwe's legal system began to emerge in 1894 when the first High Court was established in Matabeleland Province, the southern part of the country. The first judges and laws came from the Cape Colony, which is in present-day South Africa. The old Cape ordinances were the laws of what was then Southern Rhodesia. For years there were only one or two judges each in Salisbury (now Harare) and Bulawayo, which is Zimbabwe's second biggest city. Appeals from the High Court in either city went to the Appeal Court in the Cape. After Southern Rhodesia became a self-governing colony in 1923, appeals from the High Court of Southern Rhodesia were heard by the Appellate Division in Bloemfontein, South Africa—an odd situation. Southern Rhodesia did not obtain its own Appeal Court until 1964.

In 1953 a federation was established by Britain between Southern Rhodesia (present-day Zimbabwe), Nyasaland (present-day Malawi), and Northern Rhodesia (present-day Zambia). Thereafter, appeals from those three territories went to the newly established Federal Supreme Court situated in the capital of the Federation, which was Salisbury. The Court was comprised of the former chief justice of Southern Rhodesia, Sir Robert Treadgold, a South African judge, Sir John Clayden, and a British judge. It dealt with two systems of law because while Southern Rhodesia's legal system was based on Roman-Dutch principles, the two northern territories functioned under English Common Law. For this reason, one judge had been trained under the English system and the other two in the Roman-Dutch system. The major portion of litigation came from Southern Rhodesia because it was the wealthiest partner of the three countries.

The Federation was based theoretically on the concept of a partnership between the races. Unfortunately it did not work at all in practice. The two northern territories were very bitter about their experiences with the Federation and, justifiably, they viewed it as a failure. There is no doubt that Southern Rhodesia was the only territory to benefit from the federal process. Ultimately, Britain had to accept that it was a mistake. Within a year after the Federation disintegrated in 1963, Northern Rhodesia became independent as Zambia, and Nyasaland as Malawi. Although Southern Rhodesia was by far the most developed of the three countries and had been self-governing since 1923, Britain refused to grant it independence. This refusal occurred because there was a white minority government that denied the vast majority of its people political, social, and cultural rights.

In 1965, Southern Rhodesia declared unilateral independence from Britain. What followed was an absolute disaster—15 years of violent and destructive civil war. Economic sanctions were also imposed upon the country, and living conditions deteriorated. The civil war was fought not in the cities, but in the outward rural areas. Businesses were disrupted. There were continuous call-ups of whites to serve in the armed forces. Many black people were recruited and were fighting their own people. It was a terrible, disastrous situation.

Anthony R. Gubbay

Fortunately, in the middle of 1979 the party led by Bishop Abel Muzorewa, the United African National Council (UANC), began to bring the warring factions together. By the end of the year, it brokered a settlement between the Rhodesian government of Ian Smith and the two rebel leaders, Robert Mugabe of the Zimbabwe-African National Union (ZANU) and Joshua Nkomo of the Zimbabwe-African Patriotic Union (ZAPU). After the Lancaster House Agreement, a new constitution was drafted by Britain and imposed on Rhodesia, which was then renamed Zimbabwe. An election was then held, and Robert Mugabe's party won most of the seats. Joshua Nkomo's party won a number of seats as well. Bishop Muzorewa's party was totally beaten, winning only a few seats. Zimbabwe was declared an independent republic on 18 April 1980.

Amazingly, with independence came reconciliation. The Mugabe government recognized that not only was it necessary to achieve reconciliation between blacks and whites, but also among the principal black factions. It worked as far as the white population was concerned. Many whites had left the country during the civil war, and at its end there were probably fewer than 100,000 whites left. Opposition to Mugabe from Nkomo's ZAPU Party generated dissident activity in Matabeleland, which lasted for quite a few years. It was not until 1987 that Mugabe and Nkomo agreed to merge their parties under the name ZANU-PF (Patriotic Front), which has been in power since then.

At present, there are 150 members in Parliament, 120 of whom are elected. Parliamentarians serve a term of five years. Of the elected seats, 118 are held by the unified party of Joshua Nkomo and Robert Mugabe, and two are held by the opposition. The president has the right under the constitution to appoint 12 persons from any walk of life to parliament. They are recognized as apolitical because they have not won a seat. In recent times President Mugabe has brought in some expert white persons. The present ministers of agriculture and health are white, and whites have served as ministers of mines and of the public service. In addition, the governors of each of the eight provinces in the country occupy a seat. The final 10 seats are held by the chiefs of the different areas, bringing the total number in the house to 150. So although there are democratic elections and opposition parties in Zimbabwe, it is *de facto* a one-party state.

In March 1996, Zimbabwe held a presidential election and President Mugabe was reelected for another six-year term. The presidential election campaign commenced as a three-candidate race consisted by Robert Mugabe, Bishop Abel Muzorewa, and Reverend Ndabaningi Sithole. The odds were stacked heavily against the two challengers, however. Under the Electoral Act passed by the Mugabe government, a candidate's party must hold at least 15 seats in parliament to be eligible to receive government funding for an election campaigns. Only Robert Mugabe and his ZANU-PF Party qualified. Muzorewa and Sithole were at a severe disadvantage.

Less than three weeks before the election, the Reverend Sithole withdrew. On the day before the election was to be held, Bishop Muzorewa petitioned the Supreme Court for a postponement of the election on the grounds that he was greatly hampered by the lack of adequate funding. Because he had known the proposed date of the election for months, the Court considered his petition to be nothing more than a last-minute ploy to disrupt the process. For that reason the postponement was refused, and within half-an-hour Muzorewa withdrew from the race. The election therefore proceeded with only one candidate. But there was a very low turnout and a great deal of apathy—exactly what President Mugabe did not want. The last official function I performed on the day I left to come here was to swear in Robert Mugabe as president of Zimbabwe for another six years. That is the current political situation in Zimbabwe.

* * * * *

Zimbabwe's legal system is based on Roman-Dutch law, but there is also a parallel system of customary law that deals with traditional and tribal matters. Many indigenous people prefer to go to the customary law courts in disputes concerning the custody of children, inheritance rights, ownership of cattle and land, and so forth. The jurisdiction of the customary courts is limited, however. In the initial stage, these cases are presided over by a head man who lives in the rural area and knows the parties involved in the dispute. He will call the people in the immediate area together. Anyone who knows about the dispute is entitled to speak. It is like an inquisitorial procedure, yet it works quite well. The decisions of the customary law courts may be appealed to a district court headed by a magistrate and from that court to the Supreme Court of Zimbabwe. Consequently, the Supreme Court hears matters of customary law as well as general law.

Zimbabwe has about 160 magistrates comprised mostly of qualified lawyers. They have a somewhat limited jurisdiction in both criminal and civil matters. For example, a regional magistrate, who ranks just below a High Court judge, has penal jurisdiction of seven years' imprisonment for a single offense. If the accused person is convicted of three offenses, his sentence can be multiplied by three. Below the regional magistrates are provincial magistrates with less jurisdiction in criminal cases. Regional magistrates handle 90 percent of the criminal caseload in Zimbabwe. They deal with serious crimes such as rape, attempted murder, aggravated assault, and large thefts. The civil jurisdiction of the magistrates does not exceed $15,000.

Magistrates are civil servants who fall the Ministry of Justice. In contrast, members of the judiciary—judges of the High Court and the Supreme Court—are entirely independent and not part of the public service.

Currently, there are 18 judges of the High Court. Fifteen are based in Harare, and three are in Bulawayo. Zimbabwe's judges have unlimited jurisdiction: They deal with offenses that carry a potential death sentence and with large thefts, frauds, corruptions, and other very serious crimes as well as with civil disputes where the monetary value exceeds $15,000. Years ago the judges often had to try persons who unlawfully sold or acquired foreign exchange; now they deal with money laundering-type cases as well. The considerable amount of civil litigation creates a heavy workload for them.

It is extremely expensive to litigate in Zimbabwe, especially at the High Court level. Unlike the U.S. system, the loser is normally ordered to pay the costs of litigation. Whether the costs are recovered or not is a different matter. Consequently, people sometimes forego pursuing their claims. Even if they win, they may not be able to recover the costs from the other party, who may not have the means to pay. In criminal cases, the accused person has to pay his or her own legal defense costs, even if acquitted.

If a matter goes on appeal, the same situation arises. If the appeal fails, then the appellant will have to pay the costs of the appeal as well as the costs of the proceedings in the lower court. If the appeal succeeds, then the respondent will have to pay the costs of the appeal as well as the costs of the original proceedings. Anyone considering an appeal in Zimbabwe must contemplate the substantial costs that have to be paid in the High Court plus costs of the appeal itself. The costs associated with litigation are soaring.

Above the High Court is the Supreme Court, where I sit with four other judges. The court is racially mixed: two whites, one Asian, and two blacks. We hear appeals not only from the High Court, but also from the Administrative Court, the Labor-Relations Tribunal, the Special Income Tax Court, the Water Court, the Rent Appeal Board, and so on. We hear criminal appeals from the High Court if the presiding judge grants leave to do so. If not, then the appellant may apply to a judge of the Supreme Court for leave. Sometimes we overrule the refusal and grant the appellant leave. In civil matters there is an absolute right of appeal from the High Court. Thus, the Supreme Court deals with many appeals, even those with little chance of success. There is nothing we can do about that process. We also hear appeals from the Magistrate's Court in certain instances. The Supreme Court has a large variety of appeal work.

The Supreme Court also hears cases involving alleged contraventions of the constitution. Those occupy a large portion of our time. Anyone who considers that his or her fundamental rights have been infringed or threatened may immediately petition the Supreme Court for relief. The complainant need not go through the normal channels. That is a good system because it is designed to achieve finality expeditiously. Another provision stipulates that if a constitutional issue arises before an inferior court and if the parties to the dispute request a Supreme Court ruling, the judicial officer is enjoined to refer it directly to the Supreme Court unless he feels the matter is frivolous or vexatious.

Anthony R. Gubbay

Constitutional disputes are always difficult and sensitive, and a strict set of procedures is followed. When constitutional issues are at stake, all five judges of the Supreme Court sit to hear the arguments. If a constitutional issue involves one of the government ministries, then the appropriate minister is cited as a party and the attorney general must be notified. The attorney general is entitled to intervene in any constitutional dispute, whether civil or criminal. It is the policy of the Supreme Court not to hear a constitutional dispute that can be resolved on a basis other than invoking the constitution. If there is some other remedy available, if a question of fact may decide the matter without necessitating a constitutional decision, we refuse to hear it and the case is sent back to the lower court. The reason for this policy is that every constitutional judgment that goes against the government has the potential to spark a conflict between the judiciary and the executive. Thus, only as a last resort do we decide these issues by rendering a constitutional judgment.

Zimbabwe has a fairly active legal profession. From the foundation of Southern Rhodesia until 1981, there was a divided system of lawyers similar to that in England. "Barristers" were called "advocates," and "solicitors" were called "attorneys." I used to practice as an advocate. We were permitted to be briefed only by the attorneys and could not take work directly from members of the public. Judges were appointed from the members of the bar association—from advocates who had attained the rank of senior counsel, the equivalent of the Queen's Counsel in England. Following Rhodesia's unilateral declaration of independence in 1965, one had to apply to the minister of justice instead of the governor to be accorded that status. Normally, after three or four years of practice as a senior counsel, one would be offered a position on the High Court bench.

Until 1980, Rhodesia had an all-white judiciary. In the High Court today, six of the 18 judges are white, which is a high figure considering that the white population is small. We have had one black chief justice since independence—my predecessor, who was appointed to the High Court in 1980 and became chief justice in 1984. He held that office for six years until he attained the age of 70, when under the terms of the constitution, he had to retire. I was appointed to succeed him. It is unusual in Africa to have a white chief justice, but that is the situation. I am much indebted to President Mugabe for having appointed me.

QUESTION: The United States has 70 percent of the world's lawyers, due in part to the American insurance industry and insurance litigation. Could you discuss Zimbabwe's insurance industry and the degree of litigiousness of the society?

CHIEF JUSTICE GUBBAY: Zimbabwe does not have the same problem with insurance claims that America has, as most of the claims are settled satisfactorily. Unlike the United States, Zimbabwe does not have the system of contingency fees. I must confess that I do not approve of that system. Not much litigation involving insurance companies actually comes before the courts in Zimbabwe. Roughly 90 percent of malpractice suits and similar litigation cases are settled out of court.

QUESTION: What is your personal assessment of whether Zimbabwe's transition to black governance has worked? Many white people emigrated during the early 1980s, particularly young people. Are people now returning?

CHIEF JUSTICE GUBBAY: I think the transition has worked very well. The black people in Zimbabwe are exceptionally nice; they are good-natured. There is virtually no racial tension. I believe full credit must go to President Mugabe because he insisted on a policy of reconciliation. Racially, it is a very happy country.

Attracting whites back to Zimbabwe has been hindered by the current policy that makes it extremely difficult for any person, white or black, who has been out of the country for more than seven years to return as a settler. It matters not that he or she may have been born in Southern Rhodesia or Zimbabwe. The individual is no longer automatically entitled to return; he or she is put on the same basis as any person and may face grave problems in applying to immigrate. If a person has been out of the country for less than seven years, however, he or she is entitled to return as a settler. For example, a former Zimbabwean resident who has been living in

Britain or South Africa since 1989 may return to the country and import a motor vehicle and other assets duty free. Although this policy is not written into the constitution, it is the practice adopted by the immigration authorities and is unlikely to change.

Zimbabweans have experienced some difficulties in the way immigration authorities treat different groups. For example, if a male Zimbabwean citizen is married to a foreigner, she is automatically entitled to reside in Zimbabwe and may apply for citizenship, but if a female Zimbabwean citizen is married to an foreigner, he does not have the same rights. In fact, the immigration authorities have been deporting these alien men. They are being refused the right to reside and obtain employment.

The Supreme Court was faced with this issue because the constitution guarantees a Zimbabwean citizen "mobility" rights—the freedom to permanently reside in any part of the country. We held that prohibiting an alien male from living with his citizen wife was tantamount to denying the citizen wife her right to permanent residence. The practice, in effect, left her with a dilemma: whether to enjoy her right to remain living in the country to the detriment of her marriage, or to give up that right and go to live in the country of her alien husband. The Supreme Court's decision was very unpopular, and the government is in the process of amending the constitution to avoid the ruling.

One of the great drawbacks of Zimbabwe's Constitution is that there was only a limited ten-year period during which the Declaration of Rights could not be diminished or eroded in any way. With the end of that period, amendments to the constitution are permitted with a two-thirds parliamentary majority. Several amendments have effectively overruled previous rulings of the Supreme Court with respect to fundamental human rights.

QUESTION: You mentioned Zimbabwe's 30 percent unemployment. Since more private investment is coming into the country, has the level of education reached a point where the unemployed can take advantage of job opportunities?

CHIEF JUSTICE GUBBAY: The policy of the government since 1980 has been to make the cost of education as little as possible.

As a result, many people have become highly educated but now cannot obtain employment. In addition, there is only one major university in Zimbabwe, together with an engineering college in Bulawayo and a small Methodist college in the Eastern Highlands. The University of Harare is so full that it is extremely difficult to get a place, even for students who have very high grades. The solution to this unemployment problem is to attract more foreign investments, which unfortunately has been occurring far too slowly.

QUESTION: When you say 30 percent unemployment, are you including subsistence farmers in that figure?

CHIEF JUSTICE GUBBAY: I am talking about 30 percent of the total work force, which does not include subsistence farmers. Zimbabwe has always had a large number of people who live off the land, and that way of life will continue. Most urban people maintain their rural homes, and many families continue to live off the land while the breadwinner goes to the urban areas to earn an income. The level of wages is extremely low, and with the high cost of commodities and the depreciation of the currency, I do not know how Zimbabwean people are able to survive. It is a real problem.

QUESTION: What effect has the civil war in neighboring Mozambique had in the last 20 years other than closing off that route to the sea?

CHIEF JUSTICE GUBBAY: That route to the sea is no longer closed. For many years after independence in 1980, there were acts of sabotage to the oil pipeline from the Indian Ocean port of Beira to Mutari in the eastern part of Zimbabwe. With the continuation of the civil war in Mozambique, Zimbabwean forces had to guard the essential pipeline for many years at a cost of $1 million a day. Fortunately, the situation has improved, and now peace has been achieved in Mozambique. Some white South African farmers have settled in Mozambique and are developing farm operations there. This is a good sign. Peace in Mozambique has made a tremendous difference to Zimbabwe, just as democracy coming to South Africa has done. Unfortunately, the South African government has placed large duties on Zimbabwean goods to protect its domestic producers. Being shut out of the South African market has caused the bankruptcy of quite a few companies.

QUESTION: What is the mechanism for appointing judges?

CHIEF JUSTICE GUBBAY: I chair the Judicial Service Commission. The other members are the most senior judge of the High Court, the attorney general, the chairman of the Public Service Commission, and two leading practitioners from the private sector. After the minister of justice proposes a lawyer as suitable for appointment to the bench, commission members meet and consider whether or not to accept the nomination. If we do so, the president is notified and then makes the final decision on the appointment. Thus, judges are appointed by the president. If the commission rejects the nominee and the president wishes to appoint him or her anyway, he has to explain to parliament why he has not abided by the recommendation of the Judicial Service Commission. That situation has never happened as far as I know.

Prior to 1984, the Judicial Service Commission would select someone suitable to be appointed as a judge. That procedure was preferable because members of the Judicial Service Commission are in a better position than the minister of justice to know who is meritorious and who is not. Fellow legal practitioners know best whether a particular man or a woman is worthy of a judicial appointment. Regrettably, the power was taken away from the Judicial Service Commission. The result is that although we may find the nominated person suitable, he or she may not be as qualified as other candidates.

QUESTION: Is there a strong bar association?

CHIEF JUSTICE GUBBAY: There is a bar association, but it has no say in judicial appointments, save that two of its members sit on the Judicial Service Commission.

QUESTION: How long does the process take from nomination to confirmation?

CHIEF JUSTICE GUBBAY: It takes a week or two for the Judicial Service Commission to approve or disapprove a nomination. The process thereafter takes some time. It depends on the person's availability. Three judges were appointed recently, and I think the overall process took about three months.

QUESTION: You spoke of large numbers of people coming from the countryside to work in the city. How do such large numbers of people commute into and out of the city?

CHIEF JUSTICE GUBBAY: There is an extensive national bus service, but because it cannot cope with the number of commuters, there are also privately owned commuter vehicles that transport people back and forth. They are known as "emergency taxis." The construction of a rail system between Harare and this large area 25 miles away is under consideration. The cost factor, however, is delaying its implementation. People do manage to come into the city and work, but they spend long hours en route. There is such congestion that some people have to leave their homes in the very early morning and return at 8:00 or 9:00 p.m.

QUESTION: How do you think history will judge Ian Smith?

CHIEF JUSTICE GUBBAY: He was never a favorite of mine, I can tell you that. He continues to live in Harare and no one interferes with him. He is perfectly safe. As far as I know, he still has his farming interests. He is a bit quieter than he was a few years ago. He is regarded with bitterness by the black politicians, but he carries on. I do not believe that history will judge him at all favorably. After all, he involved the country in a long civil war to entrench a white oppressive regime and resist black advancement.

QUESTION: Does Zimbabwe have rail lines to the sea?

CHIEF JUSTICE GUBBAY: Yes, a rail line extends from Harare and Bulawayo to South Africa, with connections to the ports of Durban and Cape Town. There is also a rail link to Beira, the nearest port, and to Maputu. I believe there is now a rail link, via

South Africa, to Walvis Bay in Namibia. In the past, problems have occurred at Beira; goods were often found to be lodged in the warehouses there for an inordinate length of time. Since the Durban and Cape Town ports are the most efficient, most of Zimbabwe's imports and exports are shipped there.

QUESTION: Zimbabwe has some wonderful tourist attractions. Does tourism figure very prominently in Zimbabwe's foreign exchange earnings?

CHIEF JUSTICE GUBBAY: Yes! Yet I feel we could publicize our tourist attractions much more. We have some beautiful places— Victoria Falls, the Eastern Highlands, and the lovely islands on Lake Kariba. Zimbabwe has excellent hotels, a good road system, and good services. Now that South Africa has opened up, we are attracting more attention. People visiting South Africa often come to Zimbabwe as well. Our currency is low compared to hard currencies, so tourists from other countries find the hotels, restaurants, and everything else not only very inexpensive, but of outstanding value.

NARRATOR: Thank you, Chief Justice Gubbay, for sharing this most interesting account of Zimbabwe with us.

CHAPTER EIGHT

The Role of Christianity in the Transition to Majority Rule in South Africa*

PETER WALSHE

NARRATOR: Aubrey Peter Walshe is the director of the African studies program and a professor of government and international studies at the University of Notre Dame. He received his primary schooling in Johannesburg, South Africa, and his secondary education in Bulawayo, Rhodesia. He received his bachelor's and master's degrees in the Honours School of Philosophy, Politics, and Economics at Oxford, where he also pursued his doctorate. He has held a number of fellowships, including an Oppenheimer Fellowship at St. Antony's College, Oxford, and most recently a MacArthur Foundation Grant in International Peace and Security. Mr. Walshe has been a fellow of various institutes, such as the Helen Kellogg Institute for International Studies and the Joan Kroc Institute for International Peace Studies at the University of Notre Dame.

Professor Walshe is the author of numerous articles and several books. These publications include *The Rise of African Nationalism in South Africa* (1971); *Black Nationalism in South Africa: A Short History* (1975); *Church versus State in South Africa* (1983); and *South Africa: Prophetic Christianity and the Liberation Movement, 1912-1993* (1995).

---

*Presented in a Forum at the Miller Center of Public Affairs on 4 March 1994.

THE ROLE OF CHRISTIANITY IN TRANSITION TO MAJORITY RULE

MR. WALSHE: I have two themes to pursue. First, I will discuss the difficult political transition in South Africa. Second, I want to weave into that story the phenomenon of prophetic Christianity and liberation theology, or what in South Africa is thought of as contextual theology. The central theological argument, considering that the commonwealth or kingdom of God starts in history, is that people ought to be working on issues of justice. This they cannot do unless they undertake a fair amount of social analysis in order to understand the particular context within which their biblical values have to be applied. Such an indigenous contextual theology has emerged in South Africa. Although some differences exist, it is comparable to liberation theology in Latin America. This theology, which produced a politically activist ecumenical movement in South Africa, has played an important role in the country's current transformation.

The struggle against apartheid and segregation in South Africa has been a long one. The African National Congress (ANC) was formed in 1912. Thereafter, for almost half a century it relied on moral appeals—begging, pleading, signing petitions, and sending delegations to the white power structure. It did not achieve any progress. Rather, in 1948 the white electorate put the Afrikaner National Party into power to tighten the hold of segregation and to give an added twist—separate the economic and political development of whites and blacks. Separate development was the theory underlying apartheid; its practice was characterized by ruthless economic exploitation of the black majority and severe repression of political dissent.

Four years after the National Party came to power, passive resistance broke out in the Defiance Campaign of 1952—300 years after whites arrived in South Africa. Under the leadership of Albert Lutuli, who was the first African to receive the Nobel Peace Prize, blacks tried for almost a decade to resist the apartheid government. The result was the banning of the African National Congress after the Sharpeville massacre in 1960, when police opened fire on an unarmed crowd. In other words, the white state sought to crush the anti-apartheid movement.

That first upsurge of mass black protest was followed by a second major wave in the 1970s, the Black Consciousness Movement, led by a young medical student named Steve Biko. This time the pattern of brutal repression emerged when thousands of school children marched from Soweto into Johannesburg in 1976, protesting their segregated and inferior education. Hundreds of school children were killed over the next few months, as the state again sought to crush any mass opposition, banning the Black Consciousness Movement in 1977. In short, two major waves of nonviolent protest were dealt with by the white state with increasing ferocity.

By the late 1970s, after the crushing of the Black Consciousness Movement, the South African regime was concerned that there would be a recurrence of internal black resistance. It was alarmed also about political changes in its southern African hinterland. The cooperative security relationship between South Africans and the Portuguese had given way to problematic relationships with newly independent Mozambique and Angola. Rhodesia was on the brink of becoming Zimbabwe, and the South African military had to keep over 100,000 troops in Namibia to maintain its illegal occupation of that territory. Hence the government of South Africa was having to focus not only on internal dissent but also on potential conflict with the emerging frontline states.

In that context, particularly after the opprobrium following the shooting of the school children in Soweto, a move toward serious international sanctions against South Africa began. The divestment movement grew in the United States and Europe, accompanied by the prospect that Western governments might apply formal economic sanctions against South Africa, possibly taking their case as far as the United Nations Security Council.

With its internal, regional and international predicaments in mind, the South African regime decided to pursue a double strategy in the 1980s. It set out to reform apartheid and co-opt an element of the black community into the white power structure. In other words, it sought to share power on white terms. At the same time it repressed those who would not cooperate with the process of co-optation.

An example of this attempt to reform apartheid was the desegregation of public places—cinemas, restaurants, hotels, and government offices. In addition, African trade unions were legalized for the first time in South African history and were allowed to engage in collective bargaining. Township councils were also created in the ghettos of Soweto and elsewhere, so that organs of local government might be elected by Africans within their own segregated residential areas.

The capstone of this strategy was the 1983 constitution, which sought to divide Africans from the country's Colored (that is, racially mixed) and Indian populations. Africans had been given representation in their so-called homelands, as with the tribal parliament of the Transkei, and they could also elect organs of local government in their segregated townships. Now, however, the central structure of the South African government was changed. What had been the all-white parliament became a tricameral legislature, with the white's chamber dominating the new chambers created, one for Coloreds and another for Indians. A powerful executive presidency was elected by this tricameral legislature, within which white votes were dominant. Thus, the new constitution was an attempt to draw the minorities—Coloreds and Indians—into an alliance to strengthen the white power base. Simultaneously, the government hoped that by drawing Africans into an elective process in the townships and, as apartheid had always done, giving them the vote for their tribal homeland governments, the Bantustans, it would offer Africans a political alternative to taking to the streets.

Statutory refinements to the Internal Security Act constituted the other, overtly repressive side of the policy. This act destroyed the rule of law in South Africa and contained the provision that people could be detained indefinitely at the pleasure of the minister of justice. It also nurtured the emergence of a national security state that produced a state security council and regional joint management committees. These committees were composed of the police, the military, and the civil service and were empowered to take over from the civilian government in a state of emergency. The regime was clearly gearing itself up for further internal repression, which intensified in the course of the 1980s. Torture became endemic in South African prisons, as key antiapartheid leaders were systematically murdered by death squads. In 1986 a state of emergency was declared.

Peter Walshe

In the buffer zone around South Africa, the situation became comparably brutal. RENAMO (the Mozambique National Resistance Movement), an African equivalent of the Nicaraguan contras, was sustained by the South African state as a means of manipulating the Mozambican government. RENAMO had been started by Prime Minister Ian Smith during his struggle to maintain white authority in Rhodesia. When that struggle failed, RENAMO was taken over by the South Africans and used to destabilize Mozambique. UNITA (National Union for the Total Independence of Angola), Jonas Savimbi's outfit, was also taken over by the South Africans and supported in part by the CIA in order to pressure the Angolan regime. This scenario created devastating civil wars in the frontline states around South Africa. Almost two million people lost their lives as a result of a policy designed to keep the frontline states on the defensive so that they could not support any guerrilla movement against the apartheid state itself.

The internal co-optation strategy failed when, rather than stabilizing the country, the constitution of 1983 produced a massive backlash—a major resurgence of black resistance. This tidal wave of protest was the result of many forces. One was the gathering strength of the African National Congress, which had clung to existence in exile. It infiltrated South Africa with its armed wing, *Umkonto we Sizwe*, the Spear of the Nation. Although this guerrilla force had no prospect of toppling the South African regime, *Umkonto we Sizwe* was involved in what it termed "armed propaganda." By the middle 1980s it was attacking the South African military and police in 300 to 400 engagements per year. This symbolic presence in South Africa was very important for the younger black generation in the townships, who were encouraged not only by the collapse of the Portuguese regimes in Angola and Mozambique and the white regime in Rhodesia, but also by the fact that a guerrilla movement was operating against the hated apartheid state.

In addition to the ANC's activities, a United Democratic Front (UDF) was formed in 1983 to oppose the new constitution. The United Democratic Front was exactly what the title suggests, a front composed of hundreds of organizations, including cultural and political organizations, local civic bodies and trade unions, all fundamentally opposed to apartheid. It is worth noting that the UDF's patrons involved people like Desmond Tutu, who was to become the Anglican archbishop of Cape Town, and the Reverend Beyers Naudé, the preeminent dissident in the Dutch Reformed Church. Like a great Jewish prophet, Naudé stood up, shook his fist at his own people, and told them that although they were trying to save themselves through apartheid, they would actually destroy themselves through its injustices. The Reverend Allan Boesak was also a patron of the UDF and perhaps South Africa's leading black theologian.

The United Democratic Front (composed *inter alia* of hundreds of civil bloc organizations formed within the townships throughout South Africa) was able to bring together a swelling grass-roots movement that opposed the co-optative reforms, including the black township councils and the new constitution. Thus, as Africans, Coloreds, and Indians were being invited by the regime to join the process of co-optation, a ground swell of opposition arose to boycott the elections to the local councils and to the Colored and Indian chambers of the new South African legislature. The UDF was extremely successful in organizing these boycotts.

As the ANC infiltrated back into South Africa and the UDF consolidated opposition to the regime in the 1980s, black trade unions were also gathering strength. The South African government had tried to control the black trade union movement through legislation, the fine print of which barred the unions from politics. The unions defied that provision, and the state could do little about it. By 1985 a new federation, the Congress of South African Trade Unions, COSATU, had coalesced and enjoyed massive support, for example, from the National Union of Mine Workers. Black labor was beginning to flex its muscles.

As these renewed forces of opposition to apartheid gathered strength, the demographic time bomb was ticking away in the background. By the 1980s, about 300,000 additional African laborers were coming onto the market every year, pushing the rate of unemployment to approximately 50 percent in the cities. The regime therefore had to deal with persistent political ferment driven in part by economic desperation. With each passing year, the unemployment problem grew worse as the rate of urbanization in South African cities became the highest on the planet. The huge industrial complex around Johannesburg in the Vaal triangle will hold 18 million people by the year 2010. The cities of Cape Town and Durban, for example, are now doubling in size every decade and each will soon have populations of eight million. The economic and political context within which the repressive apartheid state was trying to maneuver was, to put it mildly, becoming problematic.

International sanctions then began to bite. When the regime tried to reschedule its foreign debts of over $23 billion in 1985, it found that the Western banks declined because of alarm over the country's instability and pressure by the divestment and anti-apartheid movement. Shortly thereafter, the U.S. Congress overrode President Reagan's veto in 1986 and passed a moderately tough South African Sanctions Act.

The regime therefore had a choice: It could make one last attempt at destroying this third major wave of protest, or it could negotiate. It opted for repression. In February 1988, it banned the United Democratic Front and COSATU as well as a number of other organizations. It was at this moment of crisis in the late 1980s, as the apartheid regime tried again to round up key political leaders, lock them away, and crush the liberation movement, that the role of prophetic Christianity became important. It is to that theme I now turn.

When the African National Congress was banned in 1960 after the Sharpeville massacre, the World Council of Churches held a conference in South Africa at one of the residence halls of the University of the Witwatersrand. The name of the residence was Cottesloe Hall, and so the gathering came to be known as the Cottesloe Conference. That conference drew together the member churches of the World Council in South Africa, which at that time included the white Dutch Reformed churches, supporters of the regime. At the end of the conference, a statement was signed that was critical of the practice of apartheid. It made clear that the majority attending the conference did not feel that apartheid could effectively bring justice from a Christian point of view and that the policy ought to be reconsidered. The white Dutch Reformed Church had a delegation at the Cottesloe Conference, and one of its most outspoken members was the Reverend Beyers Naudé, a young Afrikaner minister, who had experienced something approximating a Pauline conversion. He was not exactly knocked off his horse, but he had been exposed to the realities of the black townships and gradually came to the conclusion that apartheid was a grotesque injustice that had to be dismantled. He was one of the white Dutch Reformed Church ministers who signed the Cottesloe declaration criticizing the regime and its apartheid policies.

This declaration resulted in an uproar within the Afrikaner community. Prime Minister Verwoerd went on the radio condemning it. The white Dutch Reformed Church consolidated itself through various synods and likewise condemned its representatives for having criticized apartheid. It also put great pressure on those who had signed to withdraw their signatures. Most did, but not the Reverend Beyers Naudé. Consequently, he was ostracized by his own people, defrocked, and expelled from his Church. He then formed the ecumenical Christian Institute of Southern Africa in 1963, dedicated to dismantling apartheid.

The Naudé story is interesting because one could not have been closer to the core of the white power structure than Beyers. Incidentally, he had been named after a die-hard Afrikaner general who had rebelled during World War I against the new settlement in South Africa. Certainly, he came from a hard-core Afrikaner nationalist family. He was in the inner circles of *Broederbond*, the secret society that coordinated the Afrikaner power structure in the military, police, civil service, church, and the South African cabinet. He was next in line to become moderator of the Dutch Reformed Church. This ostracism was therefore a traumatic experience, not only for Beyers and his wife Ilsa, but for the entire Afrikaner community, which was shocked to find such a personality at the very heart of its power structure. Naudé, as I have suggested, was perhaps the equivalent of a Jewish prophet who stood up in the royal court, confronted the king, and declared that his own people were breaking their covenant with the Creator and hence were in great danger.

Something very interesting then happened. Naudé's Christian Institute, which was developing its own brand of liberation theology, began to interact with the Black Consciousness Movement during the late 1960s and 1970s, and within this movement a school of black theology emerged. This school was influenced in part by black theology in the United States, as well as by political theology emerging in Europe and by liberation theology in Latin America. Black theology was not a racist theology, but a theology of the poor in South Africa, who happened to be black. This theology and the whole Black Consciousness Movement influenced the Christian Institute. Close cooperation developed, for example, between Beyers Naudé and Steve Biko.

Out of this interaction, the beginnings of an indigenous liberation theology and the conscious articulation of a prophetic Christian voice emerged in South Africa. When the Black Consciousness Movement was crushed by the state in 1977, the Christian Institute was also banned and Beyers Naudé placed under house arrest for seven years. This action by the state represented a deliberate attack on prophetic Christianity by the state. Nevertheless, the South African regime could not stop the prophetic movement, which continued to spread during the course of the 1980s, particularly within ecumenical organizations. The mainline churches remained problematic. The white Dutch Reformed Church continued to support the state. The English-speaking churches—the Roman Catholic Church, Methodists, Presbyterians, Congregationalists, and so forth—remained what I call "phlegmatic" churches: They condemned apartheid but did very little to confront the state.

The Roman Catholic Church, for example, had condemned apartheid with elegant statements as far back as the 1950s. It was not until the 1970s, however, that the Roman Catholic seminaries in South Africa were desegregated and the private Catholic schools began token integration. Nor was there any massive transformation within the mainline churches; Christian hierarchies remained white-dominated. Only a minority of prophetic voices emerged within the denominations, often led by black Christians and usually ecumenical in political activism.

That prophetic voice was expressed most clearly in the South African Council of Churches, which came under the leadership of some courageous personalities. A new and vigorous leadership that was concerned with biblical values in the reconstruction of society rose to the top of this key ecumenical organization. The Reverend Desmond Tutu was one such leader. He was followed by Beyers Naudé, who became general secretary of the Council after his release from house arrest in 1984. When Naudé's term expired, he was replaced by a remarkable young man, the Reverend Frank Chikane.

Within the Catholic Bishops' Conference, several voices were also urging political resistance. Not all of the bishops were capable of social analysis or inclined toward prophetic Christianity, but a few of them were, such as Dennis Hurley, the archbishop in Durban, Natal. Other groups within what was becoming a rather loose coalition of ecumenical antiapartheid organizations were also increasingly bold in their social analysis. The Institute for Contextual Theology was led by a remarkable South Africa Dominican, Father Albert Nolan, who established a close partnership with the Reverend Frank Chikane. Various pastoral institutes, such as Diakonia in Natal, were becoming activist, prepared, for example, to support black striking trade unions. Thus, a prophetic voice that had begun in the Christian Institute and interacted with black theology and the Black Consciousness Movement became a more diverse phenomenon during the 1980s.

In 1988 the regime again cracked down on protests. It banned the United Democratic Front, tried to crush the trade union movement COSATU, declared a state of emergency, and decreed a press blackout. As the security forces made a final effort to crush the protest movement, a vacuum was created in the secular political leadership of the liberation movement in South Africa. At this point, prophetic Christian leaders stepped into that vacuum. Desmond Tutu, Frank Chikane, Beyers Naudé, Allan Boesak, and other leading figures went into the streets and led mass protests that swelled through South African cities. Up to 70,000 people marched through Cape Town and Durban, 100,000 through Johannesburg. The people in the front line leading those protests, defying the banning orders, encouraging South Africans to simply ignore the repression of the state and take to the streets in a nonviolent, disciplined way were the prophetic Christian leaders. This meshing of prophetic Christianity and the liberation movement was successful in part because the language of justice within the

African National Congress and the black protest movement had drawn heavily on biblical values, symbols, and terminology over the years.

It is not that prophetic Christianity was in the vanguard of the liberation movement in South Africa. Events were more complex. Rather, I am arguing that the grave injustices of apartheid sparked the rise of a liberation movement. That historical phenomenon became a challenge to the churches, and belatedly, prophetic groups within the churches. They had started to learn from the grotesque injustices of apartheid and the emergence of what one might loosely call the secular liberation movement. Learning from that historical context, they began to organize, usually in an ecumenical way that could assist the liberation movement. That assistance was crucial for the short period from 1988 to 1990 when the apartheid state was making its last desperate effort to crush the opposition. At this point, the liberation movement literally unbanned itself under the leadership of prophetic Christians.

So it was that the final thrust against apartheid was one within which ecumenical, activist Christians played a major role. This was in stark contrast to the Defiance Campaign of the 1950s when the churches stood on the sidelines, completely irrelevant to the struggle. By the late 1980s, however, a unified liberation movement, supported by prophetic Christianity and in conjunction with international sanctions, forced the regime to reexamine its strategy and move to the negotiating table.

Once negotiations began and Nelson Mandela was released from prison in February 1990, the apartheid government realized that it could not stop South Africa from slipping into civil war and chaos if it continued to reject negotiations with the real black leaders in preference to those who had been co-opted under apartheid. Consequently, a fraught situation arose where both black and white politics became acutely problematic for new reasons. White politics produced what threatened to become an increasingly powerful right wing, one determined to maintain racist structures. The Conservative Party and extreme fascist groups like the Afrikaner Resistance Movement tapped into a strain of Afrikaner ideology that went back to Nazism and support for Germany in World War II. This movement, which at times enjoyed almost half of the white South African vote, was in favor of a white separatist state—in other words, the partition of South Africa—and vehemently opposed negotiation with the African National Congress. F. W. de Klerk, leader of the National Party, therefore had great difficulty containing this surge of extremism.

Nelson Mandela and the African National Congress also faced a major challenge. They were backed by a huge, inchoate ground swell of support but did not have the organizational base to control it. Moreover, they also faced a spoiler: Mangosuthu Buthelezi and the Inkatha Freedom Party. In the 1970s, Buthelezi had become prime minister of KwaZulu, one of the so-called homelands or Bantustans, and he played a subtle game. He argued against apartheid while using the platform of apartheid to articulate his opposition. There was, he suggested, no alternative to using the political structures of apartheid to criticize the apartheid system. He was a complex figure: deeply resented by the Black Consciousness Movement and the liberation movement, but not simply a stooge of the white establishment. In the course of the 1980s, however, as the United Democratic Front and COSATU gained strength and the African National Congress reasserted itself inside South Africa, he lost ground in his core area of ethnic Zulu support, Natal. As his support weakened, he tried to claw it back with the use of violence. At this point, Inkatha was more firmly co-opted by the white South African state. Certainly, Buthelezi's relationship with the state had long been problematic; for example, he had refused to accept independence for KwaZulu. Now, however, Inkatha hit squads were trained by the same South African security unit that was training the RENAMO resistance movement in Mozambique. In addition, the South African cabinet not only supported the budget of the KwaZulu state, it secretly placed funds in Inkatha's pocket as well. In short, Inkatha came to be used by the white state as a spoiler to weaken the liberation movement.

The transition itself in South Africa was, therefore, problematic. Initially, the white right wing consolidated itself. Simultaneously, the ANC struggled to strengthen its organizational base while Inkatha relied increasingly on disruptive violence, assisted by elements within the white regime, the military, and the police through access to funds and arms. In that context, the negotiations were painful and protracted. I have no doubt that the South African regime deliberately prolonged them, hoping that the ANC would disintegrate in the process. This disintegration did not occur, and in the end serious compromises were entered into by both sides.

For the first time in South African history, an interim constitution will soon be promulgated, including a bill of rights. A Transitional Executive Council will oversee South Africa through the elections at the end of next month (April 1994). The constitution will be interpreted solely by a Supreme Court. Heretofore, Parliament has been supreme, and the South African courts subservient. A popular chamber with 400 members and a senate of 90 members will be elected. South Africa will be divided into nine provinces rather than the old four. Once the government of national unity is in place, it will hopefully remain until 1999. Over the next two years, both houses sitting together as the constituent assembly will be refining the interim constitution. Everyone expects Nelson Mandela to be elected president by the lower house, in which proportional representation prevails. The cabinet will be composed not only of the majority party, the ANC, but also those parties with more than 5 percent of the vote—including de Klerk's National Party.

Prophetic Christianity in this new context, this dramatic transition, has been trying to do two things. First, it has sought to nurture the process of negotiation. This process has often been in danger of breaking down, and church leaders have played a major role in keeping the discussions going. Second, prophetic Christianity is trying to think through the longer-term problems facing South Africa, not the least of which is to devise economic policies that will redistribute income in favor of the lower half of society—those devastated by decades of apartheid. It is clear to prophetic Christian leaders and many other people in South Africa that having a constitution in place will not in itself sustain the political transition. If the country fails to reverse the grotesque economic polarization that has occurred, escalating criminal violence and a revolt by the poorer half of society can be expected. The new constitutional settlement could be torn asunder in an increasingly polarized society, one triggering ethnic conflict. If step one was to accept the new constitution, step two must be to establish moral economic policies. This second step will be the really difficult one, particularly given the triumphalist and self-serving capitalist international system.

Can prophetic Christianity recover its strength and gird itself for this new struggle? Having confronted the apartheid state and supported the liberation movement, can it now help South Africa develop a political culture concerned about the poor? Can it help to bring the poor into the political process and so create a sense of the common good, of common interests, that, in turn, can produce a stable political system? As the world enters the 21st century, there is, I believe, little chance of maintaining stable political systems unless people begin to share resources more equitably. That necessity is seen most clearly in South Africa. If the prophetic movement can impart its energy to other social forces in South Africa—for example, the women's movement and the trade union movement—the cutting edge of a new radical critique could be produced, one that might generate economic policies designed to assist the poor and thereby to ensure the future of democracy in South Africa. This is a tall order, for the task is none other than to challenge the globally entrenched ideology of a value-free market system.

QUESTION: Throughout history very few radical changes in the political structure and social structure have occurred without an almost complete change of leadership. Does an alternative nonwhite leadership structure now exist in South Africa?

MR. WALSHE: A considerable quantity of the black leadership of the African National Congress and other protest groups will likely be absorbed into the new regime. The Mandelas, Mbekis, and others will move into positions of power. Nevertheless, the old white state is essentially still intact. The white civil service has been guaranteed its position in the transition. The military and the police will remain in control of a predominantly white officer corps for the foreseeable future. Attempts at integrating black South Africans into that officer corps will be made, but in the military, police, and civil service, it is a rather small group of able and well-educated blacks that will be absorbed. Insofar as their energies are taken up by matters of state, a leadership vacuum will be left at the grass roots of South African politics.

If one looks, for example, at the independence of Ghana in 1957, Kwame Nkrumah and an able group of young Ghanaians moved into the shoes of the departing British colonialists and took over the Ghanaian state. The Convention Peoples Party, which had been the vehicle that brought them to power, was drained of leadership at that point. Using this example, I am arguing that transition in the leadership of South African society will occur at the top. Beneath that level, the white state, for at least the next decade, will remain largely intact. The black educational system has been so appalling that it will be difficult to train sufficient numbers of blacks qualified enough to move into the middle echelons of society with efficiency and ease. Moreover, it will be twice as difficult to renew the sort of political leadership that Mandela and others have provided because most of the black talent will be functioning in the state sector. What South Africa needs is a new generation of young activists who will organize at the grass-roots level and draw people into the political process. This is why it is crucial that the political parties in the South African system draw the poor and the unemployed into politics. This is a challenge that will not be easily met: Hence, my argument that progressive forces, with the capability of creating a political culture that constantly raises issues of justice, are South Africa's best hope. The African National Congress needs to keep its idealism alive.

My South African nightmare scenario goes something like this: A new constitution is promulgated. Black leadership is absorbed into state structures, co-opted, and works with the established white power structure. The townships rot, levels of unemployment increase, and the level of violence, which is already considerable, escalates even further. This scenario is worrying because apartheid and the migratory labor system have undermined the structures of African family life. In addition to political tension in South Africa, African family structures have been seriously weakened in an increasingly urbanized, unjust society. Nonpolitical crime rates have escalated. That is a very nasty mix—a new black elite establishing itself in privilege and neglecting the poor. It is a recipe for chaos.

I do not think the outcome needs to be as bleak as this nightmare. The South African economy is sophisticated. Its capacity is greatly underutilized. If a new economic policy, for example, can put a major emphasis on the construction industry and the building of low-cost housing, it will be possible to assist the poor rather than neglect them. A labor-intensive construction industry can be regenerated with semi-skilled and unskilled labor and thereby overcome the enormous housing backlog that has developed because the apartheid state was not interested in building family housing for Africans in the cities. South Africa also has successful heavy industries, an extraordinary infrastructure, and plenty of indigenous raw materials. Finally, it has some fine universities and the potential to create a decent education system. All of these attributes can help produce an expanded black middle class, thereby strengthening the political processes that when linked with the redistribution of economic resources create stability.

That vision sounds utopian in the current world when one looks around the planet and sees stark class polarization. In South Africa, class and race combine to reinforce the polarization process. Comparable class polarization, of course, is present elsewhere: One sees it in Britain after Thatcher and in the United States after Reagan, although not as dramatically as in South Africa. In a sense, South Africa is an invitation to think through economic policies at a global level. Should people just let the market system reign? Or do citizens have to put market forces within some parameters of constraint that will deliberately shift resources to education, low-cost housing, clean water, and preventive medicine for the poor? If people, their parties, and leaders do not work for such goals, I do not believe democratic processes will survive.

QUESTION: The Afrikaner neo-Nazis want a separate state with 50 percent of the arable land. Do you think they will persist with that demand? How would that change affect the new constitution?

MR. WALSHE: Some elements within the white right wing would like a compromise. They will certainly accept much less than 50 percent of the best arable land. The problem is that South Africa is now so integrated a society as a result of its industrial revolution that there is no viable patch of land with an Afrikaner majority. Afrikaners are dispersed throughout South Africa. If one looks at the plan for an Afrikaner *volkstaat* (people's state), it looks somewhat like a spider: Eight tentacles spread out from Pretoria. They are actually thin strands of land gerrymandered to give Afrikaners a slim majority within such an artificial separate state. That is the level of compromise that would have to be achieved. The focus of negotiations with the white right wing has shifted in recent months, however. The question is now, How much decentralized power will the provincial state structures have? Will South Africa mutate into a federation?

QUESTION: Wouldn't the whites get one of the nine provinces?

MR. WALSHE: No. Of the total white population of just over five million, about two-thirds are Afrikaners. Of the Afrikaner community, it is estimated that no more than 10 percent are prepared to follow the civil war route to partition, and this number is decreasing in the aftermath of Mandela's irenic leadership.

QUESTION: I had not previously realized the extent to which Christian values have represented the common basis of philosophy of the two sides. What is the distinction between prophetic Christianity and Christian fundamentalism? Is Islam also a strong presence in South Africa? If so, is it of a fundamentalist nature that could cause problems for the Christians?

MR. WALSHE: The phenomenon of prophetic Christianity in South Africa is essentially ecumenical, in the interdenominational sense, which means that it is not fundamentalist. By being ecumenical in the interdenominational sense it avoids fundamentalism. It holds to a willingness to listen and explore whether common ground can be found on social and political issues in the effort to renew society. I do not think it was merely by chance that this ecumenical form of Christianity was able to relate to the liberation movement, because the liberation movement was itself a broad church—a tolerant movement with several ideological currents. That political culture was and is concerned with nurturing a nonracial society. It is also precisely this sort of ecumenical mindset that ought to set as its goal a broader cooperation between the great religions of the world. Unless people develop that capacity to work respectfully with differing religions, the 21st century may unfold as one of religious wars. The wholesome elements in South Africa's new political culture, its aversion to ethnic chauvinism and its tolerance of diversity, offer hope in this regard.

A small Islamic community is located at the southern tip of the continent. The advent of Islam in that area was not typical in Africa. Islam crept southward through the trading networks of east Africa between the 8th and 13th centuries. The new faith also came down the east coast of Africa, with Islamized Arabs trading as far south as the mouth of the Zambezi River.

The small Islamic presence within the Colored community of South Africa, centered around Cape Town, began with Malay slaves brought in by the Dutch East India Company. That Islamic group has since produced some ecumenically minded political leaders, the opposite of the late Ayatollah Khomeini of Iran. Muslims in Cape Town have been an integral part of the liberation movement and have worked closely with prophetic Christian leaders.

QUESTION: You have not mentioned much about Buthelezi and KwaZulu, which has a strong culture. I understand that he is a strong personality, while the Zulus are not as great an influence in terms of population as they are culturally. Is it possible to integrate these differing cultures into a common country?

MR. WALSHE: The Zulu, with approximately six million people, are the largest ethnic group in South Africa. The tensions that have generated the most violence in South Africa are intra-Zulu tensions—Zulu against Zulu. Polls in South Africa suggest that Buthelezi has the firm support of only about 20 to 25 percent of the Zulu population at present. Most of the Zulu support the liberation movement, such as COSATU (the trade union movement), the ANC, and the United Democratic Front. In other words, the Zulu population has been pulled into those broad currents of black political protest that built up over the decades since the founding of the ANC in 1912.

Peter Walshe

The first president of the African National Congress, John Dube, was a Zulu. Albert Lutuli, leader of the Defiance Campaign in the 1950s, was a Zulu. The Zulu community is complex, but the major current of Zulu politics has been committed to this building of a nonracial South Africa.

When contemplating whether South Africa's cultures can coexist in a single country, consider the factors that produced a black political culture concerned with nonracialism. Why didn't black opposition become black racism? The answer is complex. First, one has to look at traditional African society, which was deeply concerned with community and political participation. There are many examples of African traditional groups working across ethnic lines. Africa was not a chaotic place of barbaric, inter-ethnic conflict. In reality, a good deal of ethnic cooperation occurred. Then new factors intervened. The mission schools produced a black elite from the 1840s onward, particularly in the Cape province. African leaders coming from these schools believed that Christianity had something to say about social values and that the challenge of Christianity was to build a broader human community extending beyond clan, tribe, and racial barriers.

Then, in addition to the above, in the 1880s, 12,000 Africans were already on the common voters' roll in the Cape province and were sharing in the Cape's parliamentary system. They believed and experienced that a nonracial system was possible. Add to this the self-interest that black South African leaders have in overcoming the economic color bar to advance in the new economic order. In earlier decades there also existed a small, white, liberal element in South Africa willing to extend the hand of friendship to blacks. Finally, the South African Communist Party (never very large, but having some influence in terms of ideas) argued that the future should not be a racist one; rather, people had to think in terms of class. Under the influence of all of these factors, a black political culture emerged that is dialectically opposed to white racism and counters that racism by taking the moral high ground of nonracialism. South African history has produced an interesting and perhaps unique political culture.

In conclusion, a word of caution. This political culture could be seriously eroded. That tremendous heritage of tolerance the black opposition has bequeathed to South Africa may prove to be the priceless basis for a newly integrated, stable, and increasingly just South African society; but that heritage could be lost by increasing class polarization, the triggering of ethnic tensions, and violence. The country is precariously poised at the moment, but the situation is not without hope.

NARRATOR: It is good to hear a prophetic voice in these difficult times. We are grateful to Professor Walshe for sharing his vast knowledge of South Africa and his hope for its future.

CHAPTER NINE

The Impact of Christianity on the Struggle Against Apartheid*

LYN GRAYBILL

NARRATOR: Lyn Graybill is the principal editor of this volume. She earned a doctorate in foreign affairs at the University of Virginia, writing her dissertation on "Christian Ideology and Black Resistance to Apartheid in South Africa: A Comparison of Albert Lutuli, Robert Sobukwe, Steve Biko and Desmond Tutu." She received a number of awards while completing her doctorate, including a fellowship from the Institute for the Study of World Politics. She has also written a book entitled *Religion and Resistance Politics in South Africa* (1995) and several articles, including "Reinhold Niebuhr's Normative Approach to International Relations and its Application to Foreign Aid."

Ms. Graybill currently teaches in the Department of Government and Foreign Affairs at the University of Virginia. She has also taught at Virginia Commonwealth University and the University of Richmond. As a doctoral student, she worked as a research assistant at the Miller Center. Her discussion of "The Impact of Christianity on the Struggle Against Apartheid" is one of the most illuminating and clear-eyed papers on the subject. It reflects her contribution to the field and her unique combination of religion and politics. It promises to stimulate discussion for years to come.

* * * * *

---

*Presented in a Forum at the Miller Center of Public Affairs on 20 May 1996.

The Religious Roots of Rebellion

Christianity without doubt has been the single most important ideological influence on South African resistance politics in the 20th century. Pivotal to the formulation of Afrikaner nationalism that rationalized apartheid, Christian theology has also been instrumental in the articulation of African nationalism that arose to counter the myth of racial inferiority. It has been both a touchstone for political ideas and the vehicle for the dissemination of those ideas in South Africa.

Over the last century, African politics has tended to gravitate toward two poles, or two opposing views of African nationalism. There was the inclusive multiracial approach (associated with the early ANC—African National Congress—sometimes called the Charterist position) and the exclusivist blacks-only approach (adopted by the PAC—the Pan-Africanist Congress—and Black Consciousness Movement) referred to as the Africanist position. The former approach initially rejected violent means, and the latter tended to advocate violence in pursuance of its aims.

It was the task of the individual leader to make his position appealing in the competition of recruits, and Christianity—which claimed the loyalty of most Africans—was employed in the service of legitimating various strategies and objectives to the African masses. Leaders of opposing political organizations sought religious justification for their differing visions and strategies.

Religion was employed by both the Charterists and the Africanists to recruit members, to provide a vision of a future South Africa, and to justify methods and means of defiance. Christianity was not static but was interpreted and reinterpreted to meet new situations of oppression in South Africa. Rather than a force that pushes in the direction of apolitical escapism, Christianity, these political leaders believed, requires resolute action in the world. Albert Lutuli of the ANC, Robert Sobukwe of the PAC, Steve Biko of the Black Consciousness Movement, and Desmond Tutu of the United Democratic Front were each persuaded that religious faith had implications for politics, even if they saw those implications somewhat differently.

Lutuli, the secretary-general of the ANC in the 1950s, was a significant leader in the Defiance Campaign of 1952, which was undertaken to protest the "whites only" prohibitions at public places. A committed Christian, Lutuli advocated a moderate position based on the belief that white Christians in South Africa could be petitioned on the basis of a shared Christian morality to treat Africans fairly. Multiracialism—working alongside sympathetic whites for a new dispensation—was advanced on the grounds that God's universal fatherhood made all South Africans "brothers." Certain tactics were prohibited: One could not justify illegal methods against a God-ordained state nor employ violent means against a neighbor one was enjoined to love. Multiracialism and nonviolence were hallmarks of Lutuli and the early ANC—tactics that sprang from the leaders' Christian beliefs.

The next watershed episode in African resistance politics was the Sharpeville campaign against the hated pass laws in 1960, later to be known the world over as the Sharpeville massacre when police fired on and killed 69 unarmed protesters led by Robert Sobukwe, the president of the newly founded PAC. Sobukwe borrowed from the Christian tradition that focused on the sinfulness of man (especially the white man), which imbued him with a realism about man's unwillingness to give up power and privilege without force. He drew attention to theological interpretations that condoned violence against unjust rule, focusing on the structural sinfulness of apartheid. He stressed the need for rejecting multiracial alliances—cooperating with whites, who after all benefited from the system and who could not sincerely want to see it dismantled—and the need for promoting an exclusively African movement. Unlike Lutuli, who turned to the multiracial English-speaking churches for allies, Sobukwe sought converts for his cause within the African independent churches, which had broken off from the multiracial churches in the previous century in protest against worshipping in "European" ways and the lack of leadership opportunities. There was a clear affinity between the "go it alone" spirit of the PAC and the antiwhite mood of the independent churches. It is interesting that Sobukwe did not reject the church in toto. There was a recognition among the Africanists, who saw the struggle as a battle between good and evil, that politics had to be based on a Christian foundation.

Steve Biko, the leader of the Black Consciousness Movement of the 1970s, built upon and refined the thinking of Sobukwe and the PAC. With Biko, and especially some of his followers in the Black Consciousness Movement, the acceptance of violence to counter the violence of the state was more openly espoused. Black theology, which emphasized the belief that God was on the side of oppressed blacks, was borrowed from the United States and adapted to the South African situation and helped dissolve any moral qualms surrounding the use of violence. Biko urged black ministers to develop a black theology that was relevant to the situation in South Africa. The church all too often in his view concentrated on moral trivialities—robbing, adultery, and drinking—without attempting to relate these to the poverty, unemployment, lack of schooling, and migratory labor brought about through apartheid. The real sin for Biko was "to allow oneself to be oppressed." The youth of Soweto who rose up against the state in 1976 to oppose the use of Afrikaans, the language of the oppressor, in the schools were the embodiment of the assertive, proud, self-confident, and fearless African that Biko and his movement had hoped to produce.

A recent figure in the African opposition has been Desmond Tutu, the Anglican archbishop of Cape Town, who came to prominence in the 1980s after the organizations affiliated with the Black Consciousness Movement had been banned. (The ANC and PAC had been banned since 1960.) Tutu was one of the founders of the United Democratic Front (UDF), which was organized in 1983 to oppose the new tricameral parliament that would give rights to Coloreds and Indians, but not Africans, in their separate chambers.

Tutu issued a statement from the South African Council of Churches, which he headed, noting that since the new parliament would exclude 73 percent of the population from sharing political power, fundamental change would be blocked. He urged member churches to reject the new constitution and to urge their parishioners to boycott the upcoming elections to the two new chambers. Despite Tutu's plea, white voters approved the new constitution by referendum in a landslide victory with 66 percent in favor.

From the launching of the UDF until the first elections under the new constitution in 1984, campaigns were instigated throughout the country to discredit the upcoming elections. The UDF's boycott of the elections was wildly successful: Only 17.5 percent of eligible Coloreds and 15.5 percent of Indians participated.

The United Democratic Front did not cease to exist after the Colored and Indian elections. Rather, the campaigns opened a new chapter of resistance, and the UDF initiated the longest sustained period of agitation in the history of black resistance since the 1950s. Protests raged through the country as the UDF employed a variety of strategies: work stay-aways, rent, consumer, and bus boycotts; anti-sports campaigns; and campaigns for the unbanning of the ANC—activity that ultimately led to the unbanning of the illegal political parties and the release of Nelson Mandela from prison.

Theologically and politically, Tutu draws from the multiracial nonviolent approach of Lutuli and the early ANC. Likek Lutuli before him, he has been determined to work alongside all concerned individuals—black and white—for a nonracial democratic society. The United Democratic Front permitted affiliation of white organizations in the belief that "all the oppressed sections of the community had an over-riding interesting in the destruction of apartheid." The UDF believed that the strategy of "closing ranks" had achieved the purpose of consciousness-raising envisaged by the Africanists and that now was the time for all enemies of apartheid—black and white—to join forces.

Like the early Charterists, Tutu has argued against violence: "Because our cause is just," he wrote, "we cannot afford to use methods of which we will be ashamed when we look back." Yet even with the basically moderate Tutu, we witness an evolution over time in his thought. He had argued over the years for continued sanctions as the best possible chance to invoke change without violence. But given the intransigence of the white minority-controlled government, he came to believe that violence may be the lesser of two evils, the greater evil being unyielding oppression. He has said: "How could I commend nonviolence to blacks who know that resistance movements in Europe during World War II were praised to the skies, and who hear similar movements condemned because they are black?" He increasingly sympathized with those who called for a violent response against a violent regime. "There may be a time when we have to take up arms and defend ourselves," he explained.

While some black theology proponents associated with Biko believed blacks were morally superior to whites, Tutu was quick to denounce this notion. He wrote that God is on the side of the oppressed not because they are better or more deserving than their oppressors, but simply because they were oppressed. "We say that God is on our side," wrote Tutu, "not as some jingoistic nationalist deity who says 'my people right or wrong' but as one who saves and yet ultimately judges those whom he saves."

One gets the impression that Biko and the black theologians supporting his movement felt that suffering had made blacks more moral than whites, and hence the political order following black majority rule would be a Golden Age of justice and compassion. Tutu warned against this notion:

> We have too much evidence that the removal of one oppressor means the replacement by another; yesterday's victim quite rapidly becomes today's dictator. [We] know only too well the recalcitrance of human nature and so accept the traditional doctrines of the fall and original sin.

Tutu has refused to preach a liberation that excludes whites and fails to criticize blacks.

By the time of the release of Nelson Mandela from Robben Island, the two strands of thought had coalesced in the Mass Democratic Movement: multiracialism—working hand in hand with all persons interested in dismantling apartheid—combined with a determination to use whatever means, including violence, to win freedom. (Mandela would not renounce the "armed struggle" as a condition for his release from prison on Robben Island.)

There is no doubt that Christianity shaped the long struggle against apartheid; Christian ideals served as an ethical critique of apartheid, as a source of righteous anger that inspired action, and as a wellspring of confidence in eventual victory. Christian values of resistance leaders inspired and shaped black political protest over the 20th century and in no small measure were instrumental in ushering in a new democratic era.

The Continuing Relevance of Religion

What role remains for religion to play in a postapartheid society? Forgiveness of enemies is one of the fruits of religion vital to any possible reconciliation of the races in South Africa. The world has witnessed some remarkable events in recent months that point to the reality of forgiveness on the part of black South Africans. Mandela, for instance, chose to include and embrace his former jailers at inaugural events in a spirit of forgiveness that bodes well for national reconciliation. Observers have been impressed with Mandela's complete lack of bitterness against his former oppressors despite being imprisoned for 27 years, more than a third of his adult life. In a postelection celebration on 2 May 1994 in Johannesburg, Mandela set the tone for the incoming government: "Let us stretch out our hands to those who have beaten us and say to them that we are all South Africans. We had a good fight, but now this is the time to heal the old wounds and to build a new South Africa."

Forgiveness, however, is two-sided. It requires not only mercy on the part of the persecuted but it also demands repentance on the side of the oppressor. Beyer Naudé, head of the former Christian Institute and one of the leading Afrikaners to oppose apartheid, sees a merciful attitude on the part of the ANC leadership: "In some incredible way," he says, "God has sown the seeds of a gracious attitude, of the spirit of ubuntu, in the hearts and minds of the whole African community." Yet, he fails to see the admission of guilt on the part of the oppressors: "As far as I know, none of the leaders of the National Party ever said they were sorry about the system they created."

Significantly, during the four years of negotiations leading up to the elections, no reference was made by the National Party to the immorality of creating and maintaining a system of exploitation based on strict racial segregation. To de Klerk, apartheid was not inherently wrong. No "evil" intent had motivated its architects, he argued. Clearly, the motivation behind de Klerk's reforms was not the belief that apartheid was wrong, evil, or sinful, but simply that it had failed to work out.

Recently, de Klerk reiterated his belief that he has nothing to apologize for—that "everything in the *so-called* apartheid era wasn't bad." This refusal to come to terms with and acknowledge responsibility for fostering an evil system are constraints upon true reconciliation. The Dutch Reformed Church, traditionally referred to as the "National Party at Prayer," may help in the reconciliation process by encouraging its members to own up to the evil committed by their leaders on their behalf. The Dutch Reformed Church took one significant step in this direction in 1990, when more than 300 church leaders from 80 denominations met to produce the Rustenburg Declaration. The document said:

We confess our sin and acknowledge our heretical part in the policy of apartheid which has led to such extreme suffering for so many in our land. We denounce apartheid, in its intention, its implementation and its consequences, as an evil policy. The practice and defense of apartheid as though it were biblically and theologically legitimated is an act of disobedience to God, a denial of the Gospel of Jesus Christ and a sin against our unity in the Holy Spirit.

The declaration went on to admonish that there had to be a genuine repentance and "practical restitution" to obtain God's forgiveness.

What does forgiveness mean in the political realm? Donald Shriver in *An Ethic for Enemies* argues that the conventional wisdom of "forgive and forget" is wrong. Rather, the axiom should be just the reverse: "Remember and forgive." For without memory, forgiveness is cheap and destructive, with perpetrator and victim alike left untransformed.

To help both victims and perpetrators to remember the past, the government has authorized a Truth and Reconciliation Commission to uncover the truth about human rights abuses in the apartheid era, to grant amnesty to those who confess, and make reparation to victims and their families who come forward. The Truth Commission's findings certainly will have significance for the victims, but equally important, the hearings could be a revelation to many whites who insist they do not know much of what was done in their name. Researcher Paul van Zyl argues for the importance of public accounting of what happened, since the "Nats to this day consider apartheid a policy option that just proved unworkable, not an immoral crime against humanity." ANC MP Willie Hofmeyer believes that there may be a number of white people who are genuinely sorry and who would welcome the opportunity provided by the commission to come to terms with their consciences. They will be able to confront themselves with the questions, "What did we do?" "How were we responsible?" The Truth Commission then may be the first step toward a public apology for the sin of racism and may foster genuine repentance. The Church can not only prepare people to understand the commission and train pastors to counsel and care for the victims and the accused, but also offer its theological insights on forgiveness and repentance to a deeply wounded society.

To be meaningful, confession and repentance must be followed by restitution. Tutu argues that repentance means not only expressing regret to those wronged under apartheid but also offering restitution. He says, "Those who have wronged must be ready to make what amends they can. They must be ready to make restitution and reparation. If I have stolen your pen, I can't really be contrite when I say, 'Please forgive me,' if at the same time I still keep your pen. If I am truly repentant, then I will demonstrate this genuine repentance by returning your pen."

Genuine repentance requires making amends by accepting policies that empower blacks economically, which will inevitably occur at the expense of white South Africans. A serious constraint on white renunciation of economic privilege is that many South Africans do not consider themselves as belonging to one community. Christianity, which is the predominant religion of the majority of blacks and whites in South Africa, may be able to provide that sense of oneness that can make self-sacrifice possible. Though sinful, man is not entirely sinful, or there would be hope for the future South Africa. Reinhold Niebuhr, perhaps America's foremost 20th-century political thinker, writes that the fact that various conceptions of a just solution to a problem can be synthesized into a common solution disproves the idea that groups are consistently egoistic. If that were so, society would be an anarchy of rival interests. The ability of communities to synthesize divergent approaches to arrive at "tolerably just solutions" proves man's capacity to consider interests other than his own. Christianity may contribute to a democratic South Africa in helping to forge a just compromise by synthesizing conflicting interests.

Still, the ANC in power may be tempted as the National Party did to rationalize its own interests in terms of religious truth. It would not be surprising to see the resistance movement's theology of "prophetic criticism" that railed against the illegitimacy of government replaced by one that emphasizes the "priestly sanctification" of government, which renders blanket approval of the actions of government. Niebuhr notes that the oppressed who rise up against an unjust government may be the executor of divine judgment in history, but they are not themselves immune to divine judgment. Tutu affirms the Niebuhrian understanding of man's obstinacy in insisting he has a monopoly on truth or virtue, that his viewpoint is ipso facto God's viewpoint. "We are all created in the image of God. The problem is that we have returned the compliment by creating God in our own image," he explained in an interview. It would behoove the new government to guard against self-righteousness, keeping in mind that political conflicts are between sinners, not between sinners and saints, and that yesterday's oppressed, upon gaining power, are likely to exhibit the same will to power that they abhorred in their opponents.

If religion is to continue to play a vital, constructive role in postapartheid South Africa, it will be important that it raise up those "prophetic minorities" of which Niebuhr speaks to hold the government accountable. A prophetic faith will eschew the role of court chaplain that sanctifies uncritically state action. There is evidence that church leaders are serving that function already. Bishop Tutu was one of the first critics to speak out against the ANC's failure to take strong action against individuals within that organization guilty of human rights violations in the period leading up to national elections. And recently he has attacked officials of the ANC government for riding a "gravy train" of opulence. Cabinet members in their chauffeur-driven Mercedes are a

disturbing sight to the masses who have neither basic transportation, housing, nor jobs, he has warned.
Notwithstanding the importance of prophetic criticism, however, there is a danger of church leaders making unrealistic and utopian demands of the state. According to Charles Villa-Vicencio, the Church needs to be critical but from within the context of solidarity and support for what is good and laudable in the government's programs.

Challenges Ahead

The tasks facing the new government are formidable. Reducing unemployment and poverty are the main challenges for the ANC. Fifty-three percent of black South Africans live below the poverty line (compared to just 2 percent of whites), and 50 percent of black South Africans are unemployed. For those who are employed, comparisons with white workers are stark: White salaries are 7.5 times more than black wages. And despite the lifting of trade and investment sanctions, only a handful of the U.S. companies that disinvested have returned.

There is reason for concern also over the education system for blacks. Only 38.3 percent of black students who took the exam for a diploma in 1993 passed, and only 8.1 percent passed with scores high enough to continue at the university level. Conversely, 98 percent of white students passed the exam, 43 percent of whom qualified for university admission. These results can be explained not only by higher funding of white schools over black ones but also by the fact that between 5 and 15 percent of six-to-15-year-old blacks are out of school at any time. Mass resistance of the 1980s meant making South Africa ungovernable, and many township youths believed the political struggle took precedence over getting an education.

Clearly, South Africa embraces two distinct worlds: One that allows its white population to gain higher education at rates that occur in richer industrialized countries and the other that limits Africans to levels found in developing countries. Two economies exist side by side: one that offers a developed country's wages and lifestyle against one that like other less-developed countries can barely provide a subsistence. No government can possibly meet the expectations of both white and black South Africans, whose goals—losing as little privilege as possible for whites and gaining the good life for blacks—may seem mutually exclusive.

Another trend deserves attention. Almost as great as the income disparity between blacks and whites is the growing gap among blacks. Of the wealthiest 20 percent of South African households, about a fourth are black. Their incomes are rising faster than any other sector in South Africa. At the same time, the incomes of the 40 percent of the poorest blacks have been declining for the last 20 years. The growing black middle class is a key constituency of the ANC, and the ANC will have to choose between this more conservative middle-class support and a radical mass constituency.

There are signs that the ANC is leaning toward a more moderate economic agenda than it had espoused as a liberation movement. Although Mandela reiterated his commitment to the Freedom Charter and its socialist economic politics upon his release from Robben Island, with the demise of the Soviet Union and socialism in worldwide disrepute, he has come to reject a key tenet of the Freedom Charter: the nationalization of banks and mining. In addition, *sunset clauses*, protecting for several years 1.2 million white civil servants' jobs in a bloated bureaucracy that had been maintained by the Nationalists to provide jobs for Afrikaners, have been accepted by the ANC. This promise will go far in allaying white fears of imminent loss of privilege but will necessarily mean less funds for jobs, housing, and education that blacks have come to expect under a new black-controlled government. The government says it is committed to the Reconstruction and Development Program and pledges the construction of a million homes, electrification and telephones for 2.5 million homes, free and compulsory schooling through age ten, free infant health clinics, land redistribution, and the creation of 2.5 million jobs over the next five years. It is not clear how these projects can be paid for without reducing the standard of living for white South Africans, who already pay among the highest income taxes in the world. The

ANC, therefore, may be tempted to do less than promised for the black masses to appease the middle class.

Even if a concerted effort is made to balance the conflicting interests of social classes, some critics warn that given projected low growth rates of 2.5 percent in the coming years, it will take at least ten years for parity to be achieved between standards of living in black and white communities. (To look at just one area—housing— two years after elections, only 10,000 of the one million houses planned have been built in a country where eight million blacks are homeless.) If black South Africans see little economic improvement in this transitional period, the possibility of violence erupting is great. Township youth are impatient for Mandela to produce the goods, even though he has warned, "You must not expect dramatic changes [the day after the election], or in the first year, or even in the first several years. These things take time." The militant Pan-Africanist Congress (PAC) has potential to gain support if disillusionment with economic progress sets in among poor blacks. The PAC, although faring poorly in elections with a mere 1.25 percent of the vote, nonetheless holds celebrity status in the townships because of attacks by its armed wing, the Azanian People's Liberation Army (APLA), against white farmers. The inability of the ANC to prevent youth in its organization from chanting, "Kill the Boer, kill the farmer" at pre-election demonstration points to the possible switching of loyalties from the ANC to the PAC by young people, who comprise the largest sector of the African population.

Both the Pan-Africanist Congress and Black Consciousness Movement under Robert Sobukwe and Steve Biko had attempted to tap into the African Independent Churches (AICs) as a source of political support given their compatible visions of exclusive African nationalism. The fact that the AICs are the largest and fastest growing religious group in South Africa may signify the ascendancy of the nationalist approach over the Charterist vision in the future. Although these groups have been viewed by most observers as apolitical or conservative—eschewing violence and respecting authority—there has been some indication that turmoil in the townships over recent years has politicized them. Their numbers alone could make them a potentially important political force in the future, and it is to be expected that the Pan-Africanist Congress/Black Consciousness Movement/National Forum wing will attempt to draw upon the AICs for political support.

Given the culture of violence that permeates South African society, it would not be surprising to see notions of *just revolution* used against an unresponsive government. Even Mandela, when he is not cautioning patience, has been known to urge his activist audiences to "overthrow the government" if the ANC does not improve their lot. Liberation theology, which condoned the use of violence against an unjust regime, inspired much political protest over the last two decades. If the new government chooses to appease the middle class and to ignore the poor, one might expect liberation theology again to come to the forefront and resonate among township youth. To meet the new situation of poor blacks fighting a ruling class comprised of both blacks and whites, these righteous rebels will necessarily borrow more heavily from the Latin America school with its emphasis on *class* conflict than from the American school of liberation theology that stressed the *race* struggle.

Black South Africans became politically free in 1994, but economic liberty in any real sense has yet to be attained. To the delegates attending the World Council of Churches conference in South Africa, Tutu remarked that elections would mean the legal death blow of apartheid but the "pernicious consequences would almost certainly remain for many a long year."

Christianity can make a contribution to the continuing struggle for justice in South Africa. It can inspire white South Africans to repent for their past complicity in maintaining an evil system, foster forgiveness on the part of black South Africans, invoke a sense of unity among the races, and assist in the search for a balanced compromise of interests. It can challenge South Africans not to lose sight of the importance of the poor in any scheme of justice, and, most important, provide hope that somehow all of this is indeed possible.

* * * * *

QUESTION: I have also read Shriver's book. What is most important in South African politics—to forgive and repent, or to accept some kind of political compromise, as de Klerk did, that gets one to the next step?

MS. GRAYBILL: This problem has caused one of the most serious breaks between the National Party and the ANC now. De Klerk and the National Party are opposed to ideas of truth commissions dredging up the past. They want to move forward and focus on creating needed jobs. If people see improvement, they will not care to know who committed wrongs against their relatives.

The other position is that if the problem is hid, it will fester, and that victims have a right to know who committed crimes against them. Families of people who died in detention also deserve to know who perpetrated the crimes. This issue is very controversial.

The Truth Commission has begun despite De Klerk's pleas that the matter be buried. It is also controversial because of the decision that there would be no prosecution, which is controversial. People in the human rights movement say that there are some crimes so horrible, so heinous that prosecution of these individuals under international law is required. The government has decided, however, that in the interest of reconciliation, if people come forward and confess or come forward in response to a subpoena, they will get blanket amnesty. At least people would know the truth.

QUESTION: Does the new constitution contain much about human rights?

MS. GRAYBILL: The new constitution was finally hammered out about a week ago. It contains a bill of rights and outlaws the death penalty. There is a new separate independent judiciary, which South Africa never had before. The government is aiming for a culture that protects human rights, which is new for South Africa. There are many problems ahead—for instance, how does one build a human rights culture? The Truth Commission is one step in that direction. Victims will get some sense of closure from knowing who committed the crimes and from the acknowledgement of these wrongdoings. Many people say they are ready to forgive, but they need to know who to forgive.

NARRATOR: Thank you for a most informative presentation.